GROBAR

GROBAR

PARTIZAN PLEASURE, PAIN AND PARANOIA:
LIFTING THE LID ON SERBIA'S UNDERTAKERS

JAMES MOOR

Pitch Publishing
A2 Yeoman Gate
Yeoman Way
Durrington
BN13 3QZ
www.pitchpublishing.co.uk

© James Moor 2013

A CIP catalogue record is available for this
book from the British Library

ISBN-13: 978-1-90917-870-0

Typesetting and origination by Pitch Publishing.
Printed in Great Britain by CPI Group (UK) Ltd, Croydon, CR0 4YY

Contents

Foreword

IT happens less now that I've written more books but, when *Behind the Curtain* came out, you could pretty much guarantee the question would come up at some point in any discussion of it: why eastern Europe? There were many reasons – some of them mundanely pragmatic and financial – but the romantic strand began in 1984 when I went to Bohinj in what is now Slovenia. I was seven and it was the first time I'd ever been out of Britain.

I remember quite clearly stepping out of the plane for the first time at Ljubljana airport and being overwhelmed by the sense of heat and the scent of the pines: so this was abroad. I loved it. Yugoslavia, it seemed to me, was basically the Lake District but with better weather and more interesting food, particularly the ice cream. There was a little hut by the mini golf course in the park that served a couple of dozen flavours. Blackcurrant! Lemon! Cherry! Stuff with Italian names that I didn't trust! And this at a time when, at home, Wall's Neapolitan seemed like a treat. We went back another four times before the war began: to Bovec and Portorož, to Kranjska Gora, to Bohinj again, to Žabljak in what is now Montenegro.

Coming back from Žabljak to the airport at Tivat, the fan belt on the bus broke, forcing us to take a taxi. With missing the flight a serious threat, the driver raced along back roads through the mountains. At one point we came upon an army roadblock. There was a long discussion between an officer and the driver before they finally agreed to let us through, with the instruction not to look anywhere but straight ahead. Even so, I remember dozens of soldiers, at least one of whom was carrying a bazooka on his shoulder. 'They're training,' said the driver when we got to the other side. 'For the war.' That was 1990.

We clearly didn't quite understand the significance of that because the next year we were booked up to go to Istria, only to be forced to cancel because of the conflict. We ended up going to Wick in north-eastern Scotland instead which, frankly, wasn't as good. I never went on another summer holiday with my parents.

Looking back, I can see that Yugoslavia wasn't an obvious holiday choice but at the time, knowing no different, it felt entirely natural. My dad had been to Croatia in 1962, when Tito first opened the borders, on what was essentially a lads holiday – he had tales of going out with the fishing fleet and having to hide from port officials determined to keep tourists to the designated beaches when they came back to shore – and my mam, coincidentally, had been to the same resort a year later. Both of them had been back repeatedly, first independently and then together. My nana and grandad, my mam's parents, had also been frequently and had an etching of the bridge in Mostar on their living room wall. To me as a kid, Yugoslavia was just a place people went for their holidays; it didn't seem odd, even if, when I think about it, I don't think anybody else at school went there. My dad's father had been an engineer in the merchant navy, so perhaps he was slightly more conditioned to be adventurous in his travel choices, but essentially I think my parents liked it because it was beautiful, sunny and cheap.

But of course what that last holiday had revealed was that, beneath the surface – and not far beneath – were serious political tensions. And it was that that came to fascinate me as I became a journalist and started going back to the former Yugoslavia to cover football, particularly given the clear intersection between football and politics and the war. But there's also something about the football itself that attracted me, the combination of brilliance and mental fragility, the sense that Yugoslavia and then the former Yugoslav states somehow both overachieve given their population and yet also should have done far better historically, perpetually self-destructing at the vital moment: Yugoslav football is a litany of lost finals and semi-finals (it's tempting, but probably over-simplistic, to suggest a significance in the fact that the key moment in Serbian history, romanticised beyond all reality now, was the defeat to the Ottomans on the Field of Blackbirds in Kosovo in 1389), with one notable exception: Red Star's victory in the 1991 European Cup Final as Yugoslavia spiralled into conflict – a glorious pan-Yugoslav triumph (there was at least one player from five of the six republics in that side) achieved a little under a month before Slovenia formally seceded from the federation to announce the death of Yugoslavia.

Presumably it's because of that success that Red Star seem to be the best-known Serbian side today. Or perhaps it's because it was they who were playing Dinamo Zagreb when Zvonimir Boban kicked a policeman in 1990, or because it was their ultra group, the Delije, that Arkan led and from which he drew many of his paramilitaries during the war. Perhaps it's even as simple as the fact that after the war, they had better PR, advertising their role in the toppling of Slobodan Milošević. Whatever the reason, one of the joys of this book is seeing Belgrade football from the Partizan side of the divide.

More generally, there's something very encouraging about the fact that a book about Partizan can be published. It's only two decades since three books – Pete Davies's *All Played Out*, Nick Hornby's *Fever Pitch* and Simon Kuper's *Football Against the Enemy* – changed the face of football publishing. Those three books persuaded publishers both that good, intelligent books could be written about football and that they would sell. The result has been an extraordinary boom in football literature, much of it following Kuper in turning to international themes, using football as a means of examining another culture or society, something that, as just about the one universal cultural mode, it is ideally equipped to do. This is a fine addition to that genre, but it is more than that. Publishing is an industry beset by gloom, as bookshops close and the major conglomerates lay off staff, but if it's possible to bring out a book about the second most famous team in Belgrade, it is at least getting something right.

Jonathan Wilson, 2013

Author's Acknowledgements

SEVERAL people played a huge role in helping this book come into existence, in their different ways. In chronological order: firstly to my Mum and Dad – to my Mum for being the person who got me interested in reading and writing and told me from an early age that I could do this if I wanted to (although she might not have envisaged quite so many references to the word pička when she said that), and to my Dad for taking me to my first ever football game – Crystal Palace v Arsenal at Selhurst Park in 1989, a bustling 1-1 draw that set the tone for decades of dependence on the live footballing drug.

Thanks also to my Serbian teachers, Ana Lazarević, Dragan Milović and Mira Danilović, without whose expertise I would never have been able to understand the banter all around me.

Once I had arrived in Serbia, someone had to get me to my first match. That man was Zgro, Igor Todorović, who ensured I went to my second, third and subsequent games, imparted so much knowledge and history, and infected me with his love for Partizan Belgrade.

Without Dušan Mihajilović there simply wouldn't be a book. The main character, my matchday companion all season, a brilliant colleague and a good friend. He was the first person to know that I was planning to write something, and fed so much information into the book, pointing me to the right media and filling in the cultural gaps. Dušan was also the first person to read the original draft, and contributed over the months to the gradual editing process. Big thanks to Dušan's mates – to Uroš, Goran, Vili, Debeli, Demba, the Milovans, Gule and the rest, for accepting me in the group and creating the matchday atmosphere.

A group of friends helped out a lot in reading the opening drafts and offering suggestions and corrections. The text evolved considerably over a few months to get to the point necessary to convince the publishers it was nearly ready. So, thanks to my sister, Steph Cole, for her assiduous grammar checking and correction, without which the book would be a mess of commas and rogue speech marks. Thanks also to Paul 'Bish' Clayton, whose allergy to adverbs improved the text greatly, and to Paul Nower, Scott McCarthy, Alex Picker, Chris Pidgeon, Nick 'Engleski Grobar' Hercules and Vicky Seymour for their support and constructive criticism.

A note of thanks too to my friend, accomplished attacking midfielder and (now) fellow writer Polly Courtney, who offered advice and encouragement to me as a novice looking for a deal.

Special thanks to my friend Jon Surtees, who not only read the whole text and offered improvements, but also made the introduction to Pitch Publishing and gently advocated on my behalf. Without him, this might not have happened.

Thanks to Paul at Pitch for taking a punt on publishing this book and seeing the whole process through, to Duncan Olner for a great cover, to Dean Rockett, Gareth Davis and Graham Hales for getting the book into shape, and to Jonathan Wilson for agreeing to write the foreword. Thanks also to my colleagues in the FCO who helped ensure accuracy and avoid unnecessary sensitivity. Nevertheless, any of my views expressed in the book do not necessarily represent the FCO's position. Finally, and most importantly, I need to thank Jenny Øvreås Rød, my girlfriend. Her encouragement to me, not least when it looked unlikely that this book would ever be published, means the world to me. She is truly the best thing ever to have happened to me, and her pride in this book being published makes me love her even more than I already did, which was a lot.

Indoctrination

I HAD wanted to be a Red Star fan. Hurrying away from Partizan Belgrade's stadium after my third derby of the season, with Red Star fans lobbing fireworks at me and a hundred other Partizan fans, I initially struggled to remember how I had ended up plumping for the black-and-white half of the city over the red-and-whites. Four crackers had already gone off behind me, the noises getting progressively closer like a rapidly approaching thunderstorm. The crackers, black discs the size and shape of an ice hockey puck, looked innocent enough as they flew through the air. But for something so diminutive, they make a surprisingly loud noise when they go off. A fifth one clattered into a wheely-bin a few metres behind me, giving the sound wave of the explosion a deep metallic ring and sounding even more sinister.

But still we didn't break into a run, even if a few of us quickened our walking pace. To start running would be to admit defeat. A hundred metres in front of me was the junction in the road where I could peel off right and get out of the bombardiers' range. The police couldn't save me – they were nowhere to be seen. Their last act had been to force me into sniper range, blocking my usual exit and forcing 5,000 of us to run the gauntlet of this narrow alley, while the Red Star masses still commanded the heights of the stadium's outer balcony. I was just going to have to hang on grimly for those last hundred metres.

Bang! I turned round to see a Partizan-supporting boy of ten or 11 jumping out of the way of the device as it fragmented just in front of him. 'ZVEZDA [star], WO-O-OH!' came a triumphant call from above us. Maybe I had decided to support Partizan because Red Star fans were the kind of neanderthal cretins who thought that chucking small incendiary devices at people was fun. It couldn't have been that – some of our number do the same thing in almost equal measure.

The seventh cracker landed 18 inches in front of me, in precisely the spot where my right foot was about to plant itself at the end of this very stride. The little black disc, fizzing and sparking tiny yellow drops, looked harmless enough. But instinctively I contorted my body leftwards, stepping like a drunkard back across my own leg, all the while keeping one eye on the still sparkling puck. As I drew level with the cracker, it exploded. The flash of light was a little disorienting but not dazzling, and the disintegrating cracker's shards didn't so much as tickle the bottom of my jeans. But I did feel a sudden rush of intense heat up the back of my leg.

It was too much for my poor central nervous system. My conscious mind, desperate to maintain my credibility as a football fan and as a man, stopped me from crying out or leaping into the arms of the nearest fellow human, but the proximity of the explosion had been a bit too much for the closest sphincter, and I let out a rasping and powerful fart. In among our crowd, not too tightly packed but with not much more than a foot of personal space each, I can't bear to imagine how many people heard it. As the next 'ZVEZDA, WO-O-OH!' rang out, I was sure I heard more titters from my so-called kinsmen than I heard supportive noises against our mutual attackers above.

In an effort to try and forget my embarrassment at the flappy noises emanating from my own digestive system, I tried to comfort myself by recalling how I ended up becoming the kind of person seen as a viable target by the Red Star grenadiers – that is to say a Partizan fan.

The answer is sadly a lot more prosaic than the threat of concussive weaponry and involuntary flatulence. To be honest, it was more like the excuse that girls used to give me as to why they couldn't be my date at the school disco – because Partizan asked first.

To go back to the start, in April 2010 I was informed that I would be working in the British Embassy in Belgrade from summer 2011 onwards. I have been watching live football, finances permitting, since the early 1990s, so I was determined to continue when I got there. On paper, there was only really one choice. Red Star Belgrade.

Why? Firstly, there is the name. How many other clubs are named after celestial bodies? The Kansas City Comets perhaps, but as a European fan whose formative footballing years were the late 1980s and early 1990s, I don't really consider them in the same league. 'Red Star' has a uniqueness that few other European club names match, apart from maybe the guttural power of 'Monchengladbach', the musicality of 'Fiorentina' or the calendar-specific 'Sheffield Wednesday'. The original Serbian version of the team's name, Crvena Zvezda, has the same effect.

Secondly, the colours. I have been an Arsenal fan since 1986, so I gravitate towards red-and-white teams anywhere in the world. Except Stoke. But I have always had a soft spot for PSV and Atletico Madrid. And where a handy red-and-white equivalent doesn't exist, then I usually prefer the team with more red in any given European duopoly. AC over Inter, Barcelona over Real, Crawley Town over Hastings.

Thirdly, the history. Red Star were the most successful team in the former Yugoslavia, and their European Cup-winning team from 1991 contained some of the best players in the world at that time: Prosinečki, Savićevic, Pančev, Belodedici. It seemed like a no-brainer that, from the start of the 2011/12 season, I would transfer my resident allegiance from London N5 to the Marakana in Belgrade.

Partizan, on the other hand? My knowledge of them wasn't as poor as the little Liverpudlian boy in the milk advert, whose ignorance of Accrington Stanley taught a whole generation of kids how to impersonate an incredulous Scouser. But I didn't know much about them.

The luck of the Champions League draw gave me a chance to make their acquaintance, as they were drawn against Arsenal. Watching Arsenal's away game on TV back in London, I was impressed by the level of noise that the Partizan fans made, which just made me think, 'Imagine how much louder it will be at Red Star, given they've got more fans.' Football-wise, I don't remember much of the game, save for Denilson, one of my least favourite Arsenal players of that era, conceding one of the most needless penalties ever. Even though Arsenal won with relative ease, and Partizan's play was never that imaginative, the crowd kept up their noise throughout.

Back at the Emirates in December, Arsenal went into the game needing to win, while Partizan came to London having lost all five of their Champions League games, and were trying to avoid becoming the arcane statistic of the 11th team in Champions League history to finish the group stage with no points.

Partizan's few hundred fans, mostly made up from the Serbian community in London, but also including some who had come from Belgrade just for the match, were comfortably out-singing the 50,000 or so Arsenal fans who had ventured out on a viciously cold December night. The overall attendance for the game was given at 58,845, but it was nowhere near that many really, judging by how much of the white cannon of seats was visible in the East Stand.

The Emirates is the only ground I know where the fans actively laugh at the announcement of the attendance figures because the official figure is consistently so much higher than reality. I have always assumed that this is because season ticket holders are counted even if they don't come, but there is an inescapable Eastern bloc-era propagandist undertone. This evening was no exception.

Arsenal started the better, and took the lead through a soft penalty converted by Robin van Persie. Partizan wouldn't give up, and equalised when Cleo's shot deflected off Sebastien Squillaci and looped over Lukasz Fabianski. Even away in the upper tier, 90 metres diagonally across the pitch from the Partizan fans, the roar they produced was a surprise, and I am used to visiting fans being the dominant force in my ears. Arsenal scored twice late on through Theo Walcott and Samir Nasri to take a fortuitous 3-1 win, earning us the right to be frighteningly outplayed by Barcelona for the second consecutive year, and go out of the competition.

While the noise and passion of the Grobari, the Partizan fans, had impressed me, and both Cleo and defender Stefan Savić seemed like good players, they hadn't done enough to change my conviction that I was going to become a Red Star fan when I arrived in Belgrade.

The first seed of doubt was sown when, while learning Serbian, my teacher showed me the sports pages of a Serbian newspaper to see how much I understood. I am not the hardest-working student in the world, so I first looked at the pictures. A picture of defender Dusko Tosić, in action for Red Star in a league game, caught my eye, not least because of the logo on his shirt. My former teacher Ana is both an excellent and professional teacher, but is also the possessor of a sixth sense for when her students are not working properly. In a one-on-one lesson, I had nowhere to hide.

'Zašto ste iznenađeni?' she asked [why are you surprised?] In my still-halting Serbian, I explained that I didn't know that Red Star were sponsored by Gazprom, and that I wasn't 100 per cent sure any more if they were definitely the team for me. I don't like Gazprom. This isn't a book about geopolitics or corporate social responsibility, so I'll just say very briefly that I don't like them, and leave it at that. Read more about them if you're interested as to why – Luke Harding's *Mafia State* is a good place to start.

It is well documented that footballers and football fans have a vast array of superstitions and idiosyncrasies when it comes to the correct apparel for matches. Mine is that as an Arsenal fan, I would always wear trainers in the same colour as the shirt, and I would never wear the same shirt to two consecutive games. I never bought trainers deliberately to match Arsenal's kits, but subconsciously I might have considered that factor when buying my yellow Onitsuka Tigers.

It is not just me. Liverpool fans complained bitterly about their 2011/12 third kit, which featured blue stripes and looks too Evertonian for die-hard Kopites. There was an outcry from Spurs fans when they first had Thomson as a sponsor and carried an outsized red (anything but red!) logo on their lilywhite home shirts. In 1992, the Italian company Kappa added a thin white piping to Barcelona's home shirt, shorts and socks to an even bigger protest. A couple of white quarks or other sub-atomic particles would probably be too much of a reminder of Real Madrid for some Barca fans. Kappa changed the kit for the next season and never allowed the person with the white pen anywhere near the design board again.

Despite the association with Gazprom, I moved to Serbia on 5 July still expecting to become a Red Star fan. I just wouldn't buy the official replica kit.

As part of my pre-job training, I spent the first month living in Novi Sad, Serbia's second city and capital of the Vojvodina region, an hour to the north of Belgrade. I worked in the mornings at the university's Student Cultural Centre (SKC) and had a three-hour language lesson in the afternoon, with some homework to follow.

I lived with the Damjanović family – Dejan, Irena and Mikica – in their comfortable flat, meaning that I was to be completely immersed in both the Serbian language and regular Serbian culture at all times. The aim was that I should be able to express myself in pretty much any situation by the end of the month – not fluent, but not far off, either. It was a great privilege to have such an experience and become better able to do my job at the same time, even if it meant that I was forced to spend a full five weeks away from Claire, my girlfriend of the time, which was going to be tough.

I arrived at the Student Cultural Centre on my first day to find that they weren't exactly ready for me. Serbia is a typical southern European country in that the pace of city life markedly slows in July and August as people take their holidays, often their only one of the year. Coupled with the university summer holidays having just begun, it was definitely the SKC's quietest time of the year, and there wasn't really enough work to go round for all of them, let alone for a British secondee who would probably need a lot of hand-holding. Introducing me to the team, Vladimir Kozbašić, also known as Vlada and 'Pećinko' [Caveman], recommended that I take myself off to the coming weekend's EXIT music festival – Serbia's answer to the V Festival – for four days, and then come back afterwards, when they would have some work for me. Given that I was being paid by the taxpayer to be there, I didn't feel totally comfortable with this, so I decided to stay for the rest of the morning to get to know the team, practise my Serbian, and see if there might be anything a bit more constructive that I could do.

There wasn't. But we did talk a lot about football. I am used to people across the world following the Premier League even more closely than we do in England, and obsessing about the same minutiae of transfer gossip and disallowed goals. But I wasn't ready for the depth of knowledge in the SKC. I told them I was originally from Crawley. My new colleagues Igor and 'Okac' [Big Eyes] immediately dissected the effectiveness of Crawley Town's business model, praised Matt Tubbs and asked why everyone hated Steve Evans. These were serious people.

Igor was a self-confessed anglophile and football anorak. He had first been to Britain in 1987 to watch Yugoslavia play away in London and wanted to go back ever since. He had been to more games in England than I had, including one at Bamber Bridge, and had succeeded in watching most English teams who played in black and white, in homage to his own Partizan. Okac's accent, from the nearby and mostly rural Banat region, was so thick that I could only understand him when he talked about football, so it was easier to talk about his admiration for Jamie Carragher than it was to talk about the weather.

It was a good thing I liked football. It always is. It is a great leveller. Before Serbia, I had worked in a few other countries, and football chat had served me very well. Sometimes it simply broke the ice or proved I was a more regular guy than my suit or conspicuous foreignness suggested. If you've got football, you can usually count on having at least one mate. And even if he disagrees with every footballing moral you stand for, you've still got something to talk about.

Trying to bond with Okac wasn't the hairiest situation that football has ever got me out of. That was when I cadged a lift with some Tunisian peacekeepers in a remote part of Congo, a lift I'm pretty sure they only gave because I was able to name two players in their national team and one club side from Tunis. I have never been more grateful to Hatem Trabelsi. But it was a lift I badly needed if I was going to catch the only flight out that week. This was much less dramatic, but it gave me some much-needed credibility.

The next day, I had some work to do at the SKC, and I began to realise that the football chat hadn't been for my benefit. This was what they talked about every day. Jovan was a tall, slender hippy with wavy hair tied into a long ponytail and an Indiana Jones hat, who was still living an approximation of the student life 30 years after he had concluded his own studies. His every sentence had baffled me thus far – a swirling mix of poetry, song lyrics and non-sequiturs – until he started talking about football, when he became lucid enough for me to pick up what he was saying. He was still offbeat – insisting to anyone who would listen that Cesc Fabregas was about to move to Real Madrid – but for once he was mostly comprehensible.

Reprising our conversation from yesterday, Igor asked me if I had decided who I was going to watch while I lived in Serbia. I hadn't, I said diplomatically. If Igor sensed his chance at converting me then, he hid it well. But he casually mentioned that Partizan were playing the following week, and I could come with him if I wanted to.

Over the next couple of days Igor showed himself to be a very competent proselytiser as his real agenda became apparent. Every now and then, he would drop in a reason why Partizan were the better option, or more often, why Red Star were in fact the root of all evil. Over the weekend, while we were at the EXIT festival, he deployed his top envoy – Dušan – to take the indoctrination up a notch. Dušan was going to be in my team at the embassy once I started work a month later, and was a physically imposing prospect even in the context of most Serbian men being considerably taller and broader-shouldered than me. Neither of these is particularly difficult: I am 5ft 7in and shaped a bit like a cylinder. But Dušan is huge, so when he said, 'Well, you can support who you like, but I really recommend Partizan', I felt compelled to hear him out.

Dušan had an argument for Partizan over Red Star in every possible category, and where he was struggling a bit, Igor was able to follow up. I started off by wondering out loud if I had to support either. There were four Belgrade clubs, right? And what about the teams in the rest of Serbia? I supported a big club in England, so it would be good to follow someone smaller here. Nonsense. Everyone in Serbia supported one of Partizan or Red Star. Even those with a nominal 'first' team had a preference. And supporting an 'underdog' was frankly just a guarantee that you would see terrible football.

But, the missionaries argued, if I wanted to support the underdog but still have a chance of winning something, that dog was Partizan. With fewer domestic trophies, and lacking the European Cup, Partizan had statistically had fewer successes. And they had to overcome the fact that Red Star was the Establishment club, and had benefited on many occasions from the assistance of the authorities, and indeed the State itself. So supporting Partizan would be a mild act of subversion, if that's what I wanted.

Hang on though, I said. Haven't Partizan won the league four years in a row? That didn't seem like the results of a club that was a victim of oppression. And Partizan and Red Star were both formed immediately after the Second World War with President for life Tito's blessing, right? And nominally both had the backing of a major State institution – Partizan were the club spun out of the Yugoslav Army, itself formed around the core of Tito's Partizans (the Yugoslav resistance movement), while Red Star was the police team.

Ah yes, but in the early years of the club, in the 1950s and 1960s, the army was an institution respected by the whole of Yugoslavia. It was the secret police – the brawn behind Red Star – who went around intimidating the population and banging up anyone who complained about Tito, who had moved swiftly from liberator to dictator. That primacy had extended itself into the footballing sphere, and Red Star had infiltrated most levels of the State.

OK, maybe that was true, but didn't the of the day president, Boris Tadić, support Partizan, and the leader of the opposition as well? It was, but that was just the politicians. The 'Deep State', the intelligence agencies, murky tycoons and the like, they were all for Red Star. The result had been several championships, cups and transfer deals fixed in their favour, and although Dušan admitted that Partizan had benefited from rigged games too, he still saw that in the context of a wider plan to secure a bigger prize for Red Star.

If that sounded a bit like a conspiracy theory gone too far, Dušan and Igor tried to bring it back to something with an evidentiary base. Red Star was a far less inclusive place than Partizan, and would indeed be less tolerant of a foreign 'fan'. Partizan had always been based around a Yugoslav identity, while Red Star had developed along narrower, Serb lines. Historically, Partizan had had more players from across the whole spectrum of Yugoslav ethnicities and religions, and a fan base more accepting of foreign imports. The fan bases followed the identities – Red Star's was more mono-ethnic, largely Serbs from Serbia, whereas Partizan's had included more from the other Yugoslav republics, across a range of ethnicities. Even Kosovo Albanians, who despised more or less everything to do with Serbia and Belgrade, supported Partizan. As the chairman of the Kosovo FA later put it, 'Partizan was the most open club in the former Yugoslavia.'

In the troubled 1990s, as Igor and Dušan described it, Red Star was very firmly the State club. Partizan was increasingly seen as a throwback to Tito's days, and less popular, but Red Star was a hotbed of nationalism and warmongering – and all of the key war criminals known to Western audiences were either Red Star fans or had drawn many of their volunteers from that fan base. Partizan hadn't been immune, but it hadn't been as bad.

After the break-up of Yugoslavia, Partizan's fans outside of Serbia had found it harder to come to the games, though some did still make it. Big, active fan groups still existed in places as far afield as Maribor in Slovenia, and Ohrid in Macedonia. The club still tried to appeal to all of modern-day Serbia's ethnicities, while Red Star showed less interest. As an example, Red Star and its fans continued to make a song and dance of its use of the Cyrillic alphabet (which is admittedly the official alphabet in Serbia, but is seen as an imposition by non-Serb ethnic groups), while Partizan went for the more inclusive Latin version.

Red Star went out of their way to suck up to Russia, partly motivated by their relationship with Gazprom (while Partizan had no shirt sponsor at all), congratulating Vladimir Putin on election victories and going so far as to have a plaque somewhere in the stadium commemorating the fact that Putin had once graced a seat with his backside. Partizan were less of a slave to Slavic brotherhood.

Then there were the fans. The Red Star fans went around calling themselves the Delije [heroes]. Partizan's had been given the epithet Grobari [gravediggers] by Red Star, but instead of coming up with their own self-aggrandising title, they had decided to stick with Grobari, and the original insult had become a badge of honour. And admittedly, they had fought fire with fire by labelling Red Star as the Cigani [Gypsies], which had stuck too.

Red Star fans were more likely to sing racist songs, salute war criminals, and try to fight the opposition. So I would be more comfortable with Partizan too. Dušan went on to say that since the 1980s the Grobari had been pro-English to Red Star's pro-Italian in their supporters' club/firm/ultra model, inspired in part by British punk culture, but also by our hooligans.

Of course, it took me less than five minutes of cursory internet searching to find a Red Star counter-argument to every single one of these stories, as well as Partizan's rebuttals of those rebuttals. But I also found countless references to games in Serbia, especially the Red Star–Partizan derbies, having some of the best atmosphere you could find in Europe. So when Igor said that he did indeed have a spare ticket for Partizan's first match of the season, a home Champions League second round qualifier against Shkendia Tetovo, the Macedonian champions, I had to see what all the fuss was about.

And if I didn't like it, I thought, I can always go and see Red Star once I move to Belgrade. I just wouldn't tell anyone.

Kill the Albanian!

I INVESTED a lot of time in choosing my outfit for the match against Shkendia. My criteria were: something white and/or black, nothing that could be confused as supporting Red Star or the opposition (so no red then), nothing which obviously marked me out as a foreigner. At the forefront of my mind was my embassy colleague Alex, who had turned up for his first Partizan game in a Paraguay shirt, his prized footballing possession. Paraguay's red-and-white striped design is as close to Red Star's as it gets. Dušan's mate Ivan had felt compelled to give the hapless Alex his own shirt, going to the game in just a vest to avoid seeing the Brit pulped.

I dismissed an otherwise suitable white t-shirt with black trim because it had 'VOTE FOR PEDRO' written on it in red letters. Too much red, too foreign, too likely that an under educated Partizan fan would think that Pedro was some Macedonian parliamentarian rather than a character in the film *Napoleon Dynamite*. Eventually, I settled on a white t-shirt with a multi-coloured elephant on it, which I bought around the time of the African Nations Cup. In support of the Ivory Coast, it says, very subtly, 'Les Elephants' on the front of it. I left the house satisfied with my choice.

Igor came to pick me up for the drive down to Belgrade. As he opened the door to let me into the car, he said, 'What's the t-shirt?' I replied, 'Oh, just some Ivory Coast thing I got a couple of years ago.' And he said, 'Yeah, can't believe they beat us at the World Cup.'

Ah. I had forgotten that. Serbia and Montenegro (as was) had been in the 'Group of Death' in the 2006 World Cup with the Netherlands, Argentina and ... Ivory Coast. The Ivorians had outplayed Serbia and Montenegro (the first World Cup in which they hadn't played as Yugoslavia, and, seeing as Montenegro had already declared independence by that point, the only time that a country that didn't exist has featured at a finals) and come back from behind to win 3-2.

As the first time that the team, as either Yugoslavia or Serbia and Montenegro, had lost to opposition from sub-Saharan Africa, and coming on the back of a World Cup campaign in which S&M had played three, lost three, it had been a dark time for football in Serbia. And here I was rubbing their face in it.

Igor introduced me to his friends, Johnny [real name Miodrag] and Miki [full name Miroslav], and we set off en route. To avoid the traffic, Igor took a back route for the first 30km or so. About a kilometre outside Novi Sad, the road got a bit bumpy. Not in an odd-patches-of-disrepair way, more in a ten metres, bump, judder, ten metres, bump, ten metres, bump, judder kind of way.

My patience for that kind of regular torture of the backside through the worn suspension of a 15-year-old Volkswagen Golf is pretty thin, so I guess within about 30 seconds I had made some kind of unconscious harrumphing noise, just the kind you don't want to hear from your fellow passenger on an away trip. Igor explained, 'This road ... it was built by the Germans when they were occupying Serbia in World War Two.' Bump. 'We haven't repaired it since they left.' Judder. 'Vidim,' [I see] I said. Twenty minutes later, we bumped off the back road and on to the motorway, and it was quiet enough for Igor to elaborate that Johnny was a cameraman for the club, and Miki worked as a photographer for the Partizan club magazine, *Izaberi Partizan* [Choose Partizan]. Izaberi was entitled to a guest ticket, which was how I was getting in tonight.

Igor, Johnny and Miki then proceeded to dissect Partizan's pre-season and the team's chances for the year. Their rapid, colloquial Serbian meant that my brain was so occupied with trying to understand even half of what they were saying that I'm afraid my contribution, until asked direct questions v-e-r-y s-l-o-w-l-y, was just listening and frowning.

The headlines were:

Their two best attacking players had left for China. Club hero Moreira had gone before the end of the season to play for Dalian Aerbin, and top scorer Cleo, who had struck in each game against Arsenal, had gone too, preferring the sweet taste of the yuan provided by Guangzhou Evergrande to another season hauling his arse round the Balkans.

Rumours that Partizan legend and former Chelsea player Mateja Kežman was likely to make a comeback were dismissed as just rumours. Another prime attacking option, the Senegalese striker Lamine Diarra, was long-term injured and unlikely to play the first couple of games. Replacing this illustrious group were a couple of promising youngsters and Brazilian signing Eduardo, who was coming straight to Partizan having played 37 games for Sao Caetano in the Brazilian league season with no break.

Partizan had a very light central defence. Manchester City's busy spell of acquisitions had not spared the Balkans, and Stefan Savić had traded Belgrade for Eastlands. His partner at the back, Mladen Krstajić, had retired and moved upstairs to become director of football, leaving last year's reserves likely to make up this year's back four. No one particularly thought that it was too early for Krstajić to retire at 37 after a career that peaked in Germany, where he won the league with Werder Bremen and then captained Schalke 04, but many felt that a 38-year-old Krstajić could still play a role in shoring up the pairing of Bulgarian international Ivan Ivanov and returnee (from Belgium) Nemanja Rnić.

The club had been worryingly inactive in the transfer market. It wasn't clear if this was because the players weren't available – or wouldn't come to Partizan because the wages were too low, the manager was trying to promote from within, or because the millions of euros that Partizan had earned through their appearance in the previous season's Champions League had been siphoned off through the ownership structure and there was nothing left to buy new players. The consensus in the car was that there was probably a bit of truth in all three, but that I shouldn't believe everything I heard, especially on the last point. 'Us Serbs love a conspiracy theory,' said Igor, turning to address me even though I would have preferred that he kept his eyes on the road at 120 kilometres an hour. 'We're always looking for what's behind the story, and who's really in control.'

Even in my first few days in Serbia, every time I had talked to anyone about the news or they had found out what my job was going to be in Belgrade, this fascination with conspiracy theories had been obvious. The favourite domestic theory was that all of the politicians were in the pocket of 'the tycoons' – mostly people who had made huge amounts of money during the years of war in the Balkans in the 1990s (with various shades of legality, luck, and profiteering) or who had benefited from the privatisation process, either through canny entrepreneurialism, political contacts, naked asset-stripping or a mixture of some or all. Many seemed to believe that the fate of Serbia was in the hands of external forces, debated and decided in the chanceries of Western embassies, or that Serbia was a mere pawn of secret 'deals' between Russia and the US, conceived in some smoke-filled room. Even though I was brand new, their eyes said they thought I was in on it.

At this early stage in my time in Serbia, I couldn't work out if this was a subconscious way of absolving Serbia and Serbs from the many mistakes they had made before, during and after the wars, or a legacy of one-party rule, under which all the key decisions had been taken with no transparency, and only presented to the public once all the (in modern parlance) key stakeholders – the big men at the top – had agreed on what they could get out of it. Or maybe I was reading too much into it, and they just loved a good gossip.

Politics aside, it was really a question of whether Partizan would finish first or second in the league. None of the teams outside the big two had improved enough over the summer to threaten even this depleted Partizan, which left only Red Star, perennial challengers, but who hadn't really done much over the past four years. Red Star had made lots of pre-season public noise about this being the year that they ended Partizan's dominance, but the group-think that dominated our car was that Partizan's self-destruction was more likely to hand Red Star the title than anything that the crveno-beli [red-and-whites] could do of their own accord.

After arriving in Belgrade and parking, we strolled down Humska Street and arrived at the ground, about 90 minutes before kick-off. Igor remembered that as well as watching the game, he had some evangelising to do. Operation Convert James was put into overdrive. We met up with Pećinko and some of their mutual friends in the Partizan bar/restaurant, which sits underneath the Sever [north] Stand – reserved for away fans. One of them was a member of parliament, and was therefore going to be very useful as a work contact. Good start. No one let me pay for my drinks. Even better.

We wandered over to the club shop – a hole in the wall further round under the Zapad [west], the main stand housing the directors' box and all the club management's offices – and Igor had a quick word with the guy running it and a couple of pin badges were produced for me, with no money needing to change hands. 'It's OK, he knows me.' Slick.

We went into the Zapad and into the bowels of the stadium to pick up my ticket from one of the club's administrative offices. 'Do you want to go and see the trophy room?' asked Igor. I nodded my assent, so we wandered, unchaperoned, through a couple of corridors and Igor persuaded the holder of the keys, with whom he also went way back, to let us in.

The trophy room is about 12 metres long and jam-packed with trophies, souvenir pennants and gifts from away matches, and dotted with life-size cardboard cut-outs of the current squad. Dominating the room was the Serbian league trophy, with the cup beneath, reminding anyone foolish enough to be ignorant of the fact that, yes, Partizan did do the double last year.

Most of the other trophies commemorated lesser wins, in friendly competitions or celebrating the reserves' victory in the 1968 Belgrade Reserve Cup. Arsenal had given a solid chrome replica of the Emirates Stadium when Partizan visited last year. Manchester United, who played Partizan in 1966, had given a gift that looked like an equine version of the Red Devil, standing on its hind legs while holding a trident. That was one talented horse.

One particular pennant caught my eye. It commemorated a match between Queens Park Rangers and Partizan, played at Arsenal's Highbury Stadium in the UEFA Cup on 25 October 1984. I knew nothing about this (I was only five at the time, after all). Igor was on hand to tell the story straight away. I could tell before he had finished the first sentence that this was one of his favourites.

QPR had been banned from playing their home games in the UEFA Cup at Loftus Road as they were one of the pioneering clubs trying out Astroturf (or the 'plastic pitch' as it was derogatorily called at the time). So they borrowed Arsenal's ground. Partizan's star player Dragan Mance put them 2-1 up with a stunning goal from 30 yards, causing Alan Parry to choke on his words as they tumbled out of his mouth: 'Mance, haven't seen much of him so far …'. QPR played out of their skins for the next hour to come back to win 6-2.

Partizan won the return leg 4-0 back in Belgrade to go through on away goals, which then was only the second time a club had come back from four goals down in a European tie to win it. Igor, beaming, told me that this ranks up in the top five games for all Partizan fans. Even those too young to have watched it live know the scoring sequence from that second leg (Zivković 4, 64, Kalicanin 40, Jesić 46).

We went back outside so that we could then enter the Istok, the east stand. Igor had decided that the Istok was the best introduction for a new fan – close enough to the hardcore Grobari in the Jug, the south stand behind the goal to feel the atmosphere, but not at any risk of trouble. As he explained, the southern end of the Istok was effectively the retirement home for former residents of the Jug – where the most devoted fans went once they had a bit more money to afford the better view, or had lost the urge to shout themselves hoarse at every game, surrounding by the heady aromas of male sweat and cannabis smoke. I wasn't sure if it was possible for me to have been pensioned off from the Jug before I had even made my debut there, but nevertheless I agreed with the rest of Igor's logic.

The queue to get into the Istok was right next to the line for the Jug and, even if we weren't expecting any trouble, the authorities were doing their best to make damn sure there wasn't any. There were maybe 150 police, helmeted, elbow- and knee-padded, and armed with both sturdy black batons and thick Perspex shields in two solid-looking lines on the outside edge of the queuing mass. Serbians tend to be pretty tall and solid chaps in the first place, so, with all the extra kit, it was pretty intimidating, like being surrounded by a platoon of trainee Robocops. A quick glance at the Grobari entering the Jug, mostly shirtless (it was about 35 degrees), tattooed, young and shaven-headed, suggested to my relentlessly middle-class mind that the police might have had a point with the precautions they were taking.

But who were the fans going to fight, other than the police? UEFA had agreed with Partizan and Shkendia that there would be no away fans, either at this match or at the return leg in Macedonia in a week's time. The football associations of both Serbia and Macedonia, and the two countries' respective Ministries of Foreign Affairs, had also been involved, showing just how seriously this was being taken. The agreement was reached to limit the possibility of nationalist or ethnic-based violence, which was a pretty high risk given the history of Shkendia and the incendiary political climate between Serbia and some of its neighbours.

Shkendia aren't just any team from Macedonia. They are the ethnic Albanian team from Tetovo in western Macedonia. Most of their players are ethnic Albanians even now, although they did have one lone Serb among their number. In my first few weeks in Serbia, the lazy stereotypes about Serbs hating all of their neighbours, which are often repeated in the UK, had been quickly disproved by talking to ordinary people. Yes, they had been at war with Croatia and Bosnia, but most people saw this as sad, given that they felt themselves as more or less one people, just with different religions. They made jokes about Montenegrins being lazy, but again, they were brothers. Likewise with Macedonian Slavs. No one said anything much about Bulgarians or Romanians. Although the Hungarians were viewed as a bit serious, there was respect for them and their country. Serbs lamented that they had used to look down on Hungary as a backwater, but it had become a normal western European country and enjoyed much higher living standards than Serbia did now.

But they really don't like Albanians. Most people with whom I'd had any kind of regional-political conversation had spoken ill of Albanians. Chief among their gripes were dark references to Albania's pre-First World War irredentist ambition to create a Greater Albania, which included Kosovo – a country recognised as independent by roughly half the world, but a territory that Serbia still claims as its own, and which is run with significant support from the EU and UN. Serbia's actions in Kosovo in 1999 and before were the reason why NATO bombed the country in 1999. Thirteen years on, in the first half of 2012, Serbia's number one foreign policy priority was reasserting its sovereignty over Kosovo. In short, Kosovo is the most polemical topic that exists in Serbia.

The concept of Greater Albania also included bits of Montenegro and Macedonia, as well as a chunk of modern-day southern Serbia. Many Serbs still believed that Albanians still harboured that ambition. Even food was a source of political argument – the Serbian national dish, the royally-dedicated Karađorđeva Šnicla [a pork schnitzel rolled around cream cheese and ham and then breaded and deep fried] was eaten in ethnic Albanian areas but named the Skenderbeg steak, in honour of their own national hero. Although it had been quiet for a few months, tensions were ratcheting up in Kosovo, bringing with it a concomitant rise in anti-Albanian sentiment.

Few teams are better equipped to arouse anti-Albanian sentiment in Serbia than Shkendia. Formed in 1979 by ethnic Albanians in the Macedonian republic of Yugoslavia, their historic purpose was to unite Albanian fans in Yugoslavia behind one team. They rose from the Yugoslav Fourth Division to the second tier in time for the start of the 1981/82 season. But fearing a rise in Albanian nationalist sentiment on the back of the club's success and increased popularity, Yugoslavia's ruling Communist Party had them shut down. Shkendia reformed after Macedonian independence in 1991 and worked their way up through the divisions again, before reaching the top flight, winning it for the first time in 2010/11 and earning the right to play this fixture.

Shkendia's supporters are known as the Ballistet, named after the Second World War Balli Kombetar Albanian anti-communist nationalist resistance movement. In brief (because this subject alone could be the theme for an entire book), one of the chief goals of Balli Kombetar was to defend the ethnically-based frontiers of the Albanian state revived by the Italians during the course of 1941. These borders included most of today's Kosovo, as well as other bits (but not all) of the originally-conceived Greater Albania. Balli Kombetar also collaborated extensively with the Nazis in both Kosovo and Greece, and killed or deported large numbers of Serbs from Kosovo. If you were trying to add together as many historical reasons for why a Serb would dislike a group as you could, you would probably end up with Balli Kombetar.

As we walked up the steps into the stand, I wasn't exactly impressed by the stadium. Stadion Partizan [Partizan Stadium], formerly Jugoslovenska Narodna Armija [Yugoslav National Army] Stadium, and still referred to by most fans as the JNA, and also sometimes as the Humska, after the road it lies on, is a fairly typical southern European bowl, dull grey except for a shiny office bit on the outside, and completely open to the elements on three sides. It has small backless seats in Partizan's original maroon and blue colours (the kit changed to black and white in 1958). There was a worn-looking athletics track, and a scoreboard at one end that had about as much technology as a dot matrix printer. And these were the fruits of a renovation in 1998.

It was a far cry from the English grounds of the same era, like Middlesbrough's Riverside and Derby's Pride Park, which were palatial by comparison. There were maybe 15,000 inside the ground, well short of the 32,710 capacity, but the Jug was stuffed to the gills and already belting out a series of Partizan anthems. The atmosphere was powerfully charged and, for a man used to the Emirates – where the first five minutes are even quieter than the rest of the game, as people arrive late and finish their pre-match snacks in their seats – it was great.

This is what football had sounded like when I was growing up in the 1980s. There was a physicality about the support too, fans content to stand and bump into each other as the crowd swayed (even before kick-off). The man next to me, standing a foot taller than me, shirtless, biceps straining the skin of his upper arms, was clearly part of my induction too, bringing the rough and tumble of the Jug to the Istok, and teaching me an early lesson about the need to keep my feet firmly planted at all times.

As the players came out of the tunnel in front of us to line up on the opposite side of the pitch for the pre-match formalities, from inside the solid mass of fans in the Jug came dozens of Serbian flags, alongside the couple of black-and-white Partizan flags, which had been aloft when we arrived. Was this a sign of healthy patriotism or rampant nationalism? I didn't need to wait long to find out.

Partizan were patently the better team from the first kick of the game. Igor and Pećinko had both ventured to me beforehand that the standard was likely to be lower than English non-league football and, in Shkendia's case, it was definitely true. They couldn't string two passes together, couldn't kick straight, couldn't do anything. Partizan must have had 80 per cent possession in the first ten minutes, but somehow couldn't find their way to a clear chance on goal. In the 13th minute, a fortunate ricochet sent the ball into Partizan's defensive third for the first time. Partizan failed to clear properly, and a Shkendia player tried to lob the ball into the box. As the ball broke the plane of the penalty area, the furthest forward it had been for the whole game, Partizan winger Stefan Babović jumped up to block the pass, twisting his head away to avoid taking one in the chops, and brushed the ball with his flailing hands. The referee gave the penalty.

I had expected the Partizan fans to boo and whistle to put off the penalty taker. They did that all right. As the striker placed the ball and turned his back on the Jug, the main body of Grobari, on the command of an unseen man with a megaphone, upped the pressure with a booming chorus of 'ubi, ubi, ubi shiptara!' [kill, kill,

kill the Albanian!]. I can't vouch for how much Serbian Shkendia's players know, but the expression is similar in Macedonian, and the penalty taker's face became visibly paler. He gulped for air as the referee blew his whistle, stepped forward and struck the most timid of penalties, within easy reach of Stojković, who made a regulation save. Ethnic hatred had won this particular battle.

The rest of the half passed by in a blur. Not because of the football – it was 0-0 at half-time – but because I was swept along in the barrage of noise from the Jug. When they were praising Partizan, they were great. And I admired their loyalty in the face of a poor Partizan performance. Arsenal fans would have booed their team off or at least indulged in a lot of exasperated noises. Not the Grobari. But Arsenal fans would never have threatened to kill anyone, not even Teddy Sheringham. And I had never heard such open hatred at a football match before (though Celtic and Rangers supporters would later tell me that they have).

The Grobari's patience was rewarded two minutes into the second half when the pale, blond midfielder Zvonimir Vukić rounded off a decent move, ghosting into the area and stabbing the ball high into the roof of the net. The flags in the Jug waved with renewed vigour and the Grobari jumped up and down in unison in celebration, singing their version of the popular European 'He who doesn't jump is …' song. Here that unknown scapegoat was, unsurprisingly, an Albanian.

Partizan scored again through Eduardo, who had sported a pained expression until that moment, and once more through his strike partner Marko Šćepović. In a lull between the goals, the crowd had shown more of its nationalist side, with first a chorus of 'Kosovo je srce Srbije' [Kosovo is the heart of Serbia], and then a brief, less unified chant in support of war criminal Ratko Mladić, who had been extradited to The Hague only six weeks previously.

At this latest chant, Igor self-consciously looked at me and winced, 'If you think this is bad, you should go to some of the other clubs. Red Star think that we're not nationalist enough.' Most of the nationalist chanting was confined to the Jug, but some people around me were joining in too, though most confined themselves to the tamer exhortations of 'napred Partizan' [come on Partizan] and 'volim te Partizane' [I love you, Partizan]. I wondered whether this was really something I could be associated with. Igor seemed to read my mind. 'It's not like this all the time, it's just because of who we're playing.'

A 4-0 win was completed when substitute forward Vladimir Jovančić (on for a visibly relieved Eduardo) saw his cross diverted into the net by a Shkendia defender. The last ten minutes was pure partying for the Grobari, punctuated by sustained one-minute bursts of 'jebi, jebi, jebi Shiptare, Shiptare, Shiptar-e-e-e-e!' [f***, f***, f*** the Albanians!]

In among all the exuberance, a small scuffle broke out in the Jug. It wasn't clear if someone had accidentally jumped on someone in celebration, or someone had started something with malice. The fans in the rest of the ground made their disapproval known loudly, denouncing the fighters as 'Cigani' (meaning Red Star fans rather than literally Gypsies), the worst insult that could be dished out in this stadium. The Grobari recovered their unity and at the final whistle beckoned the players over to them, so that they might salute their efforts with another mighty roar before sending them down the tunnel. No one tried to 'beat the rush' and get away before they had completed the final part of the matchday ritual.

On the way back, we talked (well, actually the others talked, I mostly listened) about what this year's line-up had looked like on the pitch. Goalkeeper Stojković wasn't popular and hadn't been tested apart from the penalty, but he was a decent keeper. At the back, young full-backs Vladimir Volkov and Nikola Aksentijević looked sharp, and decent prospects. This probably meant that they would leave next year, but it was good for now. Ivanov and tonight's central defensive partner Aleksandar Ranković had faced little, but even then hadn't inspired confidence. In midfield, skipper Saša Ilić still had a lot of class and vision but not much pace. Medo [Mohamed Camara], a Sierra Leone international and Partizan's only black player in tonight's squad, was easily the man of the match. He had distributed the ball well and played the 'Makélélé role' of shielding the back four with ease. On the wings, Vukić had scored the crucial goal and generally done OK, but Babović was the kind of 'skilful' winger that I always hated. Lots of technical ability but not good in a game situation, taking too many touches and hogging the ball when team-mates were better placed. Lank, straggly hair, which probably looked little better after an hour with straighteners and hairspray, added to my instant dislike. Up front, Šćepović had scored but not impressed, and Eduardo looked good but tired. Sub Jovančić had looked pacy and dangerous. All in all, the team looked to be in OK shape despite its summer exodus. But this was only one game against an obviously poor opponent. Greater tests were to come.

We stopped at a service station on the way back to Novi Sad to get a late-night snack, pausing to look at the poor guys who were going all the way back to Subotica on the Hungarian border, who wouldn't get to bed before 2am, and the policemen deployed to escort them all the way back (with a ratio of about one cop for every four fans). That was going to be a long old night.

As we got back into the car, Johnny handed me a bag from the Crno-Beli Butik [Black-And-White Shop] with my own Partizan 'Dupla Kruna' [Double Crown] double-winners t-shirt. No-one had even remotely cared about my Ivory Coast t-shirt, but now I had something that would definitely make me fit in. The Cyrillic print would make me look completely authentic. 'From us. So, did you enjoy it?' I could hardly have said no anyway, and I am such a sucker for football-related merchandise that I was totally bowled over and probably gushed a bit. How could I possibly not support this team, given the effort that its fans had made to win me over at my first game?

'I did. Everything except some of the chants.'

'They're worse at Red Star, you know.'

The next day at work, everyone was keen to know how I had found it. There was a degree of disbelief that the stereotyped genteel Englishman and diplomat, who supported Britain's quietest club, could possibly have enjoyed it among those rough and noisy Serbs. The sole truly neutral colleague in the SKC, Nemanja, only neutral because he doesn't like football, was keenest to know what I thought. So, James, did you enjoy the match?

'Yeah, the game was fun, the atmosphere was intense, but I wasn't comfortable with some of the chanting.'

'Oof, and that was Partizan? They're not the worst, you know. You should hear some of the others.'

I wasn't sure if I could use 'least-racist option' as valid grounds for supporting Partizan, but I figured I would definitely give it another go.

Love Partizan, Hate Yourself

A T the game against Shkendia, Pećinko had worn a t-shirt featuring the slogan 'Volim Partizan, mrzim sebe' (I love Partizan, I hate myself). On the front of the t-shirt was an angry-looking man in Partizan colours, and on the back was a list of Partizan's worst defeats against weaker opposition, including European exits against Artmedia Bratislava and Maccabi Petach Tikva, who aren't even the third-best Maccabi in the Israeli league. It was an island of self-deprecation in a sea of 'Double Crown' and 'Four In A Row' hubris printed on white cotton. Was it still a valid criticism of the club, considering their run of recent success? Definitely. One after another, Igor, Pećinko and Dejan (who, after a week of me living in his house, felt comfortable telling me that he was also a big Partizan fan) all assured me that Partizan's capacity for throwing matches away far outweighed their current and indeed cumulative success, and that it was only a matter of time before I found this out for myself.

Before the second leg against Shkendia (to which no Partizan fans would come from Belgrade as the reciprocal UEFA measures were taken in Macedonia), the draw for the next round of the Champions League was made. Partizan would face Belgian team Genk, a challenge according to UEFA's rankings and the relative wealth of the clubs, but not one which daunted any of my colleagues. Victory against the Belgians would earn Partizan the right to play one more game (the fourth qualifying round – at which Arsenal, Udinese and Bayern Munich would enter) to make the group stage. Defeat would carry the parachute payment of entry into the Europa League.

The second leg against Shkendia was my first chance to watch football on TV in Serbia. Despite not being confident about my level of Serbian, I understood the programme better than any other I had watched thus far. The key to this high level of comprehension is that football commentators (with a couple of exceptions – in England, I like Jon Champion and Peter Drury) trot out the same trite platitudes in every country I've ever watched it. I found myself predicting what the commentators would say before they did.

It helps greatly that the Serbian football vocabulary is so heavily based on English, more so than in other European languages that I've studied. Words where the influence is clearest are the following: out [throw-in], gol-out [goal kick], šut [shot, also as the verb to shoot, šutirati], centar-šut [cross], bek [defender], štoper [centre-back], golman [goalkeeper], rezultat [score], and penal [penalty]. The words for goal, corner, foul and offside are all directly lifted from English. This means that there are fewer non-English expressions to memorise, like lopta [ball/pass], and napadač [attacker] and the false friend of start [tackle].

The game itself was a routine 1-0 win for Partizan, who were rarely threatened by Shkendia despite vocal support from the 'home' crowd, which had transferred from Tetovo to play in FK Vardar's newly redeveloped home ground in Skopje. Dejan remarked that it was embarrassing that the stadium in Macedonia, looked down upon as one of Serbia's poorer neighbours, looked so much more modern than Partizan's. Jovančić scored the only goal of the game, running on to a through-ball and thumping a crisp, low shot past the Shkendia keeper. He looked the sharpest of all the players, some of whom looked like their brains were still in pre-season. The atmosphere in the ground seemed rather jolly, with the hardcore Ballistet outnumbered by Shkendia-supporting families enjoying a night out in the capital city and a chance to cheekily wave Albanian flags in the centre of Skopje, where they wouldn't normally be allowed.

After the game, Partizan coach Aleksandar Stanojević complained that, far from enjoying the party atmosphere, his players had been intimidated in the first half by nationalist chanting from the Albanian fans, urging the killing of Serbs, venerating dead former Kosovo Liberation Army leader Adem Jashari and proclaiming the independence of Kosovo. Stanojević might have been right, but his memory for the first leg was failing him – the Shkendia fans' themes were exactly the same as Partizan's.

Before the first leg against Genk, to be played in Belgium, European football came to my temporary home town of Novi Sad. Local team FK Vojvodina, last year's third-placed side, had a qualifier against FK Vaduz of Liechtenstein. Having beaten the Liechtensteiners 2-0 in Liechtenstein, it should have been a formality for Vojvodina to go through. Igor and I, short of anything better to do after work on a late Tuesday afternoon, went to the stadium to find enormous queues for the first home game of the season. An enterprising man, having spotted that there was only one ticket office counter while the stadium was being redeveloped, had bought up dozens of tickets, and was offering punters at the back of the queue 300 dinar tickets at 400 dinars each. Faced with the prospect of waiting 20 minutes and missing kick-off, we paid the 90p premium and sustained the market for touting. I seemed more bothered about this than Igor.

After the relative grandeur of Partizan's ground and the 15,000 crowd for a game in July, Vojvodina's stadium was a reminder of the real popularity of Serbian football – the club was delighted with a crowd of 5,000, barely filling a third of the stadium, but making it much fuller than normal. Vojvodina's main set of ultras, the Red Firm (not translated – they refer to themselves in English, like many fans groups in Serbia), were trying to drum up some atmosphere, but the bulk of the supporters were casual fans sitting in the shade of the main stand and were either chatting or munching their way through bags of sunflower and pumpkin seeds. Igor was greeted by many people as they came past us, and he pointed out to me who was a Partizan fan, whose main club was Red Star, and the few for whom Vojvodina were their main club.

Here was one of Serbian football's main problems in microcosm – the duopoly of Partizan and Red Star is such that even in Novi Sad, Serbia's second city, the bulk of people support one of the two big Belgrade clubs, and follow them on TV or in person, and only go to the occasional big game of their home town team. I couldn't imagine the same thing happening in England – three-quarters of Manchester, for example, supporting one of Arsenal or Chelsea, and just a few die-hards going to United or City. The advertising hoardings on one side of the ground tried to invoke a sense of civic duty to combat this effect: 'Budi pravi Novosadjanin – Navijaj za Vojvodinu' [Be a real Novi Sad-er – Support Vojvodina].

But even in autonomous Vojvodina, an area of the country with a more Austro-Hungarian than Ottoman past, a significant ethnic Hungarian minority and a long history of autonomy from Belgrade, the draw of the big Belgrade clubs built up in Tito's era was still too strong. Before the increase in nationalism and subsequent Balkan wars of the 1990s and the break-up of Yugoslavia (and its football leagues), it had been even harder for the smaller clubs, with strong support for the Big Four of their day – Partizan, Red Star, Dinamo Zagreb and Hajduk Split – across the six republics. But the erection of borders and general deterioration of travel connections post-war made it harder to support a club now in a different country, so more fans were forced to go local for a footballing fix.

Vaduz had not read the script, which pointed towards a comfortable home win. They re-wrote the first act, starting well and scoring within ten minutes. The crowd seemed relaxed despite going a goal behind. There was no way that these part-timers could score again. Vaduz continued to defy the scriptwriters and, midway through the second half, they did exactly that. With the score at 2-0, the match was heading for extra time and penalties, too much of a lottery for the superior Vojvodina team to want to risk. Vojvodina were sparked into life and, with seven minutes left on the clock, it looked like they had seized the pen from the Liechtensteiners and roughly scribbled in a happy ending, scoring a scruffy goal after a host of missed chances.

In injury time, Vojvodina missed a golden opportunity to seal the match before Vaduz ran down the other end to miss a similar chance, which would have given them the win on away goals. This was turning into an Ionesco farce, without the wordplay. With nearly six minutes gone of a designated five minutes of injury time (more having been added for substitutions and an injury), Vaduz got a free kick on the edge of the area. A scuffle broke out in the wall between opposing players. The ref showed a red card. No one left the pitch. From farce to slapstick comedy, Vaduz's keeper sprinted 50 metres to join the melee in the box, changed his mind and retreated to the edge of the area, and then charged back into the middle once everyone had settled down.

When the free kick did come in, it didn't beat the first defender, and was cleared to about 25 yards out. Surely it was over, after 97 minutes. The referee didn't blow the whistle and the second cross was flicked by the head of Moreno Merenda past the keeper and in. The Vaduz team, who had won four European games in their entire history prior to this match, all jumped five feet in the air. Vojvodina heads slumped. The referee went through the motions of bringing the game back to the centre but blew immediately after kick-off. Vojvodina had lost at home to a team from Liechtenstein and gone out of the Europa League.

The chants of 'uprava napolje!' [management out!] erupted around me immediately, aggression and fury accentuating the consonants to give a real impression of intended malice. I have never wanted less to be foreign than at that moment. I muttered 'užas' [horror] and 'sramota' [shame] repeatedly, because those were the two words that everyone else was saying and I knew what they meant. That way I wouldn't get found out. To mix it up a bit, I added a 'neverovatno' [unbelievable] to Igor on the way out. No one could suspect a man who knew three ways of expressing shock at a football result as a non-Serb.

We waited in the car park for a journalist friend of Igor's, whom he was giving a lift to. He was apoplectic. 'They sold the game! They f***ing sold it!' I asked what he meant by 'selling it'. 'The bookmakers. Illegal betting. They were paid to lose it 2-1 or something like that but they weren't supposed to go 2-0 down and then they couldn't get it back. Loads of people were saying they must have sold it. And the ref! He sent a Vaduz player off but he didn't leave. Cheats!' I had neither the Serbian language skills nor the inclination to get involved in an argument, so I left it there.

Partizan played away at Genk the next day. Dejan promised two things as the game started on TV. 'Partizan will play better today. They always play as badly as the bad teams they're up against,' and 'If they do play well, they'll still make a mess of it. They always do.' This was 'Volim Partizan, Mrzim Sebe' at its apogee. He was right on the first count straight away.

Partizan sprinted out of the blocks and took the game to Genk. Helped by Genk's immaculate pitch, this was a completely different Partizan. These guys could pass, for starters. An even first half swung Partizan's way when Ngongca of Genk was shown a straight red card, but they couldn't capitalise and it was 0-0 at half-time. Three minutes into the second half, a Genk player challenged Babović, but a foul wasn't awarded against him. Babović decided to take justice into his own hands, charged towards another player and hacked him down despite the ball having gone a full second earlier. It was a clear yellow card. Unfortunately it was Babović's second and he was off. I couldn't believe it. 'Why did he do that? It was just osveta [revenge]?' 'Pa, nije osveta. To je glupost [stupidity].'

Numerical equality took away Partizan's swagger, and it also looked like a couple of players were already tiring. One of them was Eduardo, who had 30 more games under his belt in the season than his team-mates. 'Is Eduardo injured?' I asked. 'He seems really slow.' Eduardo heard me. He ran on to a through-ball, outpaced the defender and shot against the onrushing goalkeeper, where the ball fell for midfielder Nemanja Tomić to pass it into the unguarded net.

Tomić's moment of glory lasted five minutes before he tripped a Genk attacker in his own box and Jelle Vossen converted the penalty. But as the game went into injury time, this was still going to be a very good result. Dejan wasn't sure yet. 'They can throw this away, watch.' Two and a half minutes into injury time, he was more specific. 'Watch this,' he said as Genk launched a long ball. Neither Ivanov nor Rnić went for it first time and it bounced into the box where substitute Marvin Ogunjimi nipped in to flick it over Stojković. 'Told you.' I had taken a shine to Rnić before that point – a stocky chap, and several inches shorter than his partner Ivanov, his build was more like mine than what I expected of a professional footballer, so I felt a certain fat man's empathy. This was a reminder though as to why people like us shouldn't play at centre-half.

A week later, the mood among the Partizan fans at the SKC was positive ahead of the return leg. Partizan had been the better team in the first leg, and Genk's threat had been limited aside from their two goals. Both Igor and Pećinko were away, so Miki had sorted me another free ticket and was going to take me to and from the game.

On the way down, as we entered the outskirts of Belgrade, Miki stopped to get some beers at a service station. We weren't going to be particularly early at the game and, as a photographer, Miki had to take shots of the warm-up and other pre-match action so there was probably only going to be about an hour's drinking time before we had to make our way into the stadium. Miki bought a sack of beers and passed them to me in the back of the car.

I should confess to something here. I don't like beer. I really don't like it. I try it every few months to see if I've changed my mind in the meantime, but thus far I've found every time that I still don't. There are beers that I dislike less than others, the less malty the better, but even with them I still wouldn't want to actually have a whole one. And I like other booze, from cider to gin to wine. And in the UK if you don't want to drink beer, you don't have to. Even beer festivals have dedicated cider stands. So I generally get away with it, and now that my friends and I aren't teenagers anymore, I don't get called 'gay' every time I order something that isn't a beer. It's still quite tough explaining that I don't like it though. As my friend from school Phil Arber said, 'You don't drink beer because you like it. You drink it to get p***ed.' My argument that I could get equally p***ed on other things didn't wash with him or anyone else in 1996 at the Half Moon pub in Crawley. But it got me by these days.

It wasn't going to wash in Serbia, where most of male society hasn't transcended the beer barrier yet, and the two main brands, Jelen [Stag] and Lav [Lion], are enormous institutions that have their own political and cultural significance. Sometimes the men would start off an evening with Serbia's ferocious national spirit, rakija, but they would have a couple of beers to wash that down.

I tried explaining that I didn't like beer a couple of times, but it was met with the same bafflement as trying to explain vegetarianism in countries where meat is considered a staple (a bit like Serbia, again). I can drink a beer if absolutely pushed, to avoid embarrassment for my host. But embarrassment for me, I can live with, and I will take any alternative drink if I can, with no sense of shame. Anyway, I was very grateful to Miki, who had only met me once before, for organising the whole trip and getting me in for free for the second time. It would have been pretty churlish to turn it down, and I guess frowned upon if I'd asked him to mix me up a caipirinha on the way to the football.

So I drank the beer, which wasn't fun. But I nursed it skilfully to ensure I wasn't offered another one before we arrived. We parked up next to the stadium, and Miki packed the remaining beers in a rucksack and told me that we would have to head to a park somewhere to go and drink them. The police were imposing a 500-metre alcohol exclusion zone for tonight's game, and anyone caught with booze would either be asked nicely to move further away, have their drinks seized, or arrested.

The police were on high alert for this game, in part because fresh unrest had broken out in Kosovo on 25 July after a stand-off lasting a few weeks. Trouble there had in the past translated into violence in Belgrade. The most prominent example was in February 2008, when Kosovo declared independence, and hooligans with alleged links to right-wing groups and football ultras from both halves of Belgrade broke into the US Embassy and set parts of it on fire, and tried to firebomb other embassies too. One of the attackers had died in the US Embassy, having been burned by the fire he had helped start.

On this occasion, Kosovo special police had been sent to take control of the border between Serbia and the northern part of Kosovo. This part is dominated by Serbs, who fiercely resist any attempt by Kosovo to assert its independence there. For them, the territory is an integral part of Serbia. The aim of the police mission had been to implement a recently-imposed trade embargo, but it did not go smoothly. One Kosovo policeman was killed, and then Serb elements torched a border post. The situation on the ground calmed down a few days later when the Kosovo police withdrew and NATO troops took over the operation of the border. But this was the first football match since then, and the mood of the fans had not been tested. In short, we didn't want to mess with the police on this of all nights.

Miki had chosen a drinking spot maybe 400 metres away from the stadium, which was probably far enough. When he had said park, I had in mind one of Belgrade's many leafy and grassy expanses, but this was a scruffy kids' playground, with already smashed Partizan fans lounging on see-saws and swings while consuming more beer. Two policemen came by almost immediately and paid little attention to the group we had joined, most of whom looked like they were at least in their late 20s. But they had a threshold in mind, and shifted a group of kids who were singing too lustily for their liking a full hour before kick-off.

Fifteen tranquil minutes later, a group of seven officers, arms linked, strode down the hill in formation ready to 'sweep' the park clean. We decided that this was a good time to leave, and upped sticks. Those brave few who stayed were dealt with pretty brusquely, the police crocodile pausing briefly to give them a stark choice between leaving without their remaining beers or facing arrest, despite them not causing any trouble. And those who didn't take the first option found themselves on the end of a robust frog-marching.

Miki fished out an envelope with the tickets in it. There must have been a mistake. I didn't have an actual ticket. I had a press pass. 'It'll be OK,' said Miki, reading my furrowed brow, 'you can just use that to get in and go to the Istok like you normally do.' We got to the entrance for the Istok and met two of Miki's colleagues from *Izaberi Partizan* magazine, one of whom was a very attractive red-haired girl. The steward let Miki's other colleague in but turned us two back. 'You need a ticket, that's not valid here.' Miki made a quick couple of calls, which I couldn't fully understand, but his face told a depressing story. We weren't getting in here. He asked the steward again, who looked bemused. 'Why do they want to come in here anyway, they've got a press box in the Zapad.' Oh. So we did, box number one in fact. Me and her. The fit one. The club was trying *really* hard to make me a supporter.

I still wasn't convinced that I was going to get in. The girl, Jasmina, had a press card to accompany her press pass. I didn't have anything apart from my British driving licence, which wasn't going to fool anyone. And I was wearing a Partizan t-shirt. As we walked around the ground, I fretted that I wasn't going to be allowed in. Jasmina was much more sanguine. 'Not everyone there will be journalists anyway, and you're foreign so they won't argue with you.' I figured I would come up with a back story anyway, and decided that I would impersonate Jonathan Wilson, writing a follow-up to his excellent *Football Behind the Curtain*. Which steward on the gate could possibly refuse a famous British writer who spoke such surprisingly good Serbian? No one, surely. My back story was completely superfluous, as it turned out. They just waved us both in, and we climbed our way up to the top of the stadium to find our box.

As we corkscrewed up the last narrow flight of stairs, Jasmina told me that her (unpaid) job was to write the match report on tonight's game for the magazine, so she might not be that talkative during the match. 'It's OK,' I said. 'As a famous British writer, I should probably take my own notes too.' I was joking, but this was the point when the idea that I might write this book first entered my head. I had read Tim Parks's *A Season with Verona*, and loved it. You have probably guessed that already. I thought I could do a Serbian version. *A Year with Partizan*, or a much better title. The Shkendia game alone was worth a chapter. I reckoned I could justify a couple of paragraphs just on the rigmarole involved in getting this far into the stadium. That only left 75,000 more words on the rest of the season. The average diplomatic cable has about 1,000 words in it. I would easily write 75 of them in a year, so why not write the same amount about football?

Thinking about it some more, Claire was not due to come out to live in Serbia until near the end of next season and we could only afford to commute for weekends so much, so I would be bored, possibly lonely, and have lots of time to kill. There would be plenty of free weekends to go on more than a few of the away trips and I was going to live within half an hour's walk of Stadion Partizan. I would probably make some friends through football. And in some ways it was even good for my job – I would see lots of the country this way and get to hear a lot more from ordinary (if Partizan-obsessed) people than I would by living in a diplomatic bubble the whole time. I would have to drink a few more beers, but that would be a small price to pay for being published for writing about my favourite sport. And if I didn't get published, well, my mates would read it. Some of them. Well, two of them, at least.

In the box, we found two fat policemen in uniform and a man in plain clothes holding a video camera and smoking a cigarette. The policemen looked disappointed when we showed them our tickets, although probably only as disappointed as me when I realised that press box 'seat 1' was in fact a folding chair. And it wasn't really high enough to see over the wooden desk at the front of the box. They huffed and puffed a bit but then left the room, leaving Jasmina and me with the plain-clothes guy. Aside from breathing smoke over me for a full 90 minutes, this man spent the entire match periodically filming the 50 or so Genk fans below to our left, but he spent the majority of the time with his binoculars trained on the Jug. He didn't say anything more than good evening to us, and his demeanour, bland clothing and complete seriousness suggested to me that he was either police intelligence or secret service. I made a mental note not to ask him any questions or claim to be a famous British journalist.

The stadium was humming, alive with the electricity of anticipation and bouncing along to the nervous rhythm of the Grobari choir. Sitting up in the gods, way above the fans and at the opposite end of the ground to the packed Jug made no difference to the noise level. The ground was three-quarters full and, for tonight, the Serbia flags displayed against Shkendia had been replaced by black-and-white Partizan flags, hopefully setting the tone for a much less nationalistic evening.

Partizan attacked from the start. Again, up against decent opposition, they looked like a real footballing side. They weren't wasting the ball, either. Babović being suspended was proving to be a good thing. Genk, having weathered a difficult first ten minutes, started to strangle Partizan's rhythm, slowing the game down wherever possible, nibbling at the boundaries of legal time-wasting and deftly falling whenever there was a hint of a foul. When they had the ball, they passed slowly and precisely, and could have scored after receiving an indirect free kick in the penalty area.

In other countries, the manager's advice to his visiting team would be to 'quieten the crowd' so as to increase the pressure on the home side. That wasn't happening here, the raucous singing from the Jug accompanied by what Jasmina said was an unusually vocal Istok and Zapad, and industrial quantities of firecrackers – five times more than had been set off at the Shkendia game. Partizan responded well to their indefatigable fans, and with half an hour on the clock, they had built up a head of steam, forcing a couple of good saves from the Genk keeper and several consecutive corners. 'Dolazi' [it's coming] I said to Jasmina, who looked remarkably pleased, to the point of affectionately at me. This was the first time I had ever felt that my footballing proto-punditry had got me emotionally closer to a woman.

For all Partizan's pressure, Eduardo looked to be struggling again. He would periodically waddle after the ball but be outpaced by the defenders or lose the ball trying to turn them, all the while sporting the same pained expression he had displayed against Shkendia. The team weren't helping him by thumping the ball into the channels, instead of playing into his feet and looking for Jovančić long, which would have suited their respective styles better. Jasmina, as an employed watcher of all of Partizan's games and connected to the club, would know the truth about Eduardo's condition. 'He's injured, isn't he? But they have to play him because of his wages?' 'No, I don't think so. He might be a bit tired. I think he's doing OK.'

Partizan hoofed a long pass into the left-hand channel again. Eduardo lumbered after it, but he was hemmed in against the touchline. He sucked in the defender before jinking past him and moving away down the touchline, his speed as deceptive as that of a frightened giraffe. If you've ever seen a giraffe run, it was a bit like that. His low cross was behind its target, Jovančić, and too far in front of Vukić, but evaded one, then two, then three defenders. The ball trickled across the face of the penalty area, rolling past a fourth defender.

Tomić, though not the fittest of players and occasionally guilty of waiting for the ball a bit too much, sniffed the chance and sprinted in from the right wing, then hit a solid shot, but one too close to the keeper. Instead of catching it, the keeper went to parry, and it squirmed off his gloves and bobbled over the line at the near post. Up where we were, the celebration was so loud that it felt as though noise, like heat, was capable of rising. Partizan would go through on away goals if it stayed like this.

The second half was pretty dull. So much the better for Partizan. Technically, the Genk players were very adept, but they lacked imagination and seemed to be creating little. But a moment of Partizan stupidity midway through the second half gave Genk the lifeline they needed. An aimless cross from 40 yards out was drifting out of play when defender Miljković, a nervous-looking fellow with more experience but half the talent of Aksentijević, handled in the box. The Jug was furious, booing the decision as loudly as it could. Watching the highlights of the game again on YouTube, the RTS commentator shows significant partiality, first declaring it 'impossible' to be a penalty, then moderating this by saying that handball has to be intentional, so this couldn't be a penalty. At the match, I said 'penal' to Jasmina as soon as he touched the ball. The TV replay shows that Miljković looks round at his hand as the ball goes past his head and makes sure he brushes against it softly, but hard enough to ensure it goes out of play.

The real question is why did he do it? The Genk player on the left wing would have to have performed an astonishing first-time lunging volley-cross of van Basten proportions to have had any chance of creating danger. Most likely, it would have just gone out for a goal kick. Studying the replay some more, it almost looks like the whole manoeuvre was premeditated. As we had seen against Shkendia, a penalty didn't necessarily mean a goal. Vossen stepped up with over a hundred decibels of booing and whistling ringing in his ears, but no genocidal threats towards Flemings, and calmly slotted in the penalty.

There was still half an hour to score the goal(s) to take it to extra time or win the tie outright. But Partizan, apart from one shot from distance and a stabbed effort into the side-netting, never really got close. I couldn't believe such a flat performance in such an important and still quite promising position.

'This is terrible,' said Jasmina. 'I know. I would say "dolazi" again, but I'm not sure that it will come.' Jasmina's face told me that either my football analytical charm had worn off or she didn't like the truth. A couple of minutes before the end, I asked Jasmina how she was going to write up the game: 'Are you going to be critical of the team? They've been awful since the goal.' She looked at me guiltily and explained that she couldn't do that even if they lost 5-0 at home to a fourth division side. *Izaberi Partizan* is a semi-official magazine, and receives so much benefit-in-kind from the club that it has to maintain a pro-Partizan stance at all times. Some Communist-era practices die hard.

Despite having had more possession, more shots and contributed more to the two fixtures, Partizan were going out, giving in the process a very good example of why supporting Partizan is an exercise in self-loathing. 'Love Partizan, hate yourself, right?', I asked Jasmina. 'Yeah, something like that,' she said coolly.

In trying to take positives from the game, I was pleased that the Partizan fans had kept their nationalism to themselves during this match. Maybe it had just been showing off in front of the Albanians. And they had cheered the team right to the end, like loyal and sporting supporters. At the final whistle, though, they proved that they weren't quite so magnanimous, booing the Belgian victory and chanting Ratko Mladić's name again. And on the footballing front, they had shown they could compete against European opposition, so maybe they could have a good run in the Europa League.

The Genk players celebrated their victory in front of those few brave Belgians who had made the trip to Serbia, and the policemen there to hem them in/protect them, who outnumbered them two to one. We trooped back downstairs to meet Miki, and I promised Jasmina that I would be checking her report for editorial independence the following morning. Her studied frown told me she really wasn't finding me funny anymore.

The Old South

I MOVED to Belgrade in time for the league to start on 13 August, the same day as the Premier League back in England. I had just two games under my belt, and a nagging worry that I might have to disassociate myself from the club at some point if I risked being guilty by proximity of endorsing some of the chanting. But I was genuinely more excited about Partizan than I was for Arsenal's first game of the season. Arsenal were a club seemingly in freefall before a ball had been kicked, and there was a bit of me glad of the thousands of kilometres separating me from the mess.

Partizan, meanwhile, had a comfortable home fixture against Novi Pazar, the team everyone expected to finish bottom of the league. My good pre-season mood had been improved still further by the experience of buying my season ticket a couple of days before, a smart, scannable, silver-grey plastic number that entitled me to go to all 15 home league games and the Europa League qualifier in two weeks' time, against as yet unknown opposition.

At the stadium, I was able to select my seat on a computer screen, although Dušan, who as a Belgrade resident and my colleague at the embassy, had taken over from Igor as my chief chaperone and indoctrinator, told me that this meant nothing – seating at Partizan was purely indicative except for Champions League group games, which wasn't going to be an issue this year. Even at this late stage in the pre-season, I could still choose from any section of the ground. The best part, though, was the price. My seat in the Istok 'wing' section, which came under the middle price band, cost 3,000 dinars. Three grand might seem like a lot but with an exchange rate of about 112 to the pound, this equated to about £26.50.

I did some maths and £26.50 would have bought me about 55 minutes in my seat at the Emirates, but the other 35 minutes of that first match (I work on the basis that injury time is free), and the 24 other games would still have to be paid for. £26.50 also represented about a third of the cost of this year's increase in Arsenal season ticket prices for my category of seat. Watching Partizan for the next 45 years would cost less than one more season at the Emirates. I had probably given Arsenal three times that amount just for chicken balti pies the previous season. But I could live with that. I just love those pies.

Out of interest, I looked at the price of an executive box for the season. At 75,000 dinars (£700), it was still less than my season ticket at Arsenal. But it would have been excessive, mainly because I didn't have enough friends in Belgrade to fill it yet. And no pies were included.

My Saturday before the game was entirely dedicated to football – I spent most of the day watching the Premier League (justifying it as 'educational' because the commentary was in Serbian) before heading to the stadium. With four Serbian SuperLiga games taking place on Saturday, I checked all the domestic channels to see if Serbia had a *Soccer Saturday* equivalent and whether host Džef Stelingović was as good as his British namesake. It did, but it consisted of a guy in a studio speaking to bored-sounding journalists over tinny mobile phone connections. I gave up on that. There is only so much I can take for the love of the game.

Dušan had said that he and some friends would be meeting in a pub before the game. I was planning to go, not least to get some more opinions on what the season had in store, but then Newcastle v Arsenal started and I changed my mind. Clearly I hadn't quite transferred my full allegiance to Partizan just yet. The name of the pub – Romantika – didn't sound like a pre-football kind of venue in any case.

I was living at that time in a temporary flat on the outskirts of the suburb of Dedinje, which is about a 20-minute walk away from the main road which links Stadion Partizan and the Marakana. Dedinje itself is the richest part of Belgrade, with the nicest houses, widest streets and best air quality. The two football grounds, and the motorway close to them, mark the boundary between the land of the rich and the rest of the city. En route to the stadium I noticed that even in this, the wealthiest suburb of Belgrade, there was a heavy police presence on the streets, more than the usual few deployed to look after the resident ambassadors. It had to be for the football, but surely the authorities didn't fear hooliganism from the tycoons and diplomats of Dedinje?

They didn't. The policemen on foot and the numerous motorcyclists were there as an escort for the Novi Pazar fans, one group of whom came through in a convoy of seven buses, topped and tailed by three or four police vans and a couple of outriders at each end, sirens blaring to the bemusement of the few people driving round that part of town or visiting the supermarket that sits on the junction nearest to Red Star's ground.

To understand why the police were so concerned about the trouble requires a little bit of history. Novi Pazar is the main town of a region called Sandžak. Sandžak straddles the border between Serbia and Montenegro, from the south-eastern edge of Bosnia-Herzegovina to the north-western edge of Kosovo. In the Serbian part of Sandžak, the majority ethnic group is Bosniaks, who are Muslims – Slavic people who converted to Islam when Sandžak was an important region in the European part of the Ottoman Empire, and Novi Pazar was a significant trading centre. When the Ottomans were expelled from most of the region following the Balkan wars in the early part of the 20th century, Sandžak was one of the regions that the Turks stayed in the longest, finally being liberated from the Ottoman Empire in 1912. Even today, *Lonely Planet* describes Novi Pazar as feeling 'more Turkish than some pockets of Istanbul'. In the aftermath of the wars that accompanied the break-up of Yugoslavia, many people worried that Sandžak, and not necessarily Kosovo, would be the next flashpoint. It didn't explode, although it came closer than was comfortable at times.

Today's Sandžak is one of the poorest parts of Serbia. The discrepancy in living standards between Sandžak and some of the rest of the country is a source of discord in the region, as is the under-representation of Bosniaks in state and public institutions and perceived bias towards Orthodox Serbs. One example given to me was that only five per cent of the firefighters in Sandžak are Bosniaks, despite them accounting for around 80 per cent of the population. Such examples, and the perceptions caused by them, continue to make Sandžak a fragile region and cause resentment among locals towards the central government.

The Serbian government is at least aware that the current state of affairs in Sandžak is unsustainable and unfair, and, under pressure from the EU, OSCE and others, is starting to do something about it. But some incentives have been used to strengthen favoured people and groups at the expense of others, rather than for the common good. A volatile mix of local politics and battles for regional supremacy within the Islamic community means that even some well-intentioned actions have not helped to bring durable solutions, nor significant investment from the rest of Serbia or beyond.

Serbs can be pretty racist about Bosniaks too. Some of this is animosity generated by the atrocities committed by both sides during the war between 1991 and 1995, but there were lots of 'Bosniak jokes' featuring perennial buffoons Haso and Mujo even in the former Yugoslavia, during periods in the 1970s and 1980s when most Serbs' anecdotes would have you believe that it was the best, most harmonious country in the world. It was not inconceivable to imagine a situation in which Partizan fans started chanting Ratko Mladić's name, only for Novi Pazar's fans to invoke the name of Naser Orić, a Bosnian war criminal indicted at the International Criminal Tribunal, and for this to lead to trouble within or outside the ground. The political climate in Serbia had still not drifted into its usual summer lull at the beginning of August, with the aftermath of the July events in northern Kosovo still being played out.

Partizan were 'doing their bit', treading what seemed to me like a fine line between nationalism and humanitarianism, with the club allowing charities to collect money, ostensibly for food to be distributed to ethnic Serbs affected by the unrest in northern Kosovo. However, some media commentators had speculated earlier in the week over the true end use of that money, and the possibility that it was financing the barricading of roads and other activities that were not contributing to peace. No one offered any convincing evidence that there was any kind of food insecurity that required this charitable response. Partizan also displayed their humanitarian concern on special t-shirts worn by the players as they entered the field.

Novi Pazar's inclusion in the league for this season was controversial in itself, though not likely to cause any ethnic tension. Novi Pazar had finished third in the Serbian First League (second tier) last season, with only two teams going up automatically. When

BASK Belgrade, the champions, had declared themselves unable to take up the promotion they had earned, they offered up their promotion spot to interested teams. The team who finished 15th in the SuperLiga, Indjija, said they should be allowed to escape the drop and stay in the top flight. However, the league, after an extraordinary meeting, decided to award the place to Novi Pazar. BASK, it was announced, would be relegated to the Belgrade Regional League, and BASK chairman Bojan Radovanovic would become a member of the Novi Pazar board.

The league did not even try to disguise it as a decision based on merit. It would have been a tough sell, as Novi Pazar are a perennial second tier team, not having featured in the top flight during the days of the Yugoslav First League, and then continuing to stay moored to the second tier despite the overall standard of the league dropping when the Croatian, Slovenian, Bosnian, and then Macedonian and Montenegrin teams all left to form their own new national leagues. Twice, in 1994 and 1995, Novi Pazar had been in the play-offs to get promotion to the top flight, and failed both times.

Instead, the league presented their decision as one of restoring geographical balance to the league, in which last season over half the teams had come from Belgrade, Novi Sad or somewhere in between. Introducing top flight football to Novi Pazar (and indeed to Sandžak/southern Serbia as a whole) would encourage the development of football in the region, one of the Serbian Football Association's stated aims. Noble enough sentiment, but hardly meritocratic.

Conspiracy theorists saw it less charitably than that. Several people I spoke to about the decision felt that money had changed hands to swing the decision Novi Pazar's way, up to €2 million according to the most generous estimates, with Sandžak 'notables' buying top flight football for their region as a gesture that they hoped would bring them influence, and eventually votes. Indjija made an official complaint to the Serbian FA, which was considered briefly and then rejected, the FA unable to find any evidence to back up the allegations of wrongdoing, and sticking to their line about bringing regional diversity to the top flight.

The ground was noticeably less full for this game than it had been for either of the two European games. The Jug in particular was practically empty when I arrived, although it filled quickly just before kick-off, as the fans scampered from their drinking places outside the police's 500m exclusion zone to take their places.

I was introduced to Dušan's regular group, self-styled as the Stari Jug (the old south). For the most part, they were life-long Partizan fans who had grown up enough not to want to watch games in the fug of cannabis smoke and casual racist remarks in the Jug, or play a cat-and-mouse game with the police on away trips, but still bled black and white. Even in their late 20s and early 30s, they had decided to retire gracefully from the Jug, leaving its pleasures to a new generation of kids. With one or two exceptions, these were professional people: a photographer, someone who worked for the OSCE Mission in Serbia, a banker. This also influenced their desire not to be associated too closely with the Jug, which they assured me obliquely, 'had some dodgy types in it'.

As it was the first game of the season, Dušan's whole group had made it to the game – quite an achievement given that Belgrade empties en masse in August and heads for the coast, either in Montenegro, Croatia, or further afield. Everyone was friendly enough, and made the usual polite remark about my Serbian being good. But they still looked at me with scepticism. I reckoned this wasn't the first time that Dušan had brought an embassy colleague who said 'oh yeah, I'll come and watch a game', and then never returned, either scared by the atmosphere or the firecrackers, or bored rigid by the low standard of football. Dušan sensed this and emphasised that this was already my third game, which lent me credibility.

There were a lot of names to get my head round: Dušan's 'kum' [best man] Milovan, instinctively cynical about Partizan and with a dry sense of humour; the 'kids' (they are about 27), Uroš, Goran, Gule and the other Milovan, bouncing around with excitement like it was the first game ever, not just of this year's domestic season, and determined to practise their English with me; 'Debeli' [the fat man], actually called Nemanja and not carrying a gram of unnecessary pork, placed in the middle of the group, dominating the discussions and outright refusing to believe that I spoke Serbian (over the course of the whole season he only ever called me 'mate'); the more mature and taciturn Demba (actually called Srđan) and Vili; DJ and musician Dario, chattering nervously and always the one most likely to turn the conversation over to violence, whether past or future rucks, and then finally, standing shyly just behind us, Dušan's 17-year-old cousin Milan, who had been subjected to enough family peer pressure to skip the initiation phase in the Jug and start claiming his pension in the Istok straight away.

It was, frankly, all a bit too much to take in. I was still finding it tough to follow conversations between Serbs, but my surroundings were still unfamiliar, and I was adjusting to a third different audio-visual experience in three games. Today's match featured something very exciting: away fans. Novi Pazar had brought over 1,000 fans, the most I had seen so far from an away side and by Serbian league standards a substantial following – most games not featuring either of the big two Belgrade sides can be lucky to attract more than 1,000 fans in total.

The fans who had travelled from the south-west had been supplemented by Sandžak natives living and working in Belgrade. The rumour swirling around us in the ground was that a prominent government minister from Sandžak, Rasim Ljajić, had paid for the fans' buses to Belgrade as a gesture to shore up his political support back home, relying on the enduring popularity of the local football club to perhaps make up for the improvement in living conditions that he and his fellow politicians had failed to deliver. Despite Novi Pazar FC's traditional blue and white colours, and their yellow away kit, the Novi Pazar fans were decked out in green Sandžak scarves. Whether the Islamic green was just to wind up the Partizan fans or a regular part of the attire for travelling Novi Pazar fans, I didn't know. The Sandžak flags, featuring both an Islamic crescent and a Bosnian fleur-de-lys motif, were almost certainly only brought along to be provocative.

Unlike in previous games, the pre-match atmosphere was provided by a CD of Partizan classics rather than the Grobari themselves. This wasn't quite the powerful atmosphere I had signed up for. The stadium, which had swirled with noise and seemed alive with colour at the previous games, was suddenly a cold, utilitarian concrete bowl, with no creature comforts and dusty seats. The streaks of urine on the interior walls, which had seemed like part of the festival atmosphere in the first couple of games (Leeds or Reading, not Glastonbury), were now just urine on stone. Perhaps 3,000 dinars wasn't going to be the bargain I had thought. This doubt was compounded a few minutes before kick-off when Dušan ventured that the opposition's standard of play would be lower than that of Crawley Town. Crawley Town pre-2010, as well.

How right he was. The opening ten minutes were easily below Conference South level. Partizan were obviously substantially more able footballers, but weren't able to string more than five or six passes together, while Novi Pazar were just chasing shadows. Partizan started to create a couple of chances and it was no real surprise when Eduardo scored a header after a quarter of an hour. The rest of the half was similar, until a stinging shot by Novi Pazar (and decent save from Stojković) in first-half injury time woke them up.

Partizan ran down the other end, and were awarded a free kick, which Tomić was about to take. Dušan was furious. 'Why is he taking it? He's done nothing all game.' Someone behind us shouted encouragement for Tomić, triggering Dušan into looking round accusingly for the culprit. As he glanced back, defeated in his brief manhunt, Tomić curled a beautiful free kick over the wall and under the bar to give Partizan a 2-0 lead at the break. 'Good free kick,' I ventured to Dušan, who stonewalled me and turned to converse with his other neighbour.

Captain Saša Ilić (not the former Charlton goalkeeper), back at Partizan for a second spell after having had several years away at Celta Vigo, Galatasaray and Red Bull Salzburg, scored a third goal for Partizan that was much more warmly received than either of the first two. With the match almost certainly won, Partizan slipped back down the gears and proceeded to pass it around for half an hour, pausing only to draw a rash tackle from a Novi Pazar midfielder, who picked up a second yellow card and was sent off.

I hadn't noticed any dodgy chanting in the first half, but as the game got more boring in the second half, with Partizan playing out time and Novi Pazar hoping to keep the score down, the fans started to look for something else to sing about. The Ratko Mladić chant came first. It was even more offensive this time than it was against either Shkendia or Genk given Mladić's role in the genocide committed at Srebrenica in 1995, where over 8,000 men and boys who were mainly Bosniaks were executed. That and other atrocities are the reason why he is currently being tried in The Hague. Then came a song very similar to the one first heard against Shkendia, just with one word different. 'Jebi jebi jebi Balije, Balije-e, Balij-e-e-e!', boomed the Jug, with strong backing vocals from the Istok and Zapad.

I was confused – I understood a bit of it, but also that something wasn't right, because Dušan and his friends weren't joining in, as they hadn't for the Mladić chant for any of the Kosovo-related ones. 'Sorry Dušan, who are they telling to f*** off?' I asked as politely as I could. Dušan looked sheepish. 'Er, Balija is a derogatory term for a Bosniak. Hadn't you heard that before?' No I hadn't. I asked Dušan if there had been any other nationalist chants other than this one that I hadn't picked up so far – to me they had all sounded like regular Partizan songs that I had heard against Genk. I was right. If telling the opposition fans' predominant ethnic group (though the Novi Pazar team contained both Serbs and Bosniaks) to go forth and multiply was as bad as it got, then, wrongly intentioned as it was, this wouldn't be as bad as it might have been.

With about ten minutes to go, another chant rose up from the Jug, and looking around the Istok stand I could see few people joining in but plenty more shaking their heads. This was probably not good. Before I could open my mouth to ask Dušan for a translation, 17-year-old Lazar Marković got the ball in the penalty area. 'Hajde sine!' [come on son!] urged the crowd, the first time I had heard a phrase directly translated from Cockney to Serbian, and Marković obliged, jinking past his marker with the agility of a gazelle, his collar-length hair bobbing with him, and then slotting home to make it 4-0, scoring his first ever senior goal for the club.

Three minutes later, Babović, also on as a sub, got in on the act, scoring what even I had to admit was a pretty good goal. I still couldn't forgive him for consistently wasting the ball and his lank hair, but it was a decent finish. 'This proves how easy this game's been,' said the guy behind me to his mate. 'If Babović can score then this team must be crap.' Dušan got a text from Igor, who was in the Jug, bemoaning the fact that Babović's goal would keep him in the team. I looked to my left and spotted him immediately, in a bright orange shirt that would have sat easily on the shelves of Top Man or River Island in the mid-1990s, a beacon of colour in an otherwise monochrome picture.

Igor was heading back to Novi Sad straight after the game so I texted him to ask how come he had not come to the Istok, where he had led me to believe that discerning fans like he and I should locate ourselves. Igor, at 36 and three-quarters, was hanging on to the vestiges of his youth, and decided on 'just one more year' in the Jug with the younger, more vocal crowd. Admittedly, he was standing in the section near the flag denoting the 40+ sub-group, a small collection of fans over the age of 40 who occupy a corner near the fence separating Jug and Istok. 'I just can't bring myself to sit down during football,' he texted back. I admired him for doing it, mostly because my knees (at 32) couldn't really deal any more with 90 minutes on my feet, let alone 90 minutes interspersed with jumping up and down to prove my loyalty to Partizan.

The crowd departed happily, and the columns of gendarmes outside the stadium were stood in a more relaxed formation as the crowd dispersed in search of a late night pljeskavica (a hamburger served with salad in a roll the size of a man's head) or the tram home. I followed the crowd out to the swarming Autokomanda roundabout, looking incongruous in smart shirt (black and white, obviously) and jeans in a sea of nylon shirts and shorts and got a taxi into town to meet some friends in a bar swankier than any I'm accustomed to. As the police tried in vain to prevent the fans from swarming across the main intersection, the taxi driver asked me if it had finished 3-0. 'No, 5-0, Marković and Babović scored.' 'Babović? Awful.' He asked if there had been any trouble, and less fluently I said I had heard a couple of songs but not seen anything bad.

There hadn't been any fighting, but the next day it was reported that Novi Pazar fans had destroyed some seats in the away end, and were claiming that they had been racially abused by chants from the Partizan fans (and therefore provoked into the violence). It was an unsavoury story to start Sunday with, but the overall epilogue seemed to be positive when Red Star travelled to Subotica to play Spartak and lost 2-0, with a performance that the B92 website, one of Serbia's leading news outlets, described as 'anaemic'. So Partizan were already a win ahead of their closest rivals, who were hovering just above the relegation zone. The Novi Pazar match hadn't yet played out its last dramatic act, though.

League table after the first round
1. Partizan 3 (+5)
2. Rad 3 (+3)
3. Spartak 3 (+2)
13. Red Star 0 (-2)

Simultaneous Broadcast

DUŠAN and I sat in on a meeting between some respected Serbian journalists and our mutual boss the ambassador on the Monday morning. I had expected that they would give him a rough ride over recent events in Kosovo and the perceived collusion between the West and the Kosovan government, or at least have a bit of a dig about the riots taking place in the UK. Neither happened. They were moderate, respectful and hugely knowledgeable. While I felt that I had learned a lot from the meeting, it hadn't featured either the controversy or the cut and thrust that I had expected (and secretly hoped for, especially as, as a new boy, I knew I could sit tight and not have to say anything). So I had a lot of pent-up verbal aggression in me, and quite fancied saying something provocative.

So on the way back to the embassy I thought I would prod Dušan. Were the media similarly considered and thoughtful in reporting on football, or did certain papers obviously take sides for one team or another? Before I had finished my question, Dušan was bristling. Very much so. Red Star, as the 'Establishment' team, benefited from the 'Establishment' media, that is to say, all of them. 'You'll see,' he said. 'As soon as there's an opportunity to criticise us, they'll take it.'

The media scene in Serbia suffers from a variety of ailments. Its chief problem is an opaque ownership, with two groups owning significant stakes in four out of five main TV companies and limited transparency as to who owns what in the print media. Political and political-business interference in all media is common, and not surprising when around 70 media outlets across the country depend to some degree on state (and therefore politically-controlled) funding. The chase for ratings in a competitive market had also led to standards dropping across the media scene too.

Even B92, the famously independent radio station turned TV station and web portal, which was shut down repeatedly by the Milošević regime during the 1990s and famously won the 1998 MTV Europe Free Your Mind prize, was by mid-2011 carrying fewer items of investigative journalism and more tired repeats of *Friends* and *Two and a Half Men*. The media were, and indeed are still susceptible to the manipulation that Dušan had outlined, not least because, logically, any ratings- and advertising-chasing station would go with the team that had the most fans, which was Red Star.

I am capable of seeing conspiracy theories against my club in most things. Whenever I watch top ten goals programmes or other such clips reels on TV, I always count the number of times that the goals are against Arsenal, to see if the editors are unfairly doing Arsenal down. Sometimes I really think they are. But I didn't really buy what Dušan was saying. If the whole system, down even to the journalists, was so against Partizan, how had they won the league four years in a row and taken the league and cup double last year? The president supported Partizan. Several other clubs could probably point to a degree of victimisation in favour of the big clubs, but not Partizan.

My faith in the fairness of the system lasted about six hours. That evening, the Serbian FA announced that Partizan were to be banned from playing in their home stadium indefinitely. The entire announcement read, 'In today's session, disciplinary proceedings were begun against FK Partizan and FK Novi Pazar, because of the unsporting behaviour of both clubs in their match on Saturday in the first round of the SuperLiga. Also, for the same reasons, the members of the disciplinary committee decided to suspend Partizan's stadium from all first-team matches in domestic competitions.'

No example was given in the statement, an omission that was picked up by the media. No matter how favourable they could possibly have been towards Red Star, the absence of any proof was too glaring for any journalist to ignore. Partizan, sensibly, merely announced the decision on their website with no comment. The discussion forums on B92 and other websites seethed with Partizan fury and an equal amount of Red Star gloating.

'What are they doing? We didn't do anything! Those b*****ds ripped up 500 of our seats and we get punished? Someone in the Federation wanted to equalise for the gypsies being so sh** in Subotica', fulminated miki83, along with about 800 other black-and-white commentators on B92, including Bora, who asked 'is this the start of Zvezda's "Project Europe?", referring to the Red Star board's statement of intent at the start of the year to bring Champions League football to the Marakana.

A few fans were more phlegmatic: 'I don't know why we're surprised. I heard all that nationalist stuff on TV. Even though I'm a Partizan fan I hope that the punishment stops that singing' said another Miki. Butragenjo proved that even logicians are Partizan fans, pointing out: 'How can a stadium be guilty? People are guilty. Punish them, not the stadium.'

The underlying nastiness between Partizan and Red Star does not take long to surface online. Whenever a question even tangentially linked to fan behaviour and stadium safety comes up, Zvezda fans are quick to recall the tragic death of Aleksandar 'Aca' Radović, who was killed during the 113th derby match on 31 October 1999 by a distress flare fired by the Partizan fans. This is an excerpt from the article that appeared in the weekly *NIN* news magazine, long highly regarded in Serbia (and before that in Yugoslavia). Anything written during the Milošević era, as this was, is likely to have been subject to some degree of editorial control by the government, but it is the most reliable account that I could find.

'But before the derby, around the stadium there were police at every step. – Have you got anything, asks a policeman of a fan as he lightly touched his pockets. – I don't have anything, says the guy. – OK, good, on you go says the policeman and starts to check the next in line.

'Later, next to the fence that separates the north from the west stand: beside a policeman in uniform and stewards, a girl brings forward an overly full rucksack and passes it across the fence to a boy in the north stand [where the Red Star fans stand for the derby at Partizan]. No-one asks what's in the bag. A moment later rockets and smoke bombs start falling on the north stand.

'Fifteen minutes after the scene at the entrance to the stadium, after Partizan's goal, a distress flare flies from the south to north and falls among the Zvezda fans. Then it kills seventeen-year-old Aleksandar Radović from Opovo. Several more rockets then fly over the stadium and land behind it. As claimed by eye-witnesses, help for Radović did not come until twenty minutes later, when fighting had died down between the police and the enraged Delije. The boys in blue, it seems, thought that the reason for the commotion was a fight between the fans, so they attempted to restore order by drawing their batons. Those present say that they called out in vain to the police for help in those first moments …

'The police on Tuesday stated that they had found that the rockets and distress flares had been brought into the ground by Grobari leader and FK Partizan kit man Branko Vučićević, known as Gavran [The Raven]. "It has been established that Zoran 'Čegi' Živanović, another leader of a Grobari group, bought 60 rockets and 10 distress flares from an unknown person, whose identity is being established," said Miodrag Gutić, head of the department for prevention of homicide and sexual offences.

'These items were brought to the Partizan stadium on the day of the derby around 15:30, and given to Časlav Kurandić, who, with the help of kit man Branko Vučićević, brought the bag into the stadium with Partizan's sports equipment. The bag was taken to the dressing room, and then packages from it were given, through the window of the Partizan junior team's dressing room, to Goran Matović and Dragan Petronić. Before that, it had been agreed with Živanović that the rockets and distress flares would, via the east stand, be brought to the south. The pyrotechnics were transferred to the south stand across the metal dividing fence to an unknown person, while Nikola Dedovic distracted the attention of the stewards. In the meantime, Živanović had arrived in the south stand, where he took control of the goods and divided them up.'

What still angers Red Star fans is perhaps not so much the act of the firing of the rockets, or even that club figures were complicit. The same happens at Red Star. Rather it is the fact that when the case eventually came to trial, the justice meted out to the perpetrators was so light. In March 2001, nearly two years after Aleksandar's death, Majk Halkijević, who fired the fatal rocket, was sentenced to one year and 11 months, having not been tried for murder, but on lesser charges of public order offences and 'general endangerment'.

Zoran Živanović and Časlav Kurandić were sent to prison for a year and a half, as was Mirko Urban, accused of selling the rockets in the first place. Branko Vučićević, the club insider without whose help the rockets could arguably never have got into the stadium in those numbers, received no conviction. Though not the leaders of the modern-day fans groups, I was reliably informed that most of those involved in the incident are still regulars at Partizan games, home and away, and the number of flares entering the stadium is nearly as high.

The following day I asked Dušan whether Partizan's new punishment was serious. Surely an indefinite ban was unjustified and impossible to impose. I wondered out loud whether the league was so keen to have Novi Pazar as part of it given that insulting them was now illegal, or whether the league wanted to lay down a marker to avoid 29 further weeks where anti-Bosniak chanting featured heavily. I fundamentally disagreed with the Partizan fans choosing to sing nationalist and racist songs, but I couldn't believe that the Serbian FA were going to shut every stadium in the country down once each club's fans had (inevitably) sung something rude about Bosniaks. It felt like Partizan were being made an example of.

Dušan was calmer about the punishment than I was. 'It's only an indefinite suspension because the disciplinary committee hasn't had a chance to decide on the final punishment yet. They'll probably meet next week and give a much smaller punishment, maybe a fine, maybe a one-week closure. What's going to be more interesting is what happens when Rad visit Novi Pazar this weekend.'

Rad are one of Belgrade's many lesser (but still top flight) teams, and finished fourth the season before, behind only the Big Two and Vojvodina. Their 'firm', United Force 1987 (using English), is feared as one of the more violent and right-wing groups in Serbian football, and travel in decent numbers, despite the club's small support base. If nominally left-wing and inclusive Partizan were able to get themselves banned, what would Rad do?

The suspension moved off the back pages and towards the front over the course of the day, as Interior Minister Dačić got involved. Dačić's Socialist party featured heavily on the club's board, so he had many equities at stake in sorting this out. Dačić said that the police had not been informed of the measures that would be taken against the clubs for alleged nationalist and religious insults, and that it was a matter for the footballing authorities.

Without reference to potential violations of Serbia's anti-discrimination law in the stadium, Dačić added 'slogans were recited by both sides, I was there at the stadium so I can say so. There were no incidents, only verbal incidents, not physical contact or any element of violence.' He added 'I didn't hear a mention of Srebrenica, maybe I didn't hear properly, but I don't think it was mentioned.'

Dačić did however go some way to appeasing Partizan fans by saying that matches featuring Novi Pazar would be closely followed by the authorities 'because it's completely logical that some extremist groups could exploit these situations to voice various slogans'. I hoped, for the sake of ethnic reconciliation, more so than for Partizan's sake, that this would happen.

Before the next league game and my first away trip, Partizan played in Dublin against Shamrock Rovers in the final round of qualifying for the Europa League, a small consolation for being knocked out of the Champions League. My commitment to Partizan didn't stretch far enough at that point for a trip to Ireland, so it was another chance to watch on RTS. Or so I thought.

On my way home from work, I had seen a few Red Star fans at the bus stop near my house, in replica shirts from throughout the past ten years. The first thought that went through my head was that it was a shame that Toyota weren't still Red Star's sponsors. I haven't got anything against them.

It then dawned on me that Red Star and Partizan's games were kicking off at pretty much the same time as each other, the first time this had happened all season. It's OK, I thought. RTS have two channels. Or maybe one of them will be on Eurosport or one of the Sport Plus channels. Watching the news on RTS 1, about half an hour before kick-off, RTS promised live coverage of both games in a 'kombinovan prenos' [combined programme]. Did this mean some kind of split-screen deal, or cutting between the two? It was the latter.

Red Star's game against Rennes kicked off first, ten minutes before Partizan's match. Red Star immediately put Rennes under a lot of pressure, and had threatened to score three times when Partizan's match in Ireland began. Thirteen seconds in, before the commentators had even finished reading out the Partizan line-up, Red Star got a penalty, and we cut back to the Marakana. Red Star scored, and RTS stayed with the game for another four minutes before heading back to Ireland. This time we got nearly 40 seconds before Red Star had the ball in the net again, only for the goal to be disallowed for offside.

The next time that the coverage returned to Ireland, viewers were treated to about six minutes, in which absolutely nothing happened at either end. So the directors cut back to the Marakana, where Red Star had a free kick in a dangerous position. While the Rennes goalkeeper was lining up the wall, Partizan scored. RTS had missed two out of the three most exciting incidents so far. Tomić swept in a controlled right-foot shot from the edge of the area, continuing his good run of goalscoring form, after a flowing Partizan move. Dušan was in Maribor in Slovenia, watching Glasgow Rangers' away game there with some colleagues from the embassy. I texted him to tell him that his best mate had put Partizan 1-0 up, but he flat out ignored my provocation. Within minutes, Tomić came close to adding a second that would have been a carbon copy of his goal against Genk, and Eduardo shot wide when well placed.

Partizan were not playing well, partly because Stanojević had put out a below-strength team, bringing in defenders Ranković and Stanković, and bringing Milan Smiljanić into the midfield, who had barely featured so far this season. Smiljanić, more often known by his nickname Lola, was one of the more interesting players in an otherwise fairly dull Partizan squad. He had made his first-team debut for Partizan in 2005, when he was only 18, and was made club captain before he was 20. He had then earned a transfer to Espanyol, but had come back to Partizan after three seasons, two less than he was contracted for.

Smiljanić's main problem seemed to be that he featured more often in the middle pages of the paper – the Zabava [entertainment] section. I saw plenty of pictures of him out and about in Belgrade, where he often frequented the floating pontoons and barges on the river Sava, known as splavovi, which serve as the city's nightlife headquarters in the summer. He had been linked with many of Serbia's most glamorous women, including the leading light of the turbo-folk era, and widow of assassinated war criminal Arkan, Ceca Raznatović, 13 years his senior (although he denied it). The latest one had been a contestant in *Serbia's Top Model*.

Dušan told me that Smiljanić was a great player, it was just that he spent too much time on the booze. Worse than that, he was the leader of Partizan's version of the old Arsenal 'Tuesday Club', which in this case seemed to involve dragging fellow midfielder Nemanja Tomić round Belgrade and getting him hammered. The provincial Tomić (known as Šumadinho – combining his faux-Brazilian skills with Šumadija – the west/central 'real' Serbia of Tomić's birth, and a byword for peasant traditions) was apparently in awe of the metropolitan Lola. Regardless of who was the ringleader, a rumour had been going round that both Smiljanić and Tomić had been forced to go through extra fitness training at the start of the season as they had both come back in poor shape after eating, drinking and smoking their way through the close season (Tomić was alleged to have been 10kg overweight). And shagging. Without that, maybe Tomić would have tipped the scales even further.

But against weak opposition in the form of Shamrock, Partizan's hybrid first-reserve team, including a fit-looking Smiljanić, were not really threatened in a dull match. The RTS directors decided to stay with it nonetheless, missing a slick Rennes equaliser in the process. Maybe my Serbian was improving, or maybe the commentators that night were particularly blatant, but the level of bias was astonishing. It was probably the most one-eyed I've heard since I watched Formula One on Italian TV, where the commentary is about Ferrari, whether those cars are in the lead, at the back, not on screen or out of the race. The other 22 cars are just a colourful background.

The commentator in Partizan's game endlessly praised the superior quality of the Partizan team in comparison to Shamrock. He wasn't necessarily wrong, but as successive passes were misplaced by both sides, and Partizan failed to create any further chances in the first half, the performance didn't match the hyperbole.

That commentator was a paragon of impartiality compared to the guy covering Red Star, who squealed his way through the first half every time Red Star got the ball. Completely seriously, he claimed that Rennes' goal was 'borderline offside', when the player was at least a yard and a half onside, and appealed for offside a couple of other times even though the Red Star players didn't. I imagined him with a microphone in one hand and the other arm raised, like a journalistic Tony Adams. He delighted in telling viewers that Red Star's disallowed goal had 'certainly upset the Rennes players' and frequently exclaimed 'šteta' [shame] every time that a Red Star player failed to connect with even the most mundane of passes or aimless of crosses.

As the ref blew for half-time at the Marakana, the directors showed a couple of minutes of highlights before switching over to the last ten minutes of the first half in Ireland. My initial frustration (and shouting – alone in the flat like a madman – to change back to Partizan's game) quickly turned to hope: statistically, showing pointless footage in one game had mostly led to a goal in the other. The hope was false. It was still only 1-0, and the half petered out with the score the same.

In the second half, with Rennes looking like they would come away with a draw, the commentator in the Red Star game decided that the time for neutrality was over, and really pinned his colours to the crveno-beli mast. He proudly declared that there was 'still time for a Red Star triumph'. I checked later to make sure that I wasn't over-interpreting this, and 'trijumf' isn't simply a synonym for victory or winning, it carries the same grand meanings of glory and magnificence as it does in English.

In the 72nd minute, Red Star crossed dangerously from the right, and as the ball agonisingly squirmed away from striker Borja, he emitted a noise of such strangled excitement and pain that I can only equate it to the sound that I imagine is made at the point of expiry by those poor men who have died masturbating with an orange in their mouths and a pair of tights over their heads.

I digress. While another pedestrian passage of play by Partizan was on screen, Rennes took a 2-1 lead. All the air escaped the commentator's lungs, a lot less erotically than ten minutes before. As the replay was shown, I thought I heard him say 'jebi ga' [f*** it] as the pictures showed the Red Star defence standing aside as Colombian forward Victor Montano rifled home. But as my brain processed the Serbian, I realised he had actually just said 'evo ga' [there he is]. Nevertheless, I had started to understand why Dušan was so adamant that the media's favourites were Red Star.

Faced with such a barrage of hyperbole, and RTS spending more time on the Red Star game in the second half, I had lost focus on Partizan's game and had subconsciously assumed they would just see this one out. In any case, Shamrock, despite their best efforts, didn't seem to have a goal in them.

With just over ten minutes to go, the first sign of a potential self-destruction materialised when one defender missed his kick defending a fairly harmless cross and it bounced squarely onto Rnić's arm. The ref didn't award the penalty, not least because it would have been unfair on Rnić to have assumed he could predict such a mal-coordinated air shot from his team-mate. Shamrock's tails were up, and I could hear Dejan doom-mongering all the way from Novi Sad. For the second consecutive away European game, he was right. Shamrock put together a swift set of passes and their slightly rotund but skilful winger Gary McCabe deftly poked the ball through the gaping chasm of Ivanov's legs and prodded past Stojković to equalise.

The closer it got to the end of the game, the more Partizan seemed to want to lose. In injury time, their collective paranoia nearly got the better of them. The defence failed to clear a corner not once, but twice, with only some desperate lunging preventing a Shamrock goal. Partizan counter-attacked, and Babović received the ball in a promising position. As Jovančić and Eduardo both made runs into scoring positions that would have seen them outpace the tiring Shamrock defenders, Babović took two touches more than he needed before passing weakly into the legs of a defender, having characteristically dithered. A minute later, Jovančić committed a completely needless off-the-ball challenge that earned him a yellow card, a suspension from the return game, and an immediate substitution.

It was highly fortunate that the final whistle went 30 seconds later. I was additionally happy as my brain couldn't keep up – I didn't have the maths skills to compute what exponentially more crass error Partizan might have committed had the match gone on for another minute. A 1-1 draw seemed like a very good result in the context of those last four or five minutes, with the return match to come a week later in Belgrade.

Baps With Mashed Brains

HAVING played on the Thursday, Partizan's next league game was pushed back to Sunday at 5pm. On the Saturday, Rad had won 3-0 away at Novi Pazar (with no reports yet of any trouble), and Smederevo too had picked up their second win. To stay clear at the top, Partizan needed to win by two goals. More important than heading the standings on goal difference while it was still August, winning at one of the league's sterner opponents would put more pressure on Red Star, whose first home league game of the season, against Javor, immediately followed Partizan's.

Igor had told me that the match against Sloboda Point Sevojno in Užice was one of the away games that he wouldn't be going to this year, not least because it took all day to get there from Novi Sad. But if I was going to do this season properly, I really had to. I borrowed a car for the weekend, and Dušan organised tickets through his mate Goran, who is from Užice. The match briefly wasn't top of my agenda on Friday, as it occurred to me that I hadn't driven a left-hand drive in about four years, so a 400km round trip on a route I didn't know might not have been the cleverest debut on the Serbian roads.

Resolve tested, on Saturday I ventured bravely on to the roads. I picked up Dušan and his friend Milovan at the entrance to Belgrade's artificial city beach island, Ada Ciganlija. Even at half past nine, people were arriving in their dozens to swim and sunbathe, with the temperature already 27 degrees Celsius. Milovan was a few minutes late, but he was let off because it was his birthday. Dušan explained that we were going to celebrate the occasion mainly through the medium of meat. Our 'brunch' on arrival was going to be the famous Užice speciality, the komplet lepinja. A lepinja is a largeish bread roll, baked in the oven and then, to turn it into the komplet version, spread with kajmak [Serbian cream cheese], beaten egg and lamb dripping and returned to the oven. It sounded delicious, if heart-stoppingly calorific, to me. After that, we would head for a birthday-inspired main course of some jagnjetina [roast lamb], and then to the ground to make the 5pm kick-off.

The drive down took about three and a bit hours, including a stop for snacks, which seemed a bit excessive, even as a warm-up for our pre-match gluttony. The bulk of the journey was down the Ibarska Magistrala, the main road following the route of the Ibar river, a waterway more famous these days for being the unofficial dividing line between north and south Kosovo in the middle of the town of Mitrovica. The road took in some spectacular scenery, climbing high over thickly forested hills in central Serbia before hugging the river Morava through a steep gorge and corkscrewing our way back out over some more hills, past the city of Čačak and through to Užice. It was single carriageway all the way, allowing me to reacquaint myself with just how terrifying overtaking is outside the safe confines of a simple switch of lanes on a British motorway.

Dušan and Milovan read the papers on the way down, acting as a personal *Reader's Digest* for me. There was no mention of any trouble at the Novi Pazar–Rad game despite our belief to the contrary. Goran phoned while we were en route to say that the police presence in Užice, some six hours before kick-off, was already huge, and that many of the police had been deployed to Novi Pazar to supervise the game against Rad, before heading north to look after Partizan once the Rad buses had been safely deposited into central Serbia. Perhaps the sheer volume of security personnel had curbed some of Rad's worse instincts.

The only report that even alluded to any banter, let alone anything more severe, said that Novi Pazar fans had taunted their right-wing visitors with a chant that the upcoming Gay Pride parade was 'the pride of Belgrade'. Pazar fans were unlikely to be pursuing a genuinely liberal agenda, but even in jest, theirs was the most positive comment about the annual Pride celebration so far this year, with government politicians queuing up to disassociate themselves from it while grimly admitting that they probably should try to prevent right-wing thugs from attacking the parade, as they had tried to in 2010. Some right-wing groups were making 'pro-family' public statements, while their members sprayed graffiti on walls across Belgrade threatening gays that they were coming to get them. There would be more of this to come, with possible spill over on to the terraces, as the parade, scheduled for early October, came closer.

Another story featured the head of Partizan's Užice fan club. Partizan fans might outnumber 'home' fans today, so he was an important local figure in the context of today's game. His most famous gesture had been a couple of years ago, when he had signed a legally-binding document committing his organs to FK Partizan in the event of his death. Quite what the club would do with the liver of an unfit fan wasn't quite evident, but when asked why he had made the gesture, he explained, 'The club has already taken all my nerves, so I thought I'd complete the set.' The one exception to this full-body donation was his penis, which apparently would be going to Red Star.

We got to Užice to find that our planned culinary assault wasn't going to be as easy as planned. Goran said that we wouldn't be able to get anything roasted, grilled or barbecued after three, so we should do that now, and get a lepinja en route to the stadium. Fine. But nowhere was open. After visiting three closed hostelries, one after a 'sure' tip from a friend, the faffing was starting to get a bit annoying, especially as my stomach had received clear promises of meat on arrival. After a couple more false starts, a place was found on the other side of town, and an order phoned ahead for two kilos of mešano meso [mixed barbecued meat] for the three of us eating. We nailed it. It was Milovan's birthday, after all. But the lepinja would have to wait until after the match as we didn't have time. Or space.

Goran handed out the tickets. We were in the east stand, theoretically on the halfway line, but in practice where we could find a space. 'So we're in among the home fans then?' I nervously ventured. In theory, yes, but Dušan was sure that we would be mostly surrounded by fellow Grobari in any case, and there wouldn't be any issues. As we had decided late to make the trip, all the Partizan tickets for the south stand had been snapped up, so this was our only option. The ticket cost 300 dinars (£2.60), so even if I did get beaten up, it wouldn't be an expensive shoeing.

On our way to the stadium we had already seen one of the Partizan fan groups, Opcija Dva [Option Two], being escorted by the police as they walked down Užice's main street. A safe distance away, the Sloboda fans began their own march into town. A hundred metres behind us, they sounded impressive, creating a wall of noise that rolled down the hill with them, drums accompanying a deep and constant array of chants. The acoustics had flattered them. As they arrived alongside us, the reality of 250 lads, mostly teenagers, was a lot less intimidating. They were flanked by about 50 policemen, all of whom were in full riot gear, minus shields.

I asked Dušan if the number of police was really necessary. As well as all the officers babysitting the fans' groups, there was a group of policemen on every street corner, and hundreds more ringing the stadium. Would there really be trouble had the streets not been flooded with police? 'For this game, yeah, probably. There's enough troublemakers between our travelling fans and the Freedom Fighters.' The Freedom Fighters are Sloboda's firm, not renowned for being among the most troublesome in the league but proud of being Užice's only group and preserving the unity of the town, meaning that they have more time to concentrate on fighting the enemy rather than among themselves.

Partizan's support was much more fractured. Their two main groups were going through a bad period in relations, and the 'civil war' had claimed some political victims before today's game, with the Opcija Dva group, who we had seen walking to the stadium, denied entry en masse and put straight back on buses to Belgrade by the police. Opcija Dva, mostly made up of teenagers and guys in their early 20s, were discovering the hard way that the dominant, and older, group, led by the 'Alcatraz' faction, were going to defend their position as the alpha males by fair means or foul. The allegation from Opcija Dva was that Alcatraz leaders, in conjunction with Partizan officials, had tipped off the police in advance and agreed with them that their rivals shouldn't be allowed entry.

This was the first game at the redeveloped Begluk Stadium, which had been refurbished, mostly at the expense of the Serbian FA, to bring it up to standard. When FK Sloboda (who were in the Serbian third division) merged with Sevojno Point (who had just been promoted from the second to the SuperLiga) to form Sloboda Point Sevojno in 2010, Sloboda provided the stadium and the catchment area – Užice being a much bigger town, while Sevojno had provided the registration, enabling the team to compete in the SuperLiga. But neither had a ground up to top-flight standards, so the team played last season's home games a few miles away, in Lučani.

A special edition of the respected daily newspaper *Danas* [Today] carried an eight-page special supplement heralding the new stadium, described with no irony on page one as the Užički Vembli [Užice's Wembley]. From the front, the stadium looked like a tidy enough English Championship League 1 ground, with a capacity of about 12–15,000 and freshly painted in red and black. Perhaps Užice's The Valley then, but smaller. As we walked round to the entrance for the east stand, the comparison with The Valley became grossly unfair on Charlton. The back wall of the stadium was unpainted and the mortar looked suspiciously fresh, and there were still steel rods poking from the concrete pillars that towered above the uncovered stand, possibly destined one day to hold a roof. 'Look at the other buildings here,' said Milovan, 'they're the same – if you don't finish building a house, you don't pay as much tax.' Maybe there was a stadium tax being evaded here.

The queue to get in the ground was huge, and there was only one entrance, for a stand supposed to hold 5,000. The crush to get in, as the minutes ticked by towards kick-off, was getting to the point where I was starting to wonder if this was really worth it. The surges were the kind that my Dad was used to on the terraces, but, for a post-Taylor Report boy, something I had only experienced during a foolish foray to the front of the crowd during a Foo Fighters gig ten years before.

Eventually we made it into the ground, before the queue was narrowed even further for a pat down. 'Baci upaljač!' [get rid of your lighter] said the security guard, guessing at the shape he had just felt in my shorts pocket. Having asked him to repeat what he had said (I was still struggling to understand people first time), I was able to explain. 'To nije upaljač. To je Blackberry.' We understood each other. We made it to our seats as the players came out of the tunnel, in the second row from the front and blinded by the bright sun shining over the top of the main west stand. Before the game had even started, my arm hurt from lifting my hand to shield my eyes. Only 90 minutes to go, though.

It became quickly apparent that Sloboda had a plan to win 1-0. 'You'd best get used to this,' said Dušan. 'This is how most away games go – the other team put ten men behind the ball and try and score on the counter.' I hadn't really focused on the football yet. I had been preoccupied by trying to work out just how many Partizan fans were in our section. The 50-50 split that Dušan had predicted seemed more like 80-20 in Sloboda's favour (or as Goran later explained, 80-20 in favour of Sloboda and local Red Star fans enjoying a day shouting abuse at Partizan). I noted this discovery to Dušan, who seemed surprised.

The first five minutes passed and we had not given away (other than quietly speaking English some of the time) that we were anything other than good Sloboda fans enjoying the game. Then a Sloboda player piled into the back of young Lazar Marković, making his first start for Partizan. Dušan, all 6ft 3in of him, sprang to his feet and bellowed 'Žuti mu daj', exhorting the referee to book the transgressor. Well that was my cover blown, anyway.

Ten minutes later, Sloboda produced their first meaningful attack, and their striker went down in the area under a clumsy but fair challenge from Rnić. The referee's failure to give a penalty was instantly seen as an example of big club bias and/or corrupt officials having been bought by Partizan. 'Lopovi, lopovi!' came the chants [Thieves, thieves!]. The mood around us darkened even further when right-back Aksentijević, like Marković only 17, thundered in a shot from 25 yards to give Partizan the lead. Tomić and Jovančić both missed chances to double the advantage as Partizan took control of the game despite the manager having picked a hybrid team with one eye on Thursday's second leg against Shamrock. Eduardo and Ilić were on the bench, Volkov had not returned at left-back from injury, and Babović had been given a start.

Sitting on the sidelines, the energy of both sets of ultras was impressive. Partizan had around 1,500 in their official travelling contingent (minus the 200 or so Opcija Dva, who were already en route back to Belgrade and forced to listen to the game on the radio). Despite their numerical inferiority, they were making themselves heard above the Freedom Fighters, who dominated the centre of the north stand behind the goal but didn't have the power or coordination to drown out the Grobari. The clarion call of the Fighters, with a refrain of 'Freedom' in English, 'Sloboda' in Serbian and 'Liberté' in French, was the chant that got the most noise out of the casual fans in the stands along the sides, but when combined with the English chorus, sounded a bit too much like a George Michael song from the 90s to be credible.

There is nothing as sure in football as hubris, delusions of grandeur or just plain gloating attracting their comeuppance. Dušan had just responded to some Sloboda fans' encouragement with a bold 'you can go home. We've come here, we've opened your stadium'. A minute later, the umpteenth Sloboda long ball forward found their striker Kasalica in the inside-right channel, he came together with Rnić, the ball broke kindly for him, and he slotted past Stojković to equalise. The crowd roared around us. Probably 85-15.

The second half followed the same pattern, but Partizan looked short of ideas, either trying to pass sideways for three minutes at a time or panicking and launching long balls from defence. Sloboda, meanwhile, were playing their own ballistic game, firing the ball forward to the ever-willing Kasalica, but without much in the way of laser guidance as the bulk of their efforts landed safely in the arms of Stojković or went into touch. Sloboda's first corner of the second half was met with a barrage of toilet rolls aimed at Stojković and the Partizan defence. One Freedom Fighter managed to score a direct hit on Ivanov who was standing on the penalty spot. That's Olympic discus length.

Partizan made a double change after an hour, with Tomić and Jovančić coming off for Ilić and Eduardo. Even with more of the 'A' team restored to the line-up, Partizan still looked shorn of inspiration, each player looking to the next to take the initiative rather than taking responsibility on their own. The exception was Babović, who had probably conferred too much responsibility on himself, insisting on taking three touches when one would do, and attempting crosses from impossible angles that were easy for Sloboda to block.

With ten minutes to go, perhaps sensing the need for Partizan to take the initiative to avoid inviting the same kind of trouble that had plagued the team in Genk and Dublin, Stanojević threw on Diarra for Marković, who had been Partizan's most threatening player despite his lack of experience. Diarra was a clear fans' favourite, welcomed with his own chant 'Diarra, Diarra, ubica cigana!' [Diarra, Diarra, gypsy killer]. Diarra hadn't killed any Roma people, but he did have an uncanny ability to score in derbies against Red Star. But Diarra had clearly not yet fully recovered from injury and, unlike against Novi Pazar, there wasn't quite the gulf in class to mask his own unpreparedness. He seemed off the pace of the game, and almost scared to commit to a challenge or a full-on sprint.

Partizan were tightening up, conscious that a draw in Užice was not a bad result, and conscious too that it was important to close out the last ten minutes of an away game for the first time since the second leg against Shkendia back in mid-July. Sloboda stuck to their game plan, and kept booting it clear and chasing when they could.

The referee allowed five minutes of injury time, which extended the period in the danger zone above Partizan's (so far this season) maximal level of concentration to a full quarter of an hour.

With the ball in the right-hand corner near the Sloboda goal line and the clock showing 91 minutes, Babović pursued an attempt to cross that was never going to work, and the ball broke to a Sloboda midfielder. He skipped past a tired challenge from a stretched Camara and fed Kasalica. Suddenly, it was two against three, and Kasalica, eyes glinting at the prospect that Sloboda might actually score from this chance, shrugged off the first of them. Forty yards from goal became 30 with no challenge, and 30 became 20. Ivanov and Rnić got confused by a dummy run from the other Sloboda attacker, which opened space for Kasalica. Both Partizan defenders went to shut him down on the edge of the area, and Rnić got there first, succeeding only in taking down Kasalica, whose momentum took him tumbling into the penalty area. The referee's arm pointed goalwards, but was he pointing to the spot or just for a free kick? He purposefully ran towards the edge of the area to signify a free kick rather than a penalty, attracting a cacophony of whistles from the home fans.

A minute later, midfielder Marić took a short run-up and curled the ball left-footed over the wall. I could tell it was on target as soon as it had cleared the wall, but it was neither pacy nor right in the corner. Stojković, however, remained motionless, and the ball cruised into the middle of the goal. There was a pause before the ball moved the net (it wasn't going that fast, either), and a dip in the noise level as the significance of what had just happened dawned on the crowd. They soon worked it out, and the noise level did not drop for the next three minutes, first a powerful cheer that morphed into a guttural exhortation to the referee to end the game as soon as possible, then an expectant roar as Sloboda nearly grabbed a third, into a collective whistle that accompanied the final minute as Partizan wandered in a trance around the pitch until the referee put them out of their misery to the unconfined delight of the home fans.

Dušan had already left the ground by this point, but I have a strong belief that you should stay in the stadium until the end, no matter how unpalatable the result or unacceptable the performance (even when I saw Arsenal lose 6-1 at Old Trafford, having been 5-1 down at half-time, and England lose 3-1 to Australia at Upton Park in a game so dire that Francis Jeffers was genuinely one of England's star performers). Nevertheless, I didn't stay long, more out of a desire to escape the crush rather than not having to listen to any crowing by the Sloboda fans.

The majority of the crowd dispersed happily, although Dušan and Milovan cut forlorn figures among the beaming locals. 'Not a good birthday present?' I offered Milovan. 'No' was his terse reply. I decided to let the grief die down before I spoke again. The official Partizan fans were kept back for half an hour on safety grounds, although as the comedian Bob Mills once pointed out, this could be construed as a chance for the home fans to go home to 'fetch sticks for fighting with'. While we sat in the restaurant, forced to wait nearly an hour before we could sample a lepinja, Goran came in to say that he had just seen a fight break out between two groups of Partizan fans, in which a Belgrade-based fan had landed a powerful headbutt on a local Grobar. Maybe all those police were justified after all.

By the time the lepinja arrived, I wasn't sure I was hungry any more. Those 750 grams of meat earlier might have had something to do with it, but I also felt a bit flat and without appetite after the defeat and the subsequent pall that had fallen over us. To go over the ingredients again, it's a freshly baked large bread roll with soft cheese and scrambled egg, doused in lamb dripping and returned to the oven. It smelled amazing. It looked, however, like a mashed brain in a bap. And it tasted like lamb fat in a fat sauce. In southern Georgia (the one in the Caucasus, not the one north of Florida), they have a dish called an Adjaruli Khachapuri, which is a similar buttery-cheesy-eggy baked cheese bread (minus the lamb fat), which I absolutely love. But this was too much for me. I ate about a quarter of it before giving up and braving the disapproving looks from around the table.

The journey back took a long time. I envy you, the reader, being able to skip over it in three paragraphs instead of the four hours I had at the wheel. We were stuck in traffic for most of the journey as Belgrade residents returned home from weekends away or from annual holidays in Montenegro (this being the shortest route in distance terms to the Montenegrin coast). I was kept entertained by the banter in the car, most of which revolved around impressions of the deeply nasal Užice (Oooozzhhhitse) and Čačak (Chaaaaachaak) accents and increasingly ludicrous stories of a legendary figure – part Partizan fan, part Danny Dyer wannabe, and part ghost of Chuck Norris called Tommy Johnson, whose online stories of rucks and outright insurgency against the police were generating their own mythology.

A vigorous post-mortem was conducted of today's game. Uroš, the youngest member of the travelling party, went straight for a conspiracy theory and complained of 'other forces', citing a couple of dodgy offside decisions and a perceived foul in the build-up to Sloboda's first goal. Dušan firmly corrected him. 'No, we lost because our strikers didn't get the ball. Babović touched the ball four times more than he needed and we wasted too much possession.' News that Red Star had completed a routine 2-0 win compounded the day's misery, but at least the two youngsters, Marković and Aksentijević, had played well, so it wasn't a mood of total futility.

Beating all others, the best story from Užice was a tale of the proud father of a successful footballer from the Užice area, who has gone on to much bigger and better things overseas. The father had developed a habit recently of getting blind drunk in his local, then going into another bar, revealing his member and announcing to drinkers, 'This is the c**k that made this very successful footballer.' Apparently, the first time he had done this, it had been found quite amusing, but the joke was wearing thin now half the city had seen his c**k. 'Bar da nije bila njegova majka' [At least it wasn't his mum though], I ventured, to an actual round of applause in the car. We might have lost, but I had broken through the banter barrier.

League table after the second round:
  1. Rad 6 (+6)
  2. Hajduk 6 (+4)
  3. Smederevo 6 (+2)
  7. Partizan 3 (+4)
10. Red Star 3 (0)

Your Mum's Peasant C***

WHEN I arrived in Serbia, I didn't know how to swear. I knew what the verb 'to swear' was, but all the actual rude words were beyond me. Working in the student centre taught me a bit. But I was still wrestling with the language, and so while I could tell what was swearing and what wasn't, the phrases themselves were still elusive – I didn't know my arse from my bell-end. And I certainly couldn't use any of the words properly myself. Partizan filled in those gaps.

I made a couple of pretty crass beginners' errors before the match against Shamrock that made me swear (in English). Firstly, I decided to walk to the ground, despite having moved house and not really knowing the new way. I knew the general direction, but had forgotten that there's a fairly major motorway junction between my house and the side of the city where Partizan and Red Star's grounds are. There was an underpass under the first road, but nothing to help me cross the second. The only route was across a patch of scrubby land directly underneath the raised motorway. In the half light of dusk – replete with graffiti, rust streaks on the concrete, and a noticeable whiff of urine – it looked like the ideal place to get mugged or raped. Or both. I discovered a turn of pace not seen since the 1990s in dashing across the patch of land and sneaking between two buildings to rejoin the world of pavements, houses and a less pronounced fear of immediate and non-consensual penetration.

My second mistake was to forget what competition that night's match was in. As I walked up the hill to the ground, I could already hear the crowd in full voice. That was pretty impressive considering there were still 15 minutes to kick-off. Unless, of course, there

76

weren't. Europa League kick-offs aren't dictated in the same way that Champions League ones are, so my assumption of 20:45 had been proved sadly wrong. Making my second dash of the night, I managed to make my seat with only nine minutes on the clock and no goals scored. But the crowd was buoyant, delighting in Red Star's 6-1 defeat to Rennes earlier in the night, leaving Partizan as Serbia's only representative in Europe.

Partizan were defending the Jug in the first half. First-choice goalkeeper Stojković had a slight knock, so regular sub Radiša Ilić was between the sticks. For a permanent substitute, he was being serenaded with unusual warmth and vigour as 20,000 people were belting out a chorus of 'Ti si prvi golman Radiša!' [You're first-choice keeper, Radiša] to the tune of John Brown's 'Body' – and if that doesn't ring any bells, it's the same tune Arsenal and Chelsea use when they sing about Tottenham Hotspur going to Rome to see the Pope. How come such a rapturous reception? Not because Ilić is really that great a keeper – Dušan and the other guys around me quickly confirmed that. Which brings us to our first swearing definition:

Sranje [crap/shit], as in, 'Da li je Ilić dobar golman?' 'Ne, sranje je.' [Is Ilić a good keeper? No, he's sh**]. Completely transferable from the English, used both adjectivally as above, but also as a noun.

No. The praise of Ilić was more of a protest against real first-choice keeper Stojković. Not a protest against his ability, but more against his past. Stojković started his career at, and then went back later to, Red Star, which makes him unpalatable in the eyes of many Grobari. Unfortunately for Stojković, having moved to Partizan makes him persona non grata at the Marakana too. He needs 24-hour close protection, and has minders behind his goal at all games. If this sounds a bit excessive, in the build-up to the Italy v Serbia European Championship qualifier in Genoa in October 2010 (the one which had to be called off because of crowd violence in the Serbia end, which itself was partly provoked by Partizan–Red Star arguments around Stojković), he was struck by a flare thrown by Red Star fans at the team bus. Italy coach Cesare Prandelli found Stojković trembling in the home team's dressing room when they arrived.

Having deposed Ilić as Partizan's first-choice keeper in 2010, played well for most of the season, and won the league and cup with them (including a 1-0 win away at Red Star), you could be forgiven for thinking that he might have won the Partizan fans over. Stojković even revealed a t-shirt after the away win at Red Star begging forgiveness from Partizan fans for 'his ugly past'. But no, it wasn't enough. I asked Dušan why he was still so disliked. 'Well, he's a Red Star *pička*. And that t-shirt didn't convince anyone.'

Pička (c***) – again easily translated from English. This is the crudest word in Serbian as it is in English, used both literally and figuratively. *Pička ciganska* (gypsy c***) is the strongest football-related insult that a Partizan fan can offer. Firstly, you're a c***. And secondly, your conduct reminds me, the offerer of this criticism, of Red Star Belgrade. I literally could not hate you more.

Partizan were on top, but failing to make their pressure count. The midfielders in particular were guilty of going for a killer one-touch through-ball instead of retaining possession. Tomić, maybe for the third time in five minutes, was guilty of wasting the ball. Dušan had had enough, and rose menacingly, yelling at the midfielder:

'Pička ti materina seljačka' [Your mum's peasant c***]. The final adjective seljačka can also be substituted here for another semi-offensive word of choice, such as nepismena [illiterate] or nenormalna [abnormal]. It doesn't get much worse than this. A couple of fans behind told Dušan to lay off. They weren't offended by the language – I had heard the same thing a hundred times already in the match – but they just liked Tomić.

After half an hour, Partizan had their best chance yet. Full-back Volkov got on the end of Eduardo's flick-on and shot towards the corner, only for Shamrock keeper Thompson to pull off a great save. Around the ground, 20,000 people said the same thing at once, 'Jebote!' [For f***'s sake!]. Also 'f*** you!' if aimed correctly and used as a simple retort – it's derived from the verb 'to f***', but in this sense doesn't have a literal and carnal meaning (more on that later). Used much more freely in Serbian than in English – people who outwardly appear quite respectable, including old ladies, say it on the bus to each other if they need to reflect severe exasperation.

We didn't have to wait long though for a goal. Volkov, neither especially tall nor having proved himself to be a major aerial threat, popped up in the penalty area to head in Tomić's corner. Big noise. No swearing. Just a massive cheer. No one seemed to mind that Partizan's forwards were misfiring if the full-backs were going to be this prolific. Partizan settled and played out the rest of the half in comfort, passing the ball around like a team that actually knew what it was doing. The crowd were basking in the expectation of going through to the main stage of the Europa League. But a second goal wouldn't come. When Vukić narrowly missed just before half-time, Goran said just one word, 'Artmedia.'

What did that miss by Vukić have to do with the team from Slovakia? Artmedia was one of the games on the Love Partizan, Hate Yourself t-shirt, a classic example of Partizan snatching defeat from the jaws of victory. Against a competent but limited Artmedia side, who had surprised everyone by dumping Celtic out in the previous round, Partizan had drawn 0-0 away in the final round of qualifying for the Champions League, and then dominated the second leg, creating chance after chance. But not scoring, instead hitting the post, forcing a number of saves from the keeper, and missing narrowly time after time.

In the 85th minute, the Artmedia keeper finally made a mistake, only for Partizan's striker Nikola Grubjesić to hit the bar with the goal gaping. Partizan kept up the pressure in extra time, but to no avail. Then they were 3-3 in a shoot-out with Cameroonian striker Pierre Boya stepping up to take the decisive penalty. Artmedia keeper Cobej tipped Boya's spot kick on to the post, Artmedia scored their next effort and Partizan missed and were out. Cobej would be diagnosed with a brain tumour a couple of months later after helping Artmedia beat holders Porto in the group stage, but made a full recovery and regained his first-team place the following season.

Partizan dominated after half-time too and went close a couple more times. 'Definitely Artmedia.' Coach Stanojević seemed confident enough though to take off the (reasonably busy) Vukić and bring on Babović. Babović's first action was to ignore a pass guilty of not landing precisely on his toe, leading to howls of displeasure all around me. 'Boli ga kurac!' shouted Dušan, to everyone in his vicinity.

Kurac [dick]. A sensationally versatile word. Can, and does, mean the male sexual organ. In Dušan's outburst, boli ga kurac, literally 'his d**k hurts' means he doesn't care. Svirati kurcu, [to play (musically) the d**k] means to talk nonsense. Then there's koji ti je kurac [which d**k is yours?] – 'what's the matter with you?' Ići na kurac [going to (my) d**k] or popeti se na kurac [climbing up (my) d**k] means 'to annoy'. Ode sve u kurac [everything's going to the d**k] is like the English 'going to sh**'. Daću ti kurac [I'll give you the d**k] signifies that actually I won't give you anything. Do kurca [To the d**k!] means 'go to hell!' or 'damn it!' Puši kurac [smoke a d**k] can be semi-literal – an imperative to fellate, but is more synonymous with 'f*** you!' There are many more. In a later game, Dušan would call Šćepović 'Gospodin Kurobolja' [Mr D**kache], another way of calling him lazy. What a great word.

A minute later, Shamrock had equalised. And what a goal. Full-back Sullivan volleyed in from 30 yards out, timing it to absolute perfection, the ball never going more than six feet in the air and not bouncing before it hit the net. From where we were sitting, right behind Sullivan, it was an amazing strike, simply incredible technique. On TV, it's even better. Never has a full-back who wasn't Brazilian connected so sweetly with a ball. Not even Lee Dixon. So it was 1-1, and 2-2 on aggregate – the only way the tie could end with penalties tonight. It was probably only Shamrock's third shot all night. 'Like I said, Artmedia,' repeated Goran.

Still Partizan came forward though. Jovančić went clean through and fluffed a one-on-one, then Babović missed a good chance with 20 minutes of normal time left to play. As the frustration had built since Shamrock's goal, the old guy next to me had gone from looking disapprovingly every time someone near him swore, etching frown lines ever deeper into his forehead, to muttering his own oaths. At this point though, even he lost it and joined in the coarse chorus. 'Jebem ti sestru, Baboviću, bre!' [I f*** your sister, Babović!]

Jebati – to f***. Used in the literal sense pretty interchangeably with English. But as an individual insult, a personal f***ing of the recipient's female relatives can be used for an even stronger feeling than a standard English 'f*** you' or 'f*** your mum'. Or, in contemporary youth English, just 'your mum'. Also used fairly liberally with a pronoun, 'jebi ga', to mean 'f*** it', either dismissively in everyday language (I heard quite a few pensioners use it at the market) or more aggressively to refer to a more specific 'it'.

Partizan were increasingly wasteful in possession and looking short of ideas. But Shamrock had put in a magnificent effort and were visibly tiring. Dušan, in between invitations to Partizan players to have their female relatives impregnated, summarised it: 'This lot are a pub team. A pub team!' In the last ten minutes, Partizan went close two or three more times. Goran said no other word during this period than 'Artmedia'.

In extra time, Partizan were worse than ever for wastefulness, despite having almost all the possession against a now frankly knackered Shamrock. In attack, 17-year-old substitute Marković's industry and creativity were putting all of his more experienced team-mates to shame. In defence, Volkov was still making runs and looking committed (he came closest to scoring, sliding in but seeing his effort saved). But that was it. The old guy and his son to my left had stopped saying anything other than swear words. The son, after yet another errant Partizan pass, managed a sentence that consisted only of f***, in its various forms. Babović came in for another blast, this time from the people in front of me after playing a simple pass straight into touch:

Jebeni peder (f***ing queer). Homophobia, to be honest, is pretty rife in Serbia. Peder is a strong word, worse even than expressions unacceptable in English like 'poof'. There's something sinister about it, both in the way it's used to imply that the subject is 'not normal', and also in the aggression with which it's deployed – to call someone that in Serbian means malice aforethought, or that the swearer is genuinely accusing the recipient of being homosexual. This is something which in Serbia is a bigger deal than it is in the UK, where fortunately we have got to the point where not many people actually care, and most people support equal rights.

Peder is a word you don't use lightly. I saw this too outside of football, when a colleague of mine from another embassy, in conversation over lunch, said in Serbian that one of the reasons that he didn't go to football matches in Belgrade was because he was a jebeni peder, and so wasn't welcome. Someone didn't quite hear him properly and asked him to repeat it. And he said again, more clearly 'Ja sam jebeni peder' [I'm a f***ing queer]. He seemed oblivious to the fact that the whole restaurant was now looking at him, some baffled, but some openly finding what he was saying unpalatable. You don't drop the peder-bomb in Serbia unless you're really angry. Babović's pass was pretty lazy, but it didn't merit anything quite so hateful.

It wasn't just the guys next to me who were churning out the expletives. The whole crowd was turning against Partizan as they could see the match, which palpably should have been all over by now, slipping towards the lottery of a penalty shoot-out. Even the usually ultra-loyal Jug had lost the rhythm of its chanting and was watching and worrying like everyone else. The rest of the ground was no longer supporting the team, more holding them to account. Every player's parenthood was doubted if he misplaced a pass, his fertility mocked if he held on to the ball too long, and his sister's virginity threatened with every pace below full sprinting speed.

Then it happened. Shamrock defended another low-imagination Partizan attack and launched the ball upfield down the left-hand channel. Rnić misjudged the flight of the ball and ran too directly towards it, realising his mistake only as it sailed over his head.

Shamrock's striker Ciaran Kilduff, who had only come on in extra time, but had been ploughing a lonely furrow with limited support for most of his short time on the pitch, saw his chance. Allowing the ball to bounce, he struck a good shot first time, which Ilić couldn't hold (he should really have just tipped it over) and parried into the path of Kilduff's strike partner Sheppard, also on as a sub. As Sheppard controlled the ball, the next seconds played out in slow motion, as a panicked Ilić hauled himself up from the first save and realised the danger. Desperate to make up for the first error, he hurled himself at the feet of Sheppard, whose feet were quick enough to move the ball away and allow Ilić to take him out. Penalty.

The Partizan crowd did its best to salvage something from the situation. Ilić's morale was boosted with a hearty burst of 'ti si prvi golman Radiša', but given the howler he had just made, not everyone can have been truly sincere. As Shamrock's Stephen O'Donnell, their third substitute, prepared to take the penalty, the stadium booed as one. It wasn't as intimidating as the threat of ethnic violence against Shkendia's penalty taker but it was probably louder, and the stakes were much higher: if O'Donnell scored, Partizan would need two goals in eight minutes to avoid going out on the away goals rule. O'Donnell kept his nerve and put it away. Directly opposite from us, Shamrock's 50 or so travelling fans, hemmed in beneath the executive boxes by a thin luminous line of stewards in the Zapad, managed to make their cheers heard among the stunned silence of 20,000 Grobari.

Then came the anger. Seats were being smashed around me. The crowd, having exhausted its anger on the players, turned on the management. 'Uprava napolje!', the same chant I had heard in Novi Sad when the fancied Serbian side had lost to similarly unfancied

European opposition, swelled in the throats of the thousands around me in the Istok. As one of Dušan's mates put it, the board stealing from the club was one thing if the team was successful, but the team had been asset-stripped to the point where it couldn't even beat a team ranked so far beneath them. The chanting got more specific as the crowd in the Istok called for the chairman to go, 'Đuriću, odlazi!'

Parts of the Jug joined in. Parts of the Jug didn't. Parts of the Jug chanted for manager Stanojević to be sacked. Parts of the Jug fought other parts of the Jug. Mostly it was, as football commentators say, just handbags. In a tightly-packed crowd like the Jug, it was hard to tell sometimes what was just natural swaying of a standing crowd – how I remember the Kop from TV when I was a kid – and what was a new front being opened for rucking among the fans. But there were definitely two or three distinct fights going on, while the rest of the stadium signalled its collective disapproval and booed those Grobari who were fighting their brethren.

The turmoil in the stands transmitted itself to the pitch. Partizan's spirit had wandered off into the night, and their brains were following it out of the door. Medo's composure deserted him. He committed a series of rash fouls before a five-second combination of elbowing one player, then wrestling another and stamping on his shoulder got him a red card. Crestfallen, the team didn't produce a single shot in the last five minutes, and limped out of the competition. At the final whistle, while the Irish players jumped up and down and saluted their few dozen fans, the Partizan fans let their team know what they thought of them with the final word in our swear guide.

Pičkice [pussies]. Literally, 'little c***s', this expression is used to convey a belief that the recipients of the insult have no bravery.

The chant grew and grew, until it seemed like the whole stadium had finally found something to agree on. As the Partizan team drifted off the pitch, dazed like road accident victims, the pussy chorus reached a crescendo. Manager Stanojević reached the start of the tunnel and a few hotheads in the Jug called for him to go. The rest of the south-east corner responded with vitriol for the board of directors, and more fights broke out in the Jug. This time, the 'leaders' had decided enough was enough, and sent some heavies round from their central headquarters to suppress the dissent. It worked, just.

Still on the pitch celebrating, the Shamrock players and staff seemed oblivious to the acrimony that had accompanied the Partizan players off the field. When they finally decided to head to the changing rooms, the 15,000 Partizan fans who had remained to watch or participate in the internal feuding in the Jug stopped rowing long enough to applaud Shamrock off surprisingly warmly, with an ovation that lasted a good two minutes.

Dušan, who had gone pale in what couldn't have been far off clinical shock, wasn't one of them. Despite the anger towards their own team, the fans had still recognised the magnitude of Shamrock's achievements. This was a big deal for a club side from Ireland – to come to a famous footballing city and beat one of its big names. It was one of the most sporting gestures I've seen from a crowd, and a much more heart-warming end to the night than had seemed possible three minutes before. I noted the contrast between that and the scalding abuse I got once for applauding Manchester United off the field at the Emirates after they had destroyed us in a Champions League knockout game. Shamrock's players, lapping it up, were stood in exactly the same place where the Partizan players usually receive and give their own post-match ovations. The irony was probably lost on them.

Another game could be added to the list for next year's 'Love Partizan, Hate Yourself' t-shirts. Right next to Artmedia. Serbia's participation in all forms of European football was over for the season. It was still August. We would all be 'concentrating on the league'.

Serbia's media gave the double exit of Partizan and Red Star the full Spanish Inquisition the next day. 'Shame of Serbia', 'Serbia Out Of Europe', 'Horror at the Humska'. Serbian tabloid headlines aren't any better than British ones ... but buried among the shock and horror, there were some cleverer analytical comments. One paper questioned the business model of Serbian football: the big clubs (essentially just Partizan and Red Star) gathered up the best talent in Serbia and a bunch of foreign misfits and outside bets, only to sell them to 'proper' European clubs as soon as they showed any real promise, maybe to buy them back later after they'd had their day, or their western European adventure had failed to deliver. Meanwhile, the little clubs were mostly unable to compete with the financial clout of the big two, but too often were being used as vanity projects or fronts for dubious business practices by 'businessmen'.

A journalist from the quality daily *Danas* had texted Dušan. 'Sometimes I wish I was a normal woman and didn't care about football, and could forget about what I saw in the stadium last night.' She and her colleagues had also written some interesting stuff about the game, or, to be more precise, about the fighting that had accompanied the last five minutes. As they put it, most of the crowd had been calling for Đurić's head. Those fans, who had argued that the blame should be apportioned to Stanojević, and had defended Đurić by lashing out at those around them, were 'in the pay of the club'. No attempt to dress that up, they just came straight out with it. I would have been content to put it down to a difference of opinion between fans, but no story in Serbia is complete without a conspiracy theory. The story naturally sounded better if vested interests were behind something as banal as a fight at a football stadium.

At work the next day, Dušan wasn't himself. He is a talented and hard-working colleague, but he wasn't on form. We were all busy at that time, so I wanted to make sure that his workload wasn't too ridiculous. I needn't have worried. 'No, I'm fine, it's just I'm still in shock from last night. I can't believe it all.' I made a note to check our human resources guidelines to see if football-induced illness was a valid reason for taking time off work, in case Dušan's condition worsened.

As it was, he got back to his normal self as the day progressed. Partizan, on the other hand, was just about to experience a nasty bout of internal sickness, which had its immediate roots in the previous night's dose of Shamrockitis Extratimensis.

Management Out!

THE day before the return game with Shamrock, the Serbian FA Disciplinary Committee announced Partizan's punishment for the crowd trouble against Novi Pazar. It was a fine of a few hundred thousand dinars, with no stadium ban. All the fury and rhetoric from the message boards was forgotten, although Partizan would be playing under a warning that a repeat of the same behaviour would lead to a stiffer penalty. Given that I had been made to feel uncomfortable by some of the chanting in all three home matches so far, it wasn't inconceivable that the harsher penalty would be invoked later in the year.

Anyway, Partizan fans would now be able to go to the first of many Belgrade derbies, against OFK Belgrade, from the Karaburma suburb in north-east Belgrade. Known as the 'Romantics', the club got their nickname from playing the most beautiful football in the Yugoslav league in the 1950s and 1960s. These days, the term seemed to be mocking, given that the team's fans have a tendency to hark back to the team's 'golden era' of 1953–1973, since when, apart from a couple of mildly interesting UEFA Cup runs, they haven't achieved much at all.

OFK, the week after the game, would celebrate their 100th anniversary as a club, although this was slightly tenuous. OFK view themselves as the successor club to the now-defunct BSK Belgrade (not to be confused with BSK Borča, another team in the top flight, nor BASK Belgrade – whose place in the SuperLiga had been taken by Novi Pazar).

The only slight flaw in the OFK succession theory is that there was a season in the 1950s when both BSK and OFK existed, and indeed played against each other, before OFK absorbed BSK. But no one was going to let a minor historical error get in the way of a bit of ceremony.

When I looked at the calendar for the season, this was one of the games that I had been concerned about not being able to make, as Claire was due to visit. Obviously I was looking forward to her being in Serbia, but I didn't want my attendance record being spoiled so early in the season. Tentatively, the idea of us both going to a Partizan game was inserted into our weekend plans as a touristic-cultural experience and, when it wasn't immediately rejected, I just kept repeating that we would go until it was an accepted part of the agenda. This makes it sound more like subterfuge than it actually was. It was a good chance for her to see what I actually got up to in Serbia rather than hearing about it over Skype, and to meet some of my new mates. And Claire doesn't mind football, having been dragged along to see Bradford City plenty of times when she was younger, and was then persuaded to come to the Emirates with me a couple of times too, where she has a 100 per cent winning record and Nicklas Bendtner has scored in every game she has seen. Not many people can say that.

We got to the ground quite early to buy a ticket (400 dinars/£3.50). Instead of repeating my directionless ramble from the flat to the stadium via the scary alley underneath the motorway, we took a taxi. Claire wouldn't have liked that alley. We were there a bit too early in fact. I had expected queues, but there were only three people ahead of me. It seemed eerily quiet even for 30 minutes before kick-off. Dušan had warned on Friday that the atmosphere might be somewhere between muted and tense, with the wounds of the midweek humiliation against Shamrock still raw, and the divisions among the fan groups that defeat had exposed.

He was half right. Six hours before the start of the game, club chairman Dragan Đurić took the extraordinary step of holding a press conference to address the protests against him on Thursday. In a bold move, he criticised the fans' reactions to the defeat against Shamrock. 'It hurts me that our fans have so little tact and patience that they have sought the resignation of the board. This isn't really about real fans, rather some little groups. Red Star fans have only enjoyed one cup success in four years and they don't chant about their management in a negative way,' said Đurić.

If praising Partizan's most hated rivals wasn't enough, he went on to say, 'We're not going to allow that overnight we destroy everything we've achieved in the last four years. I won't put up with posers and dozy types. Many people have been lulled to sleep by our successes in the previous period, but they have to wake up. If they don't, I'll wake them up.'

He went on to defend the club's preparations for the season, notably on transfers, or the perceived lack of inward ones, which he claimed had been agreed with 'the sporting part of the club' (Stanojević and his right-hand man Krstajić), and which he added had not had an effect on the defeat to Shamrock or other poor performances.

Unprompted, he had also given a detailed analysis on the club's finances, about how the club had reduced its debt and turned an operating profit in 2010, and claiming fixed non-wage costs for the club of approximately €800,000–900,000 a month, which had accounted for most of the money earned by the Champions League run.

For most people on the message boards, Đurić was unconvincing. It begged a couple of questions: for those inclined to conspiracy theories and the belief that the management were siphoning off club resources for personal use, did these costs really add up? And did the chairman protest too much? No one had asked him to provide a breakdown of the accounts. Why now? For those prepared to accept these figures at face value, what did it mean for a club which had failed to qualify for the Champions League (worth approximately €9m the previous season) in terms of this year – more debt or more player sales? Or both?

Later, the club management denied entry to the ground to some 500 fans attempting to enter the Jug, the majority of whom were known to be 'dissidents' who had chanted against Đurić during the last game. The police, despite the absence of a law in Serbia banning supporters from stadia on non-hooliganism grounds, assisted the club in preventing their entry by forming a cordon around them. Individuals found guilty of football-related violence can be subject to the equivalent of banning orders, but most if not all of these fans were not officially designated as such. Dušan and Igor were later told by friends of theirs that club 'spotters' had been employed at the entrance to direct the police to those fans deemed undesirable.

If my experience from Užice was anything to go by, the 'dissidents' had probably not helped themselves much by turning up in a fully-formed unit of 500. They should have tried sneaking in in ones and twos like large male groups have to in order to get into nightclubs in cities around the UK. But for them, the principles of freedom of entry and 'face' not being lost were more important than whether the fans concerned got to see the game. If they weren't all allowed in, then none of the members would attend. All for one and one for all.

Mercifully, the stand-off outside the ground did not escalate into anything worse. The group decided to launch a protest against their exclusion from the ground by walking into the city centre and gathering in Republic Square, where they chanted 'Uprava Napolje' under the police's watchful eye. No doubt they spoiled the early evening atmosphere in one of Belgrade's most concentrated café and restaurant areas, but there was no violence.

The exclusion of such a large group of fans appeared to have had a 'chilling' effect on others. While none declared that they would boycott the game in solidarity, many fans with friends in the banned group decided not to come for fear of being denied entry, and other more casual fans stayed away, fearing that the tension could lead to a confrontation. The club's officials might have thought that by suppressing the dissent, they would make the stadium a more pleasant place, and more homogenous in its support for the team. But my experience of other political disputes, censorship and other authoritarian tendencies is that not allowing a vent for criticism usually makes the situation worse.

Claire and I were driving back to Belgrade from Novi Sad while all these events had been playing out, so the unspoken menace and latent tension around the ground came as a surprise to me as we walked round the outside of the stadium towards our seats. I had chosen to sit in a part of the Istok a bit further away from the Jug than normal, as a planned concession to assuage Claire's fears about the behaviour of the hardcore. We met Dušan, who had arrived at the stadium much earlier than usual in fear that he too might be caught in a sweep of 'dissidents' if he had timed his arrival badly. Igor was there too, fearful of disturbances in the Jug. He was sure in the logic of his decision, but he looked utterly forlorn at the prospect of having to sit down during the match.

All the pre-match talk, no matter how I tried to turn it back to Partizan, was about Arsenal's 8-2 mauling at the hands of Manchester United, which had finished about an hour previously. The dissection of Arsenal's implosion was mercifully interrupted by the stadium announcer listing the Partizan team. Stanojević, under immense pressure to deliver a win in this match to revive the season, made several changes. Stojković was back in goal, both youngsters Aksentijević and Marković started, as did party boy Smiljanić, in place of Ilić. Šćepović started up front instead of Jovančić. Babović would be captain. A whispered 'O Bože' [for God's sake] swirled round the stadium like blasphemy in a library.

My hopes that Claire would enjoy the game in its own right were quickly dashed. OFK had come with the exact same 4-5-1 formation and defensive mindset that Sloboda had deployed so effectively against Partizan. They too were content to wait for an inevitable Partizan mistake and then launch their own counter-attacks, playing even longer balls than Sloboda. Mind-numbing stuff, and it came as no real surprise when Claire let out an audible yawn after only 14 minutes. With such a terrible game being played out in front of us, Claire asked a few newcomers' questions, to keep herself awake more than anything else. I was quite pleased to realise that I knew the answer to about half of them, but we had to rely on Igor for some answers. I was especially grateful for this, as it was a chance for me to do some surreptitious research, without admitting to Igor that maybe I hadn't got up to speed with the Partizan basics.

The most interesting discussion was about the players' wages. Tomić, arguably (unless you were Dušan) the best player so far this season, was only on about 2,000 euros per month. This was five times the wage of the average Belgrader, but not an astronomical sum, and less than my monthly salary – the first time I've ever even countenanced the thought that a civil servant could earn more than a professional footballer. Babović's salary details had been in the press recently and, at 10,000 euros a month, he was among the middle earners, with some additional freebies and endorsements contributing to a wage that put him among Belgrade's elite. Eduardo was on the biggest salary at the club, taking advantage of Serbian league rules that allow one 'marquee' player to earn more than the salary cap. But even his 50,000 euros a month paled into insignificance compared to what even middle-ranking players at Arsenal were earning (pretty much the same amount, but weekly).

The first rumbles of discord among the fans surfaced before 20 minutes were up, when about half the fans in the Istok responded to the Jug's 'Ajmo crno-beli' [Come on the black-and-whites] with 'Uprava napolje' instead of repeating the exhortation of support.

Finally, there was something to interest Claire, who was excited by the anti-Establishment zeal shown by those around us, and already showing a level of cynicism equal with a much more seasoned Partizan fan. 'Well, they won't be allowed in next week, will they?' She had worked this out quite quickly.

The fans in the Jug, though low on numbers and sounding less convinced of their love for the club than usual, had been resolute in their support despite the dire Partizan performance. But the Istok was already restless. Some fans sounded desperate but hopeful, like the guy five rows behind me, who appealed for five penalties in the first half alone, but others were contributing to a grasshopper chorus of tutting, like the one that made watching Arsenal in my part of the stadium the previous season such a dispiriting experience at times.

Partizan's lack of imagination in midfield and attack, and constant sideways or backwards passing, meant that the dissatisfaction became increasingly sonorous as the half wore on. After maybe the seventh or eighth attack foundered on this dearth of creativity, one fan announced that he was going home. Another urged the players, every time they got to the edge of the opposition area, to 'vrati golmanu' [pass back to the keeper] so as to avoid inevitably giving it away again.

One man in front of us had clearly decided that the game was going to be so bad that he needed to comfort-eat his way through it. He brought a carrier bag full of McDonald's cheeseburgers into the ground (I didn't know McDonald's did bags that big) and proceeded to chain eat them, at times holding one in each hand to maximise his capacity to consume. It says a lot for the first half that this was easily the most entertaining thing we saw in the 45 minutes.

Half-time, with the score 0-0, was met by a chorus of booing, whistling and 'Uprava napolje' from the Istok, but encouraging applause from the Jug. I wondered how long the Jug could keep from wavering in their support if the score remained the same, but they started the second half in good voice, maybe encouraged by the attacking substitution made by Stanojević to bring on Eduardo. I asked Dušan if he thought Eduardo was carrying an injury. 'No, he's just knackered. He's played a full season already.' 'He's definitely carrying a knock,' I said, 'he's not running properly or striking the ball very well.'

The energy and variety of the singing in the Jug started to tail off quite quickly, so much so that after three minutes of repeating one song in an almost dreary tone, Claire wondered out loud if the guy with the loudhailer had gone for a wee. Two minutes later, with the song still in full monotonous swing, she upgraded this to a poo.

Before the conversation could get any more scatological, the OFK fans let off a couple of firecrackers and launched into a heavily choreographed (by two 'conductors' in the front of their section) routine of flag-waving and banner-unveiling. In a much smaller arena, it might have been visually impressive. With only 200 members of the 'Blue Union' present in the 32,000 capacity Stadion Partizan, it looked a bit pathetic. Their message was quite acutely observed, given Partizan's recent run of bad form – the main banner displayed by the OFK fans read 'fudbalski je bio hram' [it used to be a footballing temple] alongside smaller banners marking the years 1929 and 1944. The period between these two dates was when OFK, in the guise of their predecessor club BSK Belgrade, had played on the site of today's Stadion Partizan, before they were turfed off immediately after the Second World War, the stadium was renamed the JNA Stadium and Partizan took over as tenants, their fans soon referring to the ground as the temple of football. OFK made a good point, but it also reflected badly on the fact that they had done virtually nothing since the 1960s.

The Jug had clearly been given a message to demonstrate its restlessness either more constructively or ambivalently, and was lustily singing its song about loving Partizan but hating themselves when Eduardo received the ball from Tomić on the edge of the area, turned swiftly and shot hard left-footed, slightly to the left of the goalkeeper. The keeper's parry was weak and rebounded straight to Marković, six yards out. From my angle, all Marković had to do was tap the goal into the empty half of the net, nearest to him. In the fraction of a second since Eduardo had shot, the level of expectation had risen palpably. Bums had left seats in the Istok, voices had risen in the Jug, and I guess a couple of ice creams had been dropped in the Zapad, as prawn sandwiches aren't common in Serbia.

This was the chance to lift the gloom and restart the season. Instead, Marković controlled the ball while his marker tried to recover the yard he had lost as Eduardo had turned and shot. He seemed to be suffering from the same lack of conviction as the rest of the team, briefly looking up to see if a pass was on before taking another touch. The rising voices from the Jug had tailed off, and from the Istok complaints were forming in throats about the team's refusal to shoot. The peaks and troughs of these competing sound waves were almost cancelling each other out, creating an expectant silence, for when Marković finally shot and the net billowed, the resulting cheer seemed much louder than it should have been for a crowd of only 7,000.

I felt the relief of the goal flood through me, the first time that I had really had the same feeling from a Partizan goal as I'd had from Arsenal or England in the past. But in my part of the stadium, I was in a minority. The ball had barely fallen to the ground when the most concerted chant yet of 'uprava napolje' rose all around me in the Istok. Claire, revelling in a socially-acceptable chance to act the provocateur, joined in. The dissonance in views between the Jug and Istok fans continued for the rest of the match, a fact noted by all the papers on Monday. Partizan probably needed another goal to secure the match, and then everyone would forget about the divisions. I was tempted to say something further about Eduardo's fitness, given that three times in five games I had said something disparaging about him and he had immediately provided the assist for a goal.

Diarra came on for his regular cameo, this time for fully 15 minutes, with OFK offering little threat even to this Partizan team who had been consistently atrocious after the 80th minute of every game. Diarra looked sharper than against Sloboda, and although his first shot was straight at the keeper, it was warmly applauded by the crowd, from all parts of the ground. At least there was something everyone could agree on. With seven minutes left, Smiljanić played a good through-ball, putting Diarra in the clear. Diarra surged into the box, lifted his leg back extravagantly in a dummy, forcing the keeper to make his move early, before accelerating past his prostrate form and slamming the ball into the open goal.

Surely this would heal the wounds around the club? Not at all. While the Jug saluted the completion of Diarra's comeback with their traditional Roma murdering serenade, the Istok was urging regime change again, if anything louder than before. The same contrast was repeated deep into injury time when Diarra arched his back in a footballing Fosbury flop to loop in an excellent header with the ball behind him to complete a 3-0 win and demonstrate his own readiness to play a bigger role in Partizan's season. While the players, clearly delighted for Diarra, mobbed the goalscorer, and the Jug roared its approval, many fans in the Istok were getting into position near the players' tunnel entrance to achieve maximum impact for their anti-Đurić, pro-Stanojević chanting. Stanojević, as he walked off the pitch looking nothing like a man who had just won 3-0, gave a cursory wave as the players performed their traditional victory salute in front of the Jug, but applauded the couple of hundred fans in the Istok who sang 'Stanoje, ostani!' [Stay, Stanoje!] as he approached the tunnel.

In among all the politics, Partizan had, with that win, moved back up to fourth place, with only Hajduk maintaining a 100 per cent record. The magnitude of the victory had helped keep the goal difference up, which kept Partizan two places above Red Star in the table. But the divisions in the club were about to get wider.

League table after the third round:
1. Hajduk 9 (+5)
2. Vojvodina 7 (+6)
3. Sloboda 7 (+2)
4. Partizan 6 (+7)
6. Red Star 6 (+1)

The Banned

ON my way back from the airport on Monday, after I had dropped Claire off, I bought a copy of *Blic*, a Serbian newspaper which is a cross between *The Sun* (in that it uses very accessible language and therefore has a big readership) and *The i* (in that it's a tabloid that actually covers the news and not just tits, *X Factor* and populist slogans). I bought the paper partly because the bus journey into town is pretty boring, but I was also keen to see how this game had been reported, given its smouldering backdrop. The back page covered Red Star's hard-fought win away at thus-far-unbeaten Smederevo, but the main feature inside was headlined 'Open conflict between Đurić and Stanojević'. All of the coverage, except a text box resumé of the score and line-ups, was on the previous day's verbal jousting, rather than the match itself.

After the match against OFK, Stanojević was naturally asked for his reactions to both the match and Đurić's press conference. Đurić had ended his contribution to the pre-match atmosphere with a thinly veiled threat to Stanojević's position. 'If we don't win the title with a team which has two or three quality players for every position, then we'll have a serious problem.'

The dispute between Đurić and Stanojević had been simmering for several months prior to the chairman's press conference on 28 August. The sorest recent point had been the sale of Stefan Savić to Manchester City behind the manager's back, as he put it. But this appeared to be the straw that broke Stanojević's back, and the dispute developed into what the papers described as 'open conflict'. After the match, Stanojević used his post-match interviews to criticise Đurić's judgement in calling such a press conference six hours before an important league match. He had a point there.

Stanojević also said that Đurić's support for the conduct of the Red Star fans was 'extremely hard to accept'.

Most Grobari probably agreed with that too. Then it got personal. 'What pains me the most is that it all adds up to lies and looking for excuses.' Stanojević promised that he would soon give the unvarnished truth for journalists, as opposed to the 'restrained answers' he'd given today. 'Ask me the same questions and you'll get different answers. Sometimes I've not said certain things because I've been putting Partizan ahead of all of us, but it seems that I've made a mistake.'

'He'll get sacked for this, of course,' said Dušan on Tuesday. But Stanojević kept on working through the week, trying out fringe players in a friendly against lower division side Senta on Wednesday and preparing the team for another friendly away at Cagliari on Saturday, minus the players on international duty. A few hundred committed Grobari went to Senta, a village in the middle of nowhere, to chant his name in support, as well as broader anti-board slogans. A big political effort for scant footballing reward (Partizan's subs managed to lose).

On Thursday night, one news website with a liberal attitude to printing unsubstantiated rumours was already saying that Stanojević had been sacked, and that director of football Krstajić was ready to resign too. The decision would be confirmed at 9am on Friday after the formal meeting of the Partizan Board of Management, referred to by Dušan when he explained the procedure to me as 'a bunch of useless and thieving Bolsheviks'.

A short while later, the story was gathering steam. Krstajić had already promised one website that, after the board meeting, he was going to tell all. B92, while heavily caveating their story as unofficial and 'as far as we know', put an article on their website by 9pm not only saying that Stanojević was out, but that Partizan already had a first-choice replacement in mind, Zoran Milinković, former Partizan player and recently manager of Vojvodina last season and Spartak the season before. Some sites said that it was the choice of Milinković, not the mistreatment of Stanojević, which was motivating Krstajić's threat of resignation.

The message boards were hawkishly promising a fans' demonstration outside the stadium to accompany the board meeting. In the end, not that many turned out, but the meeting itself, usually a short affair, dragged on for three and a half hours while the board debated the Europa League exit against Shamrock and the war of words between Đurić and Stanojević. At the end of it, the various board members exited the stadium wordlessly. Even club spokesman Marko Vjetrović had nothing for the press or the fans, other than a few printed sheets via which the club released a terse statement: 'The Managing Board of FK Partizan held its meeting dedicated to recent results, above all the elimination from UEFA competitions.

'It was concluded that elimination by the Irish champions Shamrock Rovers would not shake the stability and unity of any club structures and the devotion of our army of fans.

'A clear commitment and engagement was expressed to the realisation of our target, continued domination in Serbian football.'

Stanojević had held on. The statement told far less than the whole story. Pieced together from various accounts, it seems that Stanojević was told quite early on in the meeting that he would not be manager by the end of it. He unleashed a burst of vitriol at most people in the room, before storming out past the waiting journalists with a visibly reddened face.

He and Krstajić were not finished yet though. The two of them had agreed a deal with several colleagues that if Stanojević was fired and replaced by Milinković, not only would Krstajić resign, but all of the first and youth team coaching staff and some of the club's administrative and marketing staff. At points during the next couple of hours, the debate got so heated that fists were raised and physical threats made. At midday, three hours after the start of the meeting, Krstajić left the board to take their decision on their counter-offer, and with a degree of smugness scuttled across the stadium to his own office, where he was joined by supporters.

Shortly afterwards, deputy chairman and Socialist Party chief whip Branko Ružić was dispatched to speak to Krstajić, and by 12.30pm, both returned to the main boardroom. Đurić was left isolated when influential board member Nenad Bjeković swung behind keeping Stanojević, and was left with no choice but to rubber-stamp the decision to keep Stanojević as manager, and to keep the rest of the club's training staff in place. Fifteen minutes later, the statement was released.

As B92 put it, obviously the balance of power had changed within the club. Could Đurić deal with the double loss of face of being criticised by his own manager and then being refused permission to sack him? There was no chance of him being dismissed, as club rules state that the only way for him to leave the post was through resignation.

At the airport, on the way to Italy for the friendly against Cagliari, Stanojević deployed his most defensive lines, saying that he would lead the team to Italy 'as if nothing had happened'. He claimed ignorance of any move by the board to dismiss him. Imposing a complete media blackout on himself was a diplomatic gesture to avoid rubbing Đurić's nose any further in it. It was probably the right thing to do in the circumstances.

My feeling was that Stanojević's days were still likely to be numbered, and that Partizan only needed one more defeat for Đurić to have the excuse he needed. Certainly the board was not going out of its way to be seen alongside Stanojević. Not one of them accompanied the team on the trip to Sardinia, an abstemious attitude to foreign jollies that was conspicuously different to that seen in previous seasons. Only Vjetrović, as club spokesperson, boarded the plane with Krstajić, the manager and the team.

Over the week though, the balance of power did change. With the focus switched to international football (Serbia beat Northern Ireland 1-0 in Belfast and then the Faroe Islands 3-1 at Stadion Partizan), there was more time than usual for the media to concentrate on the internecine warfare inside the club rather than its on-pitch results. Within two days, the figure of Milija Babović was already being touted as the club's next chairman, to take over as early as December. Đurić's own comments were used very selectively by the media (who had turned against him too), prioritising one sentence he had said about two years maybe being enough in the job to the point where it looked like he had definitely decided to go.

Nenad Bjeković, who had been an important figure in keeping Stanojević in situ, was also apparently in the running. Babović, a successful businessman, was not exactly the first choice of many fans, not least because he is Stefan Babović's dad. Many comments on the messageboards had suggested that Babović junior was only ever in the team, and also received universally positive coverage of his performances in the media (no matter what he did), because of his rich and influential dad. This would only be exacerbated if his dad became the club's head honcho.

Several days of will-he-won't-he speculation dominated the back pages before Đurić was ultimately rescued from more journalistic torture by the combined diversionary effect of the EUROBASKET European Basketball Championship (where Serbia were among the favourites) and the US Open tennis (Novak Djoković was, on balance, probably the most powerful person in Serbia at this time). The day before the game against Jagodina, Đurić made emollient noises about the situation having calmed down, the unity of the club and the whole board attending the away game to show its support. He and Stanojević struck the same tone in their pre-match interviews, relying on the footballing staple of 'concentrating only on the next game'.

The fans did not seem ready to allow a return to business as usual though. One splinter group, now describing themselves as 'Zabranjeni' [The Banned], made a public statement declaring that they would boycott the game against Jagodina and all future Partizan games.

The Zabranjeni claimed to be the 'most numerous fan group from Belgrade', but their profile suggested that they were the guys from the Jug who were anti-Đurić, and that their membership at least overlapped with the persona non grata of Opcija Dva. Against Shamrock and OFK, they had been quite vocal, but represented only about ten per cent of the Jug, backed up by a bigger proportion from the Istok. The reason for their decision to boycott the game centred around the role of club general secretary Darko Grubor, who they claimed had been obstructing entry for members of their group. They went as far as to suggest that they would start talks with Red Star to become their fans instead.

Notwithstanding the fact that a group of Partizan converts would go down like a sack of something unpleasant at the Marakana, it was hard to believe that this was a serious threat, given the depth of love for the club that I had come across in most fans. At the Gradski Stadion in Jagodina, there were still about 500–600 Partizan fans assembled in the south stand and casual fans dotted about the three other stands, but Dušan noted that the year before, the hardcore Partizan following had filled the south and most of the Istok, so the Zabranjeni boycott appeared to be serious.

Maybe the Zabranjeni just didn't want to come to Jagodina. It's a small town of about 35,000 in the very centre of Serbia. Its main street is pretty enough, and the park near the stadium is very well kept, but other than that there's not much reason to leave Belgrade to go there. But this wasn't a message you wanted to tell the then mayor. Also a Member of Parliament and leader of the United Serbia political party, this was a colourful man named Dragan Marković, also known as *Palma* (the palm). Is he man or is he a tree?

Physically, it has to be the former. The Palm is a big lad, with a stature and look akin to Buster Bloodvessel in his early 1980s heyday. Where to start with Marković? The sheer force of his personality cannot be argued with. The US Embassy in Belgrade felt compelled to write a cable back to Washington solely about him, reflecting a national significance that outweighs his on-paper importance. Thanks to Wikileaks, this cable is available to anyone who wants to read it. I should note here that I don't approve of what Wikileaks did with the American cables, especially the second wave of completely unredacted releases that could have put many journalists, politicians and NGO personnel in physical danger, but I do find reading them very interesting.

Marković is fiercely proud of Jagodina, and he demonstrates his pride principally through his TV channel, Palma TV, which I was able to get on cable. In the summer, one of the channel's favourite features is to interview some of the tourists who visit the town. There aren't that many tourists, but Jagodina does punch above its weight, thanks to the water park and zoo that Marković has built. The tourists are asked, in the presence of the mayor, to say what they think of the town. They always say it's the best place they've ever been to and that they're beyond amazed at the splendour of the water park, zoo or main square. The water park looked all right, in that it had four or five pretty tall slides, but I've been to bigger ones on various Spanish islands, and when visitors from coastal Croatia, Montenegro and even Berlin are claiming that their homelands are put to shame by Jagodina, you have to wonder whether they're really being sincere.

The zoo is in itself a matter of some controversy. In 2008, after the elections, the Democratic Party, the core of the ruling coalition, was looking for partners to help them achieve a parliamentary majority. After some tough negotiations, Marković and his two other United Serbia MPs came on board, and the Democrats had reached their magic number of MPs. The story of how Marković was brought aboard has become a legend in Serbian politics, although never substantiated or admitted. It allegedly involved a boost to Jagodina's city budget, and a giraffe for the zoo. Officially, Jovanca the giraffe had been brought over thanks to private donors, and became one of the region's most famous ungulates, probably unaware of the fuss around her.

And there is a waxwork museum. How could I forget? Marković has added this to the roster of Jagodina's touristic attractions, and through his TV channel has made this quite widely known in Serbia as somewhere rivalling Madame Tussauds. When we visited it, the museum had two rooms featuring various Yugoslav and Serbian 'heroes' throughout the ages, including Slobodan Milošević. Dušan asked me if I wanted my picture taken with Slobo, which I briefly thought would be funny in an ironic-veneration-of-tyrants way, and then decided against. Not just for my career, you understand, but because Milosevic's actions caused so much suffering that even mock veneration wouldn't be humorous at all. Half the likenesses, particularly those of Tito and Zoran Đinđić, were pretty poor, and they ran out of ideas a bit in the second room, putting in two figures of Nikola Tesla, one of an older Tesla standing up and a younger, seated Tesla with a suspicious stain on the thigh of his trousers. I didn't feel it did justice to one of the world's greatest ever scientists.

Shortly before Partizan's game in Jagodina, Marković had helped signal the start of the pre-electoral campaign, some eight months before the scheduled polling day, with a couple of stunts designed to dole out goodies to potential voters and appeal to his core supporters, a conservative but pragmatic bunch. The first was a World Cup-style draw, complete with glass bowls and yellow plastic balls, to dish out 200 cows to farmers in the Jagodina region, with live television coverage fronted by an ample-bosomed former National Lottery presenter. Milking gags were optional. The second was a municipality-sponsored dating exercise, offering paid-for holidays in Greece to groups of singles from the region in an effort to stimulate some procreation (Serbia has one of the lowest birth rates in Europe). This initial offering proved so popular that Marković acquired several hectares of land near Jagodina's Greek twin town of Hrisopouli, so that he could start work on a permanent resort for such jaunts – Jagodina-on-Sea.

This largesse, combined with an excellent grasp of how to communicate with ordinary people (ie speak to them normally and don't patronise them), has made Marković a hugely popular politician in Jagodina and surrounds, and a national figure in his own right. He sometimes makes gaffes when speaking in public, including once suggesting that he had been a young boy when Beethoven and Mozart were at their musical peak, but ultimately most of his supporters forgive him the occasional lapse in memory. At the last mayoral election, he got 93 per cent in a pretty fair poll. In the Wikileaked cable, the US Embassy recorded, during their conversation with Marković, that he, 'adding with a chuckle', had said that his electoral success 'was even better than Saddam Hussein'.

Amid the bonhomie and generosity, the cable recorded Marković's association with the Hague-indicted (but now dead) warlord Arkan, for whom he was a Colonel in the Tigers paramilitary movement, a group responsible for many atrocities during the war in Bosnia. Marković's attitude to Serbia's gay and lesbian population, who live under pretty atrocious pressure most of the time, also hits the headlines for the wrong reasons. Although he has softened a little in recent years, Marković says he understands why the LGBT population's attempts to hold an annual Pride parade makes people angry enough to resort to violence. He has also proclaimed that homosexuality is an illness that can be contracted, and presumably also cured. Sadly, a majority of Serbs believe him.

Although he has repositioned himself as a pro-western and progressive politician, the US Embassy in their cable still described him as 'an autocratic personality', and expressed their doubts about where his personal wealth came from in the 1990s.

The stadium in Jagodina wasn't the best advertisement for the town promoting itself on billboards as 'the city of the future – one step ahead of the rest'. The main west stand was half finished, featuring an upper level that would probably one day become executive boxes, but for now looked like the foundations for a multi-storey car park. The police and press had to perch precariously in these unguarded concrete shells as they surveyed the fans and the match. Watching them, as they dizzily contemplated the drop beneath them while trying to concentrate on their jobs, was more exciting than the match itself in the first half. Partizan created no chances at all, against a packed Jagodina defence and midfield that was using the Sloboda template, absorbing pressure before launching quick counter-attacks. The two best chances of the half, both saved by Stojković, fell to Jagodina's attackers in such circumstances.

Stojković was the subject of most interest in the first half. As had been the case against Sloboda, lots of local Red Star fans had bought tickets for the game to boost Jagodina's support. They needed the help – there was no obvious 'firm' or home fans' group, apart from a small bunch of kids in the top right of the (theoretically home) north stand. They were quite loud, but squeaky pre-pubescent voices don't tend to have the required intimidating effect. A brave lad in a group of about six Red Star fans near the front of the west stand started hurling abuse at Stojković, calling him a traitor and dishing out various sweary oaths. Threatening voices from behind us urged him to stop, but the guy kept on going. Two Partizan fans decided they'd had enough, and legged it down the steps at him, running straight towards him before changing direction at the last minute – a sensible alteration to their plan, given that the whole crowd was being filmed from above by the police. Just before half-time, while Stojković was preparing to take a goal kick, the abuse started again. This time it was too much for some of the Grobari, and a scuffle started. The Red Star fan, who had been completely abandoned by his so-called mates, had his sunglasses knocked off, but in footballing parlance, it was mostly handbags.

At half-time, some of the harder-core Grobari in the south defied the possibility of arrest and scampered across to the stand where the scuffle had broken out, hoping to dispense their own form of justice, but before they got there, they were spotted by the police. All of them managed to leg it back and lose themselves in the black-and-white mass before they were nabbed. The police decided that they needed to make an example of someone, and arrested a guy who had been close to the scuffle. A morbidly obese and visibly hammered guy with a flat cap, no shirt, and a moustache that made Ian Rush's, circa 1985, look wispy. It was hard to believe that he was a ringleader or even an aggressor, considering how out of it he looked, but he was bundled out of the stadium by a group of four truncheon-wielding gendarmes.

As he was being led past us, someone yelled out 'Marković Palma!', a famous and comparable example of such corpulence, and the mood was instantly lightened around us.

Not so in the south stand, where heated negotiations went on between the stadium head of security, the policemen attached to the away contingent, and some Grobari leaders, backed up by a few hotheads. It looked (I was ten metres away) like the Grobari were trying to make a deal – if the Red Star fans are ejected, we'll acquiesce. If not ... The police weren't taking any chances, and doubled their numbers round the main body of Grobari for the second half. The police's relief when the players came out was palpable, the diversion of football distracting minds that had been focused on a possible ruck.

The second half wasn't much better than the first, and its defining feature was continued and obvious time-wasting by Jagodina, whose ball boys were clearly part of the 0-0 strategy, while their players each took a turn to have a bit of a lie down after a tackle. Stanojević finally realised the need for urgency and brought on Lazar Marković and later Ilić. After 78 minutes, Marković stole the ball off a Jagodina defender, and played only Partizan's third decent through-ball all game, into the penalty area. Diarra, making his first start since his comeback from injury, sprinted on to it, but was shepherded towards the left-hand edge of the penalty area by his marker. He was going to have to shoot from an unlikely angle, so there was little danger.

But a second Jagodina defender came haring back and half-shoved, half-bumped into Diarra from behind. It was a poor intervention, and a needless one, and it probably was a penalty. The referee gave it. Tomić picked up the ball and dismissed the polite inquiries of a couple of team-mates as to who was going to take it. 'He's going to miss it, of course,' said a visibly fretting Dušan. Tomić had been poor all game. That was the gist of it, anyway, though the message might have been diluted by the volume of accompanying personal insults.

He scored, firmly striking into the right-hand corner of the goal beyond an unconvincing dive from the Jagodina keeper. The reaction from the crowd suggested that the home fans were outnumbered by about six to one, as many people showed their hands for the first time. Dušan (who, let's be honest, had made his allegiance clearly known from the start) invited the Jagodina players to continue lying down and wasting time if they so wished. That was the gist of it, anyway. He also called them c***s.

It was the perfect time to score, given that Partizan had been unable to deliver much in the last ten minutes of any game so far this season, except the (by that stage of the game) dead rubber against Novi Pazar. As the clock ticked on to 80, Partizan's last-ten implosion clock trilled into life, as first Ivanov and then Rnić failed to clear a cross and Jagodina somehow contrived not to score from five yards. But that was as worrying as it got. Even the five ironic minutes of injury time that Partizan no longer wanted passed by nervously but without major incident. Partizan had won away, and I no longer had a zero per cent record on the road. Partizan were top again, but only temporarily, as Hajduk were due to play Borac on Sunday afternoon, and they recorded their fourth straight win to stay first. Next week's game against them would be a proper six-pointer.

The poor bloke with the 'tache wasn't going to see it though. Having been arrested at a football ground, he stood a very real chance of receiving a custodial sentence of a year or two. Having experienced high levels of football violence in the past, Serbia's punishments for those convicted are now pretty tough. And it would be hard for Mr Tache to prove his innocence against the word of half a dozen gendarmes.

League table after the fourth round:
1. Hajduk 12 (+6)
2. Partizan 9 (+8)
3. Red Star 9 (+3)

Metallica Is My Good Friend

GIVEN that this was a top-of-the-table clash, and the fact that Red Star had won earlier in the day to go level with Hajduk on 12 points, it was surprising how few people came to the game against Hajduk Kula. The away following especially was pitiful, maybe 60 people at most. Kula is not a big town, barely bigger than a village, but still. Dušan explained that Kula was in a part of the northern province of Vojvodina that was extensively resettled after the Second World War. Many of its pre-war inhabitants were ethnic Germans, who had left, been forced to leave, or killed in the closing stages of the war and its immediate aftermath. The area had been repopulated with Serbs from further south, Serbs from Croatia, and Montenegrins, who had little attachment to the local football clubs and, if they had a Serbian team, it was Red Star or Partizan. But still, 60 people? Your team's top of the league. Even I've played for a team that had more than 60 fans, and I'm a terrible footballer.

The match against Hajduk was my seventh game with Partizan. By now, a few faces and voices had become familiar in my immediate surroundings. The first one to show their hand was Dušan's vocal nemesis, the guy who always cheers for Tomić. He had good reason to crow when Tomić curled a 30-yard free kick over the wall and into the net to give Partizan the lead in the tenth minute. 'Bravo Tomiću!' he shouted, 'Ti si najbolji igrač u ovom timu' [You're the best player in this team]. I thought he had a point. Tomić's overall contribution to a game was sometimes a bit patchy, but this was his sixth goal of the season, meaning he had grabbed a third of all of Partizan's goals.

Dušan though was turned round away from the pitch and trying to stare the guy out. I asked 'does he only do that to wind you up?', but Dušan was pretty sure that actually the guy was Tomić's manager, and that his main interest in encouraging pro-Tomić noise was to help engineer a big-money move to Italy in the January transfer window.

Joining our group today was the man they call the 'Engleski Grobar' [The English gravedigger]. Nick Hercules has the best surname of anyone I have ever met and a genuine passion for Partizan. A long-term part of the conflict prevention community in the Balkans, his current job is for the UN down in the far south of Serbia, where there is a large (and discriminated against) ethnic Albanian minority. He runs a series of projects designed to make life better for ordinary people of all ethnicities in a region that's among the most impoverished in Serbia (which is itself one of the poorest countries in Europe). So he's a good bloke.

He is also respected as a Partizan fan, a real Grobar. Not least because he comes up from south Serbia every second weekend to watch the crno-beli. That's a much longer journey than even the hardest-core Manchester United fan makes from Surrey every week. So respect is due – and Nick has been the subject of a glowing testimonial in Partizan fanzines. As he came towards us, he was greeted warmly by lots of random fans, most of whom I hadn't even met. It made me realise that I had a long way to go to be accepted as anything other than a novelty. When Nick talks about Partizan, his love for the club is obvious. When I asked him about the team he supported back in England (Spurs – I forgive him because he's such a good bloke), he talked about it like it was a news item from a far away country. When he talks about Partizan, it's always 'we' and 'us'.

I hadn't got there yet, I have to confess. When Partizan played badly (like today), it was mildly frustrating, but it wasn't offending to me to my core, like it did for Dušan, Igor, or even Nick. When they played well, I enjoyed it, and goals were starting to mean something to me – like it had when Marković scored against OFK. And I cared a bit. But I was still at this stage talking about Partizan in the third person (whereas for Arsenal I would still probably have used the first). I knew I was never going to get to the same level of love (and hate) that, say, Igor and Pećinko had for the club. You can't just import decades of association with a club and the love that comes from being brought up with something.

And look, I've never had that borderline religious attitude to Arsenal either – I watch and support when I can, and I suppose I've given lots of time and money to the club. I like watching Arsenal, I like the way the club is run, I like it when they do well, and I get cross when they don't. But my life has never revolved around it, and a lot of the evocative, quasi-religious language that many fans use about faith, loyalty, ceremony, and veneration – just leaves me a bit cold. A bit how I feel about religion, come to think of it.

Nick's integration into the club was a good reference point. I was going to have three or four years in Belgrade, and I hoped that I could get to the point where the club had accepted a second Engleski Grobar, and that I had developed a bit more of an emotional bond with the club too.

Back to the match. Nick and I were saying that 17-year-old Marković wasn't having his best game, which Goran ascribed to him wearing different coloured boots to normal. He was in a sober grey pair, not the lurid yellow numbers he usually wore, which had the effect of making his feet look like they were moving faster than they actually were. In one of his few lively moments of the first half, he burst into the penalty area and crossed superbly, only for his team-mates to let him down, not one of them making an effort to get into the six-yard box. As he got into the area, another guy behind us shouted 'penal!', demanding a penalty despite the lack of any challenge.

For the first few games when I had heard him, I couldn't tell if he was joking or not. But in the game against OFK, I had sat a bit nearer and seen him in action, as it were. And he was deadly serious, standing up and gesticulating as he claimed penalty after penalty. Whether he really thought he could influence the game, I don't know. More likely, he was protesting in the irony-laden way of the Istok about the relative lack of penalties Partizan get compared to Red Star (who had got another soft one to give them their only goal in their match this weekend, which had preceded ours), and Partizan's astonishing record of not getting a penalty against Red Star since 1999, which Dušan reminded me needlessly, was not even this millennium.

At half-time, I caught my first glimpse of a Partizan legend, Miša Tumbas. The Engleski Grobar was a bit of a celebrity in the

Istok, but Miša Tumbas is a character who everyone in Belgrade has heard of. I had heard lots of bits and pieces about him, but never actually seen him, to the point where I thought he was just an urban legend, a bit like the Tommy Johnson character that the lads talked about for three hours on the way back from Užice but who appeared to be a complete fabrication.

It is fair to call Tumbas a YouTube sensation given how many clips of him there are. More on them in a minute. Miša is probably about 60 years old, greying and balding, unshaven and shambolic. He carries a similar unkempt whiff, and an impressive belly in front of him. He is always wearing an old Partizan shirt or some other Partizan-themed gear, wherever he is. He even features on the Love Partizan, Hate Yourself t-shirt. He watches Partizan's teams in every sport, and the club (like Red Star) is one of the biggest players in virtually every sport.

So Miša not only turns up at football, but he never misses a basketball match, and is a regular attendee in support of the water polo and volleyball teams. Even Partizan's ten-pin bowling, table tennis and chess teams have been graced with Miša's presence. The final part of his standard ensemble is a plastic carrier bag. I have never seen him without the carrier bag.

Dušan told me that in the bag, which always appears half-full, are rolls and rolls of cash. Partizan's players, and other well-wishers, just give him cash all the time. This doesn't mean he leads an expensive lifestyle. Far from it – this is his only income, and he depends on the kindness of a distant cousin to look after him, his other family having either moved away from Belgrade or passed away. And he wouldn't have time to work even if he was capable. Partizan play every day in some sport or another so there wouldn't be much time to work if you were as dedicated as Miša.

But Miša isn't as loved as he is because of how he looks or just because he keeps on turning up. Nor is it pity for a man who suffers from learning difficulties as well as poverty. It's mainly because of what he says. Well, shouts. He has the most incredible voice, like someone has poured gravel into his throat, and his larynx is a cement mixer. His volume is prodigious. He likes to talk to the players on the pitch, though it's often a one-directional conversation. Today he picked on Saša Ilić. 'Sale! Sale! Sale! Sal-eeeeeeee!' Ilić didn't look round. 'Sal-eeeee!' It rivalled the 'DAN!' scene from Alan

Partridge. It works better at the basketball, where he's much closer to the players.

Actually, scrap that. It is because of what he does. Miša is one of the greatest strippers in the Balkans. He likes to go shirtless quite often, especially at the basketball, but also at the football. Quite a lot of guys take their shirts off at Partizan. Not a big deal. Miša gets his c**k out too, if he's given enough encouragement by the crowd. Apparently it's quite a sizeable trouser snake. No one seemed that bothered about seeing his Johnson today, so the regular chant of 'Vadi ga! Vadi ga! Vadi ga!' [Get it out! Get it out! Get it out!] remained unsung. This predilection for whacking out his manhood has given Partizan fans another weapon in their arsenal of chants against rival fans – 'Jebaće vas Miša Tumbas!' [Miša Tumbas will f*** you], and an intimidating banner of Miša flashing behind the goal in front of the Jug.

He is also the region's most dedicated collector of kit. Part of his post-match routine is to wait outside the players' dressing room and demand their spare kit. Not just shirts, although his plaintive cry of 'Daj mi dres' [give me your shirt] is his most widely-known mating call. No. He will collect shorts, socks, shin pads, anything. One of the best YouTube clips is of him pleading with former striker Cleo at the top of his voice for over a minute, trying to get his shorts. In begging for bits of memorabilia, he's learned one word of English, to help persuade the foreign players. 'Cleo! Cleo! Pleeeeeeaaaaaase daj mi šorc!'

Miša's dedication to the Partizan cause doesn't stop at the sports events. He goes to all the concerts organised at the stadium too. He became a star in America after Metallica played at Stadion Partizan in 2004. Interviewed by a CNN crew before the concert started, Miša is asked if Metallica is his favourite band, in English. 'Metallica je moj dobar drugar' [Metallica is my good friend], he answers. He goes on to say that he hopes that Metallica can sing well and that there are lots of people in the Stadion Partizan. The interviewer, in nasal American tones, either doesn't have a clue what Miša is saying, is taking the p***, or just ploughs on regardless. 'What do you think of Slither? Is Slither your favourite song?' 'Metallica je moj dobar drugar. Ovaj je moj prvi put… Metallica je moj dobar drugar.' Miša doesn't have a clue what he's being asked, but he's definitely good mates with the band. Kids, hoping to unearth the next viral YouTube hit, are constantly going up to

Miša wherever they find him and asking him to talk, usually about Metallica. These days he just says 'f*** Metallica'.

Marković must have been listening to our conversation in the first half, because he came out for the second half in his familiar yellow boots, and within two minutes had sprinted past his marker into the box. Before our mate behind us could claim for a penalty, Marković had squared for Tomić to hammer into the roof of the net from five yards out. While everyone else cheered the goal, Dušan slumped forward, head in hands, as his least-favourite player moved five goals ahead of all his team-mates in the season's scoring charts. The guy behind us, whether Tomić's manager or not, was crowing.

Other than Dušan, the only other guy not celebrating in the stand was the man they call 'Maldini'. He is called that because of his long hair and tanned complexion. I suppose he looks a tiny bit like Paolo Maldini, but it's a harsh comparison for the AC Milan legend. When I look at him, he reminds me more of Frankenstein's monster, with big staring eyes and devoid of emotion or expression. Goals, red cards, tackles, saves, pulsating 3-2 wins and turgid 0-0 draws, nothing gets even a flicker out of him. I don't know why he comes. He just seems to prowl around looking halfway between miffed and vacant.

Partizan saw out the game comfortably, even the last ten minutes. For a team that had been top, it was incredible that Hajduk had no plan other than to draw 0-0. At no point did they ever look like their heart was in getting a goal back. A guy came round selling seeds, and I was sure he was a regular too. He was, he had been in Jagodina the week before, selling there, and we had seen him trying to hitch a ride back to Belgrade. We asked him if that had been him, which it was. He seemed a bit p***ed off having to answer the question without making a sale, having lost ten valuable commercial seconds while we tried to work it out. Lost snack-sale opportunity or not, Partizan were back at the top, albeit jointly with Red Star.

Before we left the ground, a guy walked down the steps past us. 'We used to call that guy Kleptoman in the old days,' said Dušan. Kleptoman (I have no idea what his real name is) was a regular fixture during the away trips Dušan and his friends used to go on in the late 1990s. Kleptoman's talent was to come back from every away trip with an illegal souvenir. Over the course of the season, he had managed to nick some seats, fittings from the toilet of one stadium, a riot policeman's baton, and various other things that he wasn't supposed to have, from the shops or from the stadium. He just did it for a laugh, too. Most of the stuff he swiped had no resale value. Then one day, he didn't come to the game. For eight years. The rumour was that Kleptoman had stolen one thing too far, and had to serve out a stretch before he could come back to the stadium. All I noticed about him was that he was wearing a pretty big coat for a warm September evening.

When I arrived in Serbia, I hadn't necessarily intended to go to every single game (either for Red Star or for Partizan), but having decided on writing this diary, the pressure to do so had increased. Dušan was up for going to every game, and by now I knew enough regular fans that I would always find a willing companion, or a group I could tag along with.

However, I knew that before Christmas there were going to be two league games that I was going to miss, because two of my good friends were getting married in England on 24 September, which clashed with the home game against Rad, and Claire and I had booked a holiday for the ten days immediately following that. I did a quick cost-benefit analysis of cancelling that, or modifying it so that we were in Novi Sad (where Partizan would face Vojvodina), rather than Montenegro on 1 October. Claire was going to move to Serbia at the end of the year and take unpaid leave for a couple of years, so I imagined that I would get the shortest of short shrifts if I suggested taking two days out to drive halfway across the Balkans and watch Partizan against a team that had beaten them home and away last season. It wouldn't even be fair to ask. That game would probably be on TV in Montenegro anyway.

Another complication was the start of the cup competition. The Serbian Cup isn't as all-encompassing as the FA Cup, in that the smallest clubs outside the top two divisions have to play so many qualifying rounds, for so few spaces, that by the time Partizan join in the 'first round' (actually the fifth), it is really only a 32-team knockout between teams from the SuperLiga and Prva Liga. Partizan were, therefore, only four wins from the final and it still wasn't the end of September yet.

The draw pitted Partizan against Novi Pazar, away. In order to fit into the winter break-truncated Serbian football calendar, the cup is played midweek. I had just been to Novi Pazar on a work trip, and it had taken us about four hours to get there, at a decent pace, and without too many delays. But I reckoned that in my own car, which was faster than the embassy four-by-four we had gone down in for work, and better suited to the task of overtaking slow lorries on the single-lane parts of the route, I could get that down to three and a half. It would mean leaving work bang on the official closing time of 4.30pm (we start at 8am.) in order to dash in time for kick-off and a pre-match snack of mantije – a high fat, high taste local delicacy of spiced meat mini-pastries that are difficult to get outside the Sandžak region.

It would be a crazy dash back for a 2am return at best, plus adding 500km to my car's already well-used odometer, but it was probably do-able if we really wanted to. Novi Pazar had been the best-supported team to visit Partizan so far, so the atmosphere would probably be good, and given that studying Sandžak was part of my job, I might get something professionally useful out of going too.

On Monday morning I sorted out my work diary to ensure space for a clean getaway on the Wednesday. Then the FA announced that the game was to be played at half past three in the afternoon. Bugger. I had no chance of taking the whole day off, there were meetings scheduled and simply too much to do before I went on holiday. So I was going to miss three games in a row.

As it was, the cup game was one of Partizan's most complete performances of the season so far. Admittedly, Novi Pazar at that point of the season were still rooted to the bottom of the league, and had only just scored their first league goal after four blank games at the start of the season, so it wasn't going to take a herculean effort to beat them. Partizan controlled the match, scoring midway through the first and second halves.

At 2-0 up, Stanojević even felt comfortable enough to bring on David Manga, who had signed for the club with limited fanfare a couple of months back, but hadn't made it any further than the bench so far. Manga was touted by the club as an international player to take the team up a level. Representing the Central African Republic (even a Central African Republic having one of their best ever African Cup of Nations qualifying campaigns) though wasn't exactly the kind of player the fans were hankering after. He had played in France and Germany, but his most recent experience was in the German equivalent of the fourth division. Manga was on the pitch for Partizan's third goal as Vukić completed a comfortable win.

The next game, at home to Rad, was a dour affair all round. I was congratulated by text by Igor and Dušan for having chosen to miss it. Rad fans' preponderance for a bit of trouble in the environs of the stadium and a right-wing chant or three were other good reasons not to have been there. Eduardo scored a strange goal, looping the ball over the keeper by helping on a through-ball from about 20 yards out, and that was about all Partizan did all game. Rad hit the bar and one of their strikers missed a one-on-one, and before missing might have gone down in the box for a penalty and red card, but luckily he didn't. The result was all-important, as Red Star won again, keeping the two sides level at the top. The psychological importance of not allowing Red Star to go top, whether on goal difference or in their own right, might not have been a big deal for the players, but it was for fans' bragging rights.

I was very disappointed to miss the game in Novi Sad, though, and the chance to go 'home' that went with it. And my commitment to the Partizan cause was being questioned too. Igor texted me from the ground. 'While you're swimming, we're fighting for our lives!' I felt a bit guilty for a couple of minutes, but the water in Montenegro was lovely … Vojvodina had done the double over Partizan last season and, for most of the campaign, they were genuinely in with a chance of winning the league, before fading in the last few games and coming third. They had also come second in 2008/09, and frankly had been the only real challengers to Partizan and Red Star since the late 1990s, when paramilitary/war criminal Arkan's FK Obilić won the league and otherwise mixed it up with the big two. It was likely to be one of the toughest games of the season.

It didn't disappoint. As had been the case against Genk, Partizan raised their game in response to a team who, you know, can actually play football, and were 2-0 up within half an hour with a goal each from the youthful front pairing of Marković (rapidly becoming the team's focal point and most obvious goal threat despite his limited years) and the less rapid but highly talented (if moderately lazy) Šćepović. But from then on, it was a case of grimly hanging on against a determined Vojvodina, backed by a decent crowd – a third of whom were regulars, a third Red Star fans, and a third the once- or twice-a-season mob who just enjoy shouting abuse at the teams from Belgrade.

Vojvodina's siege though only produced one goal and, despite a nervy finish, Partizan had an unexpected victory – one that bucked historical trends of poor results in Novi Sad. The win was even sweeter as Red Star were held at home by Radnički Kragujevac, putting Partizan top on their own in time for my return to action. Sloboda, who had beaten Partizan in Užice, and had now officially dropped the 'Sevojno' part of their name, were into the UEFA Cup spot, three points behind. No one seriously expected them to stay the course though – it wasn't impossible that they would get third place, but there was no way that they could challenge for the overall title.

League table after the seventh round:
1. Partizan 18 (+12)
2. Red Star 16 (+7)
3. Sloboda 15 (+4)

Save Serbia, Kill Yourself

BEFORE getting back to league action, I went to my first game at Red Star's stadium. This wasn't a reconnaissance mission into enemy territory or the first rumblings of apostasy, it was to watch Serbia's national team.

I had already had a chance to see the Beli Orlovi (White Eagles, named after the bird in Serbia's national crest) in action this season, a home game against the Faroe Islands at an oddly deserted Stadion Partizan. Just over 7,000 people bothered to attend a national team game, and neither Red Star's nor Partizan's main groups attended at all, leaving the Sever and Jug virtually empty. Serbia had won 3-1, though it had looked a little shaky around half-time after the Faroes had pulled one back. How many other people had seen Shamrock Rovers and FK Vaduz win, and the Faroes score in the same season? There really could not have been many of us.

With two games left in the qualifying campaign for Euro 2012, Serbia were in line for a play-off spot. Italy had already won the group, and Serbia were ahead of Estonia and Slovenia in the battle for second, and had a game in hand. The campaign had been spoiled by the abandonment of Serbia's away game in Italy after just six minutes after intra-Serbian (read: Partizan v Red Star) fan fighting forced the referee to take the players off the field, Serbia forfeiting that game and then being forced to play their next home game against Northern Ireland in front of just 350 people (75 'technical' personnel from each side and 200 fans from Northern Ireland who would have been inconvenienced by a full enforcement of a closed-door game).

Despite the setbacks, victory in one of the remaining two games would guarantee them second. They weren't the easiest games though

– home to Italy and then away to Slovenia. Confidence, at least in the media, was high in the build-up. The team had shown potential, beating Germany in the 2010 World Cup but losing to Ghana and Australia and going out of the tournament at the group stage. More immediately relevant was the fact that Italy were through already and would be in the mood for experimenting. Meanwhile, Serbia's team contained some of Europe's brightest talent.

As well as Premier League stars Nemanja Vidić, Aleksandar Kolarov and Branislav Ivanović, Serbia had players from Inter Milan (Dejan Stanković), Juventus (Miloš Krasić) and Borussia Dortmund (Neven Subotić). According to one survey just published in the press, Serbia's first 11 was the fourth highest-paid (by their clubs) in Europe, behind only England, Spain and Italy. The story was written neutrally, or perhaps ambiguously, but the comments underneath it on the web confirmed that most people saw the contrast of high wages and low achievement as an indictment of how little effort these stars made for Serbia, rather than a testament to Serbian sporting ability.

The match showed clearly why football is one of Serbia's most successful export industries, or causes of capital flight, depending on how you see it. Coach Vladimir Petrović's squad for this game, and the one which would follow against Slovenia, contained not a single player who plied his trade in the Serbian SuperLiga. Even the third-choice goalkeeper was playing in Ukraine rather than in Serbia. Partizan's Stojković was still considering whether he wanted to play for Serbia again after the personal attacks on him in Genoa at the abandoned game against Italy, but even allowing for that, it was the clearest explanation so far that the standards and wages in Serbian football were simply insufficient to keep the best players in the domestic league.

Some 35,000 people turned up at the Marakana for the game, meaning there was a bit more atmosphere than against the Faroes. Capacity had once been about 110,000 but had been reduced by the introduction of seating in all four stands to be more like 55,000 today.

Dušan was not among them, having impolitely declined the opportunity to take a spare ticket. In his own words he was not interested in watching 'that bunch of prima donnas wearing red shirts' and sampling what he described as 'all that nationalist piggery in a nasty nationalist hole of a stadium'.

I was at the game with eight of my mates from home, who had come out to Belgrade for a three-day stag do in honour of my friend Rob Parris. In a desperate attempt to break up the monotony of ceaseless drinking I had suggested the match as part of their tour itinerary, assuring them that the violence in Genoa had been a one-off and that they would be perfectly safe. We were in the more family-oriented east stand so I figured we would be fine. For all Dušan's denigration of the stadium as a hole, it struck me as quite a lot better than Partizan's: bigger, better designed and, with its partial roof, able to generate more noise. Only the location, stuck on a patch of waste ground next to a horrendously busy roundabout, was worse than Partizan's.

The stadium is yet another source of tension between Red Star and Partizan. For Partizan, the rapid construction of Red Star's new stadium in 1963 with, as they put it, funding and labour provided directly from government coffers, was proof that the State was on Red Star's side. Red Star argue that the way the stadium was financed, through 'bricks' bought by individual fans, just proves that they're the more popular club.

As for the nationalism, the cars parked outside the ground told part of the story – every third one had Bosnian number plates. When we got inside, hundreds of banners celebrated Serbs coming from outside Serbia to support the team. The Banja Luka fan club, and groups from other parts of the Republika Srpska – the Serb half of Bosnia-Herzegovina – like Bijeljina and Trebinje (the latter about seven hours' drive away) were prevalent. Serbs from Montenegro and Croatia had come too.

Having studied the politics of the region, it didn't come as a huge surprise to see that people supported their supposed ethnic fatherland rather than the country they lived in, or were born in. But it was quite sad. And, for balance, I should point out that ethnic Bosniaks in Serbia tend to support either Bosnia-Herzegovina, whose team has few Serb players (they elect to play for Serbia if they can) despite Serbs making up over a third of the population of the country, or Turkey, their former ruler.

I guess it was almost inevitable that Serbs outside Serbia tend to push a harder nationalist line than those inside the country, so it was almost inevitable that there was a lot of extra-territorial chanting and saluting of war criminals who are still regarded as heroes in parts of the Balkans. I had heard enough of Kosovo being the heart of Serbia (which it hasn't been since the 14th century) and of Ratko Mladić (facing an enormous stack of evidence against him for war crimes) to be able to zone most of it out. But for my mates who had not heard it before and had only really heard about the Balkans via the BBC, it was something of a shock to hear Ratko being venerated by so many people.

The guys from Banja Luka in front of us were particularly vociferous in their singing of Ratko's name. And they were equally vocal in leading a rendition of 'Spasi Srbiju i ubi se, Tadiću Borise!' [Save Serbia and kill yourself, Boris Tadić!], an invitation which hadn't been extended to a serving president since the days of Slobodan Milošević.

Over half the stadium joined in, each with their own reasons. For some of those who had come from outside Serbia, Tadić was seen as a bit of a traitor, too ready to abandon Serbs and 'Serb interests' in order to please the EU, by doing things like recognising that Serbia should apologise for the genocide at Srebrenica – carried out by Serbs – and negotiating with Kosovo. To me, these were basic acts of reconciliation that should be welcomed. For some of those residents of Serbia, Tadić had presided over a government which had allowed corruption to increase, and had not ensured that the fruits of economic growth had trickled down, meaning a drop in living standards. Either way, it wasn't the kind of message any politician wanted to hear six months ahead of elections.

On the pitch, Serbia's highly-paid stars made a bright start, Aleksandar Kolarov stinging Gianluigi Buffon's palms with a long-range shot inside the first 20 seconds. And then Italy scored 30 seconds later, Claudio Marchisio slipping daintily past a couple of weak challenges and slotting home. All the Serbia players' belief was exhaled in one big sigh, a cloud of spent hope joining the pall of smoke from the north stand's flares above the ground. There were still 179 minutes of football left to play and save the situation but no one really seemed to care. Branislav Ivanović did score a heavily deflected equaliser to save some pride but for the most part, the team was going through the motions, passing around slowly, jogging and not sprinting. Even striker Marko Pantelić's hair, usually a powerful (but ill-advised) bouffant of shiny curls aided by kilograms of product, seemed limp and lacking its usual lustre.

The team couldn't shake off their malaise a few days later in Slovenia, slumping to a lifeless 1-0 defeat. They had some good chances, but even the ultra-reliable Nemanja Vidić (the only ex-Red Star player that Dušan has any respect for) struck a feeble penalty, which was saved, and that was that. Serbia were out, denied by Estonia's win away in Northern Ireland.

Coach Petrović was sacked before we had even returned to league action at the weekend, amid the usual bitter recriminations in the media and a prolonged period of navel-gazing about the state of Serbian football. If there was consensus about one thing, it was that Serbia's players had just not put enough effort in to justify their star status, and that they were too indulged too much by the Serbian FA. Some of the comments from press and fans went too far for Nemanja Vidić, who joined Dejan Stanković in international retirement just a couple of days after his 30th birthday, arguably at the peak of his form for Manchester United. From what I had seen, Vidić was among the harder-working players in the squad, which made the job of the new coach even harder.

The Serbian FA was keen that the new coach come in and instil some much-needed discipline in the squad. So why they picked Siniša Mihajlović, former Inter and Sampdoria midfielder but recipient of UEFA bans for spitting in the face of an opponent and racially abusing Patrick Vieira, was beyond me.

It was good to get focused back on the league, where Partizan's form – five wins in a row after the travails in Užice – was promising. Partizan played at home against Spartak Zlatibor Voda on 15 October. Spartak are actually from Subotica, in the far north of Serbia, close to the Hungarian border. They're not from Zlatibor, which is a skiing/hiking resort in the west of the country, not far from Užice. Spartak's shirt sponsorship deal with Zlatibor Voda, a mineral water company, extends further than just being printed on some nylon. Like Sloboda, Spartak are also the product of a merger between a smaller successful club (FK Zlatibor Voda of Horgoš, the town right on the border with Hungary, which had a bottling plant of said mineral water) and a bigger, less successful one (FK Spartak Subotica).

Subotica is a town of about 100,000 people, the fifth-largest in Serbia and comparable in size with a town like Blackburn or Wigan. It is linked to Belgrade by Serbia's fastest motorway, so it is just two hours away by car. Spartak have established fans groups, the Marinci (Marines) and Lowland Boys. So it was quite a surprise that only 50 of them turned up. Later on, the home fans gave their own diagnosis later on in the match, chanting 'Subotica je crno-beli grad!' [Subotica is a black-and-white town!].

Having seen all the Partizan minibuses on the motorway heading up past Novi Sad, I could believe that more Subotica residents had made the journey south to support the home team rather than their 'own'. Belgrade wasn't much of a crno-beli grad today though either: Partizan numbers were down too. Perhaps this was explained by the weather – in mid-October, this was the first game of the season where it was actually cold. 'You think this is cold?' asked Dušan. 'Wait 'til the games just before the winter break.' I didn't really think it was that cold. It was more that I resented the fact that I couldn't wear shorts to games anymore.

Instead of more speculation about the manager's or chairman's future, the big talk ahead of today's game was more mundane. Partizan were getting a new scoreboard. And not before time. The scoreboard at the south end of the ground dated back to the refurbishment of 1957, when it had been quite cutting edge. Today, it looked as clunky as a valve television. The club had announced that the game against Rad had been the swansong for 'the good old scoreboard'. But when I got to the ground, it was still there, clunky as ever. Goran showed up just after me and asked another of his mates where it was. 'Coming in a month's time.' 'But I thought it was here already.' That's what the club had said, anyway. The 'high-tech' LED screen from China's delivery hadn't been uncontroversial either – the rumour was that the chairman had asked DHL, one of the club's associate sponsors, to deliver it for nothing.

The old screen, professional as ever despite it being a week past its retirement date, announced the line-up for today's game. The biggest surprise was the absence of Camara. He had been on international duty for Sierra Leone in South Africa, and been two days late coming back. The club weren't massively impressed with the reasons he had given for the delay, and this was enough for him to be dropped, or 'given more time to recover'.

The game was a straightforward 2-0 win for Partizan. It was such a routine win that no one even bothered to demand the board's resignation at any point during the match. Vukić scored a penalty after Marković had been tripped after half an hour, and then had a tap-in for his second ten minutes later after Volkov's cut-back. At half-time, there were loud complaints around me despite the lead. 'We're f***ed. If Vukić keeps on scoring, he'll cement his place in the team.' Surely if he kept scoring, we would want him to stay in the team? But for the Istok boo-boys around me, Vukić was past it, not trying hard enough, and most importantly, blocking a path into the first team for a youngster with real talent.

Holding on for the win would have been less straightforward if Spartak had ever so slightly better aim. They hit the woodwork three times and substitute Nosković missed a sitter, which Partizan's usually very dry match report described as a '100% chance'.

Lighting up the evening more than the match were the number of fireworks used. With two goals to celebrate before half-time, the fans in the south had had to let off quite a few firecrackers. They also had a few industrial-strength sparklers to go with them. More than usual, but not ridiculously so. Too many though for the club – the stadium announcer was forced to ask the crowd not to throw pyrotechnics on to the running track. 'UEFA!' shouted someone behind me, recalling that the club only usually bothered to take such preventive measures when Mr Platini's officials were in town.

At the start of the second half, the Jug gave its answer to the request. About 20 fans, all lined up at precise two-metre intervals around the curve of the front row of the south stand, all lit flares at the same time, waved them for a minute, and chucked them on to the running track, skittling the stewards. 'Please do not throw pyrotechnics on to the running track,' pleaded the announcer again. The rest of the stadium laughed.

At this stage of the season, I couldn't quite work out my feelings about the Jug. It seemed to me that the fireworks incident was one illustration of an attitude of large parts of the Jug (not all, obviously, it had been made abundantly clear that it, like any organisation, wasn't monolithic) that their stand was in some way bigger than the club. Don't tell us what to do – we run this place. I admired the fans in the Jug for lots of reasons. They kept on singing through thick and a lot of thin – both results and performances. And their volume, over 90 minutes, was impressive, and would put any English club to shame. They were loyal too, even when the team had performed badly for weeks in a row. Only the Shamrock game had shown any fissures in that façade. The fans in the Jug kept turning up – it was busier for some games than others but always had the biggest concentration of fans.

But a couple of things were nagging at me over and above the xenophobia, which still jarred no matter how many times I heard it.

One was the sense that, actually, choreography was more important than the support itself. Lots of the flags being waved, though in Partizan colours, were actually just celebrating individual groups rather than the team. The chanting too, while impressive in its noise and duration, didn't actually do the team any favours in many situations. The Jug wasn't able to differentiate between situations and modify its repertoire accordingly.

I am no fan of negativity towards your own team, but sometimes a team does need to understand if it's doing something wrong, and a targeted rise in volume can add to the pressure on the opposition. Most fans in the Jug didn't even cheer when Partizan scored, they just kept on singing, as if the songs were more important than the football. When the fans keep their heads up, and keep singing after conceding, I think that's really positive. But if the noise after you've scored is the same as the noise after you've missed, I can't see that that helps to motivate the players.

There was no real banter with opposition fans, if any were present. For me, this is one of the best aspects of live football in England; 'You've only come to see the Arsenal/United etc', 'we support our local team', 'sh** club, sh** fans', 'see you on the motorway'. That kind of thing. Thus far, the Jug, with the exception of telling the Bosniaks of Novi Pazar to f*** off, and telling every team that their town is in fact a 'crno-beli grad', hadn't engaged with their rival fans at all. Nor had there been any topical criticism of opposition players.

Another difference was that, with the exception of Diarra and bit-part goalkeeper Ilić, there was no acknowledgement of the input of individual players. Perhaps this was better than in England, where it probably grates on hard-working but anonymous full-backs that they slog their guts out every week only to hear the crowd glorying in a new chant about the creative but lazy right-winger. But there was no way to 'reward' players for a good performance by singing their name. Dušan said that in the old days, it was much closer to the English model, but with Partizan players staying for such short periods, the chanting for individuals had mostly died out.

The second thing was the loyalty itself. The dominant group in the Jug were unquestioningly loyal to the team, the management and the board. But they were getting some freebies from the club, and more importantly their superiority within the Jug, both ideological and probably numerical, was being protected through the banning of one of the other, younger up-and-coming groups.

Was their support really for the club? Or was it really for themselves, and the protection of their special status? More of a politico-economic loyalty rather than one motivated solely by the love of the club. I wasn't doubting their authenticity as Partizan fans, but I did wonder if they would turn up every week if they weren't looked after so well.

I could tell I had been in Serbia for a while – here I was inventing a political conspiracy theory about something that on the face of it had no political element to it at all …

League table after the eighth round:
1. Partizan 21 (+14)
2. Red Star 19 (+12)
3. Sloboda 15 (+3)

The Fight For Justice

PARTIZAN'S next game was against FK Javor from Ivanjica. When the fixture list had come out, Igor had this down as the game to miss, whether you were a resident of Novi Sad or Belgrade. Ivanjica was in the middle of nowhere, and it could be completely snowbound even in late October. You might get most of the way there (four hours from Belgrade) only to find the last 20km was impassable or the match wasn't on. Dušan had given other reasons too – if it didn't snow, we'd get soaked. And Partizan never won there. I talked him round – I would drive, we would check the weather beforehand, we would get three kilos of roast lamb between the two of us. Up to Friday afternoon, that was fine, but then Dušan had to pull out. No one else we knew was going or could be persuaded to go. So I had to choose between spending ten hours mostly on my own, or not going and stretching the credibility of my claim to be a fan.

So I went. I quite enjoy driving, and when else would I get to go to Ivanjica? I had been told by one of my colleagues (an Ivanjica native) that it was quite pretty really – it had a low-rise, pre-communist centre and a stone bridge. 'Like Mostar?' I asked. Not really. But on the whole a stone bridge in the Balkans is usually spectacular.

To entertain myself on the way down, I decided to combine in-journey sustenance with important culinary research. Chipsy, the Serbian equivalent of Walkers, had just launched a competition to find a new 'national' flavour of crisp. You know the kind of thing. In Britain, this means a steak and kidney pie flavour, a fish and chips one, maybe an all-day breakfast crisp. They all taste like a dash more flavouring or a slightly different spice has been added to existing standard flavours. Serbia's three-way competition was between pork loin, sarma (a winter dish made of cabbage leaves stuffed with rice and seasoned ground meat), and gherkin.

The pork loin crisps were a bit like smoky bacon Walkers. OK but nothing special. The sarma ones had a nice spiciness to them, but again, just tasted like a decent version of a standard meat-flavoured crisp. This game wasn't really as exciting as I had hoped, and I was still 100km from Ivanjica. Then I tried the gherkin ones. It is hard to express just how amazingly close to the taste of a gherkin these crisps were. The only thing missing was the dribble of vinegar as I bit into it. If anything, I thought this was a bonus. If I had to mark them down on something, it would be that they were a bit repetitive. But it was a tasty and gherkinous repetition, so they still get nine and a half out of ten. We had a winner. And despite one minor wrong turning, possibly distracted by the rising tide of pickle fumes inside my car, I was nearly at Čačak, and so only 50km from the ground.

I needn't have worried about further in-car entertainment though. Coming up to Čačak, I had just overtaken someone when I saw a car coming the other way flash its headlights at me. Maybe they thought I had got too close to them, but that was unlikely – by Serbian standards, I am an uncourageous overtaker and take far fewer risks than many deem socially acceptable. Then the next one flashed too. And the next one. The Serbs show a spectacular level of solidarity towards one another when it comes to not getting done for speeding.

As is the case in many countries, this flash is the universally-understood signal in the union of motorists (worldwide president, Jeremy Clarkson) that the rozzers are up ahead. In Serbia, union membership is close to saturation. Everyone flashes. You could never argue that you were surprised to see a policeman by the side of the road.

I wasn't going too quickly anyway, but road signs can be quite sparse so it can be less than obvious what the speed limit is. So I backed off a little further. Four corners later, there's the policeman, who sees me and waves furiously to get me to pull over. The police are allowed to pull me over – my diplomatic plates don't exempt me from that. But it is a lot of paperwork for a policeman to complete the required admin to secure a fine or prosecution against us. And all this in the knowledge that some embassies will just claim immunity and ignore it. At our embassy, we are told that a) we must obey all road traffic laws, b) we must cooperate with the police at all times, and c) that for road traffic offences (and indeed most other offences) our immunity will be waived and we will have to face the consequences. I am no rebel, so I pulled over and opened the window.

Policeman: Hello.

Me: Hello. How are you?

Policeman: I'm very well, thank you. How are you?

Me: Alright thanks.

Policeman: So we're both good. That's good.

Pause. For maybe six or seven seconds. For someone who is supposed to be a skilled negotiator, I am terrible with gaps in conversation. I feel the need to fill them. But I can only incriminate myself, or at the very least allude to a potential problem, and a guilty conscience, if I say anything. So I'm going to keep my mouth shut. Eight. Nine. Ten. Oh, come on, this is getting silly.

Eleven. I look at the policeman, who's sort of wandering off towards the back of the car. Twelve. The car that I had overtaken a minute earlier, a smoking and aged Yugo, came past, its driver openly sniggering at me. Thirteen. This policeman should work at the UN – I'm so anxious to get a move on that I may actually sign a confession for something I didn't do at this point. Fourteen. Right, that's it, I'm going to have to say something. If I ask a question, that'll work.

Me: Is everything OK?

Policeman: You were going a bit quickly. But you can go.

Me: Oh, OK, was I? Sorry. Thanks.

Policeman: I mean, not that quickly. A bit quickly. Just a bit.

Me: OK. Well, er, I'll go. Thanks.

Policeman: Like I say, just a bit quickly. Not much at all. Go on.

Maybe he wasn't such a great negotiator after all. Another two sentences and there would have been no diminutive words left to describe how small my infraction was. And I would have thanked him for it. In truth, he just looked a bit lonely, probably fancied a chat. I was allowed on my way.

Past Čačak, I took the right towards Ivanjica. As the car climbed up towards the small town of Guca, the weather was getting progressively worse. Mist, then drizzle, then the mist turned to fog, then it started raining through the fog. The road meanwhile was getting twistier and narrower as it climbed, and while most of the drops were well-protected by barriers, at some hairpins there was nothing between me and an infinite plunge through the clouds.

It was a good job I wasn't still trying to eat crisps and form cogent analysis on their flavours – I needed both hands and for my gustatory intelligence to be transferred to the part of my brain tasked with working out which direction the road was going in. It was not the worst fog I've ever driven in – that was in Yorkshire up on the Dales one night, where it was so thick that I could actually see more by turning the lights off – with them on it was like driving through a glutinous white wall. But it was probably the second worst, and enough to make my stomach feel, in Baldrick's words, 'a bit squirty', and think seriously about turning back. Fortunately, as I descended into Guča, it cleared enough for me to recover my composure and press on.

Guča is worth a quick mention. It is a small, quiet town off the beaten track, but every year, it hosts a festival of trumpet music. A massive festival, attracting, for the last two years, over 800,000 people during the main five days. By comparison, the more widely known EXIT festival has about 200,000 spectators over its four days. Although Guča gets lots of international visitors too, and the competition for best trumpeter attracts some of Europe's best musicians, the festival has a very Serbian flavour to it. The festival's annual meat consumption is a good pointer to its Serbian characteristics – over 1,000 piglets and lambs are roasted, with 50,000 pljeskavica (giant hamburgers) for those preferring a lighter snack. No data is available for vegetables. One and a half million litres of beer helps wash all this down, along with rakija, which the awesome book *How to Understand Serbs* (subtext: you can't, but this book helps) describes as being poured down people's necks like water.

The main attraction of the festival, other than the music, is the feel of a national celebration, which it achieves without being too nationalistic. There are plenty of Serbian flags around, but (mostly) in a celebratory way, combining the strong Serbian love of a party with traditional hospitality and brass music, which binds rather than divides. This sets it apart from Serbia's more modern musical export, turbo folk, which is as despised as it is loved. The fact that many of Serbia's best brass musicians are Roma people, in the main neglected by society, but wildly celebrated for their musical talents

Igor (right) and me in the PFC trophy room

Igor infuriated with the team against Shkendia

Stadion Partizan

Sloboda fans march through the streets of Uzice en route to the game

Pyrotechnics to celebrate our goal against Spartak Subotica

The three-row away stand at Javor

The fight for justice

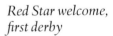
*Red Star welcome,
first derby*

Smashed seats in our section

Anti-Serb banner, Novi Pazar

Second derby – Partizan pyrotechnics

Away at Kula

Away at Rad, played at Obilic stadium

Home against Red Star – trying to intimidate the opposition

*Kosovo
is Serbia.
Except that
it isn't*

*Avram at
half-time,
away at
Kragujevac*

*The police
confront the
Zabranjeni*

Zabranjeni try to rescue their brethren from the police

Zabranjeni create a smokescreen for their attack on the Alcatraz

Proof that David Manga did indeed score a competitive goal for Partizan

Peering through the murk – a typical post-pyrotechnic view at the derby

(and in high demand for any wedding party worth its salt), makes Guča a positive affirmation of Serbian-ness. A temporary one, but it's a start.

Just outside Guča, having circumnavigated the town's maze of trumpet-adorned roundabouts, I got stopped by the police again. There was no way I had done anything wrong this time. Our conversation was much shorter, two hellos and I was told to be on my way. My guess is that he wanted to make sure that it was actually a diplomat driving the car with diplomatic plates. And while he couldn't have been able to guess from that brief exchange whether I was any good as a persuader, mediator or political analyst, he could probably tell just by looking at me that I was a foreigner. Not many Serbians have my round face or oversized forehead. Almost everyone knows I'm foreign before I even open my mouth. The police in Guča were part of the outer cordon of security for the match – I'd already seen a group of police vans waiting in Čačak as the first line of defence, to escort the Partizan groups' buses.

Around Javor's stadium, I counted probably a hundred police before I got to the ticket counter. Having wandered into the town centre, been disappointed by the bridge, which was from the 20th century and almost impossible to look at unless you were in the river itself, and wandered back, it was hard to tell why there were so many police. There were only 600 fans in the entire stadium, about 300 of each. I say stadium. Ivanjica is a small town, and it has a small ground. I played in a bigger one in Horley once (on merit – I've also played in a couple of huge stadiums, but they were specially arranged games), which made me feel sort of proud. The 'stand' I was in had three rows of seats and a wall. That was it.

A couple of hundred more Partizan fans arrived as the game kicked off – meaning that even this far from home the guests were outnumbering the hosts quite comfortably. The police numbers still seemed excessive, even given the quasi-military precision of bussing them in and out. But, as I discovered via text from Dušan, there was a very good reason for police numbers being boosted. The murder earlier that morning of a young Partizan fan, Ivan Perović, had raised tensions significantly. Perović was a member of a group known as the 'Koalicija Beograd' [Belgrade Coalition], a sub-group of the Zabranjeni, and police were treating his death as connected to the ongoing feud between the Zabranjeni and Alcatraz.

Perović was 20 years old. He and his friend Đorđe Stanojević had been out for the night and were on the streets near their home in the Novi Beograd suburb when a silver BMW drove towards them and shots were fired. Perović was hit several times in the hip and abdomen, and Stanojević in the lower leg. Although an ambulance arrived minutes later, Perović died in hospital from his wounds. Very shortly before, they had been involved in a fight with two men from the Alcatraz group, with close links to one of Alcatraz's most notorious leaders.

This drive-by was the latest in a series of increasingly violent incidents between the two supposed 'fan groups'. This season's conflict built on an incident at last year's away game in Subotica, when a fan from one of the groups that morphed into the Zabranjeni had been stabbed on a bus on the way back to Belgrade. After the close season, at the end of summer, two of the Zabranjeni had stabbed a young man at a birthday party for the daughter of a member of the Partizan administrative staff. Two Alcatraz members had then torched a Zabranjeni leader's car in September. The cycle of tit-for-tat violence had begun.

Following this, members of both gangs had indulged in a spree of breaking into the apartments of rival leaders, attacking them with baseball bats, beating up their family members, and threatening other people connected to them. Partizan official Darko Grubor, who had been accused by the Zabranjeni of being the main force behind them being, well, zabranjeni [banned], had been subjected to a campaign of low-level intimidation: stone-throwing, graffiti and verbal threats around his apartment building, which were causing his family stress. The police, in briefings to the media, said that the details of most of the attacks were only reaching them long after they had happened, as the groups wanted to settle the scores themselves, rather than rely on official justice.

Partizan isn't unique in the existence of long-standing feuds between fans of the same club. Presently, the battle was between Alcatraz and the Zabranjeni, but that wasn't always the case – the groups have had different names and many of the former protagonists have 'retired', either out of football or to a more comfortable viewing position in the Istok or Zapad. The reasons behind it aren't that unusual either – 'control' of the Jug is a lucrative business. A group leader with enough followers can exert pressure on a club.

Every big club wants to attract lots of fans – to pay for match tickets, club merchandise and, more importantly, demonstrate to the corporate sponsors that there's a big market to advertise to. Someone with a couple of thousand fans behind him can expect some privileges from the club management to keep his followers coming – and the leaders are all too ready to threaten a boycott if they don't get their way. These privileges at Partizan, as at other clubs, seemed to extend to: free tickets, for onward distribution to loyal lieutenants, resale, or to help bring in new followers; money to pay for the choreography – the loudhailers for directing the chants, and the banners; subsidised travel to away games; and a blind eye to favoured fans bringing in the fireworks and lighters. Not surprising then that other groups want a piece of the action, especially when – it was alleged – at the big clubs, the group leaders were also controlling who had the right to sell snacks or scarves outside the ground, and distribution of club merchandise in some towns, always taking a fat cut of any profits made.

Mirroring Serbia's political system, with over 100 parties and a governing coalition of 16, the fan group structure, each taking, or trying to take, their share of the cut, was pretty byzantine. Some groups were subsumed into other, larger ones. Other groups kept their identity but allied with a larger umbrella group. Sometimes a group would act like a federation, sometimes more like a central government. Groups changed sides or 'went neutral', playing one group against another in the hope of getting a better offer. Groups would indulge in their own micro-level feuds, or fight for a wider cause in their 'enlightened' self-interest. All of this is familiar to anyone who has taken a close look at football in any of a number of European countries.

What was different about the scale of the feud between the Zabranjeni and Alcatraz was that now the press were insinuating that football had really become a side issue for the gangs, and this was becoming a more classic turf war, in which football and organised crime mixed freely, and influence over large numbers of fans was linked to territory controlled in the city and creating the space for a thriving drug-dealing business. Citing sources in the Ministry of the Interior, a couple of papers were now claiming that this was the real background behind the fighting.

Media manipulation in Serbia (it's too sophisticated and not quite clear-cut enough to call it control) is a subtle business, but often when the papers start to go after a person, whether a criminal, businessman, politician, or combination of the three, it's usually a sign of government dissatisfaction with them, or a signal that something has gone too far. Effectively, the media, using information directed towards them or allowed to reach them by the government, slowly shift public opinion against the people in question, creating a situation where the government feels compelled to respond to that very same public opinion.

This looked like a warning to the groups that they were fast reaching the limit of what could be tolerated, and that the authorities were ready to act against them. Certainly the noises from the Ministry of Interior 'source' reflecting police concern that the violence might be repeated looked like the start of an old-fashioned scare campaign.

Back to the football. With the Partizan fans still coming through, and so few people in total in the ground, the atmosphere was a bit muted as the referee led the players out. One of the Javor fans, a big man who looked about 50 and had a voice as gravelly as Miša Tumbas's, stood up and yelled some exhortations at Javor and some standard accusations of thievery and subordination to Red Star at Partizan. That got it started. If the guy had intended to blend in and insult anonymously, he'd picked the wrong outfit, dressed in a custard-coloured puffer jacket. I couldn't pick out all of the oaths hurled at him, but if I had to summarise the gist of it, he was addressed as a big yellow eggy c*** and invited quite hoarsely to sit down and shut up.

And we were away. Partizan's now 500-strong contingent were making an excellent noise, magnified by the fact that the north end of the ground was just a wall, producing an echo that made them sound twice as numerous. Having driven four hours to get here, the game was terrible, obviously. I have a habit of travelling long distances with Arsenal to see poor games: an eight-hour round trip to see us scrape a 1-0 win at Sunderland in Arctic temperatures in mid-May, flying to Turin to see Juventus reserves beat us 1-0 and put us out of the Champions League at the group stage, and going all the way to Kiev and only escaping with a draw thanks to the bobbliest, shinniest equaliser from that well-known goal-poacher, William Gallas. So a dull 0-0 was definitely on the cards.

Partizan had 80 per cent possession in the first half, but only one shot to speak of. Javor's long ball tactics would have shamed rugby union. As it was, in the opening 44 minutes, the best chance fell to Javor, when one of their strikers ran on to a long ball and fell over in the box. It wasn't a penalty, but it might have been if the ref had felt like livening things up.

The lack of fireworks in the match was compensated for by a dozen fireworks lobbed on to the pitch in the first half. In a smaller ground than usual, some of them were reaching the playing area. Javor's goalkeeper complained to the referee at one point, with some justification, but the ref, like most of the security guards and police, realised that it was a lost cause trying to tackle the issue, and told the keeper to deal with it.

A few crackers would have been easy to sneak into the ground by comparison to the 15-metre-long banner that had also been smuggled through. Partizan's theme of the day was the 'Borba za Pravdu' [Fight for Justice]. As well as the big banner, which blocked half of the south stand's view for a couple of minutes, there was a second, longer and thinner one, which read '24.10, Srbija očekuje istinu I pravdu!' [24 October, Serbia expects the truth and justice!]. A court appeal process was due to begin on Monday (the 24th) against the convictions of several Partizan fans jailed for their alleged part in the killing of a French football fan, Brice Taton.

Brice was a Toulouse fan, attacked in the afternoon leading up to a Europa League game between Partizan and Toulouse on 17 September 2009. He and a small group of friends were in a bar just off Belgrade's main pedestrian street, Knez Mihajlova, when a group of about 15 to 20 thugs came in off the street and attacked the French group, injuring two of them badly and singling Brice out for a horrific barrage of blows, using wooden clubs and iron bars to lay into him repeatedly. Only the intervention of a brave Serbian patron and the imminent arrival of the police prevented them from chucking Brice over a ten-metre wall.

Although conscious when he got into the ambulance, Brice had suffered significant internal damage to many organs, and multiple fractures to his skull, injuring his brain. A fit and healthy 28-year-old, he was able to fight the injuries for a while, but fell into a coma and his condition deteriorated rapidly, before he died 11 days after the attack on 28 September. Serbia was in the grip of a bout of attacks on foreigners at the time – an Australian and a Libyan were attacked in separate incidents in the week around the attack on Brice, and an attempt to hold a Gay Pride parade had been abandoned when right-wing thugs threatened serious violence if it went ahead.

The French government naturally put immediate pressure on the Serbian authorities to bring the perpetrators of the crime, which the French Ambassador described as a lynching, to justice. Within days of the attack, the Serbian police had arrested 11 suspects, arresting more shortly afterwards. By January, 14 people had been convicted for their part in the murder. The alleged ringleaders, Đorđe Prelić (he is also the 'notorious leader' a few paragraphs ago) and Dejan Pužigaca, were sentenced in absentia to 35 and 32 years respectively. Two more men, Ljubomir Marković and Ivan Grković, received 30-year sentences. Ten more men were sentenced to between 12 and 14 years.

Prelić and Pužigaca are still at large. Earlier in 2011, Prelić was reportedly hiding out in Croatia, lying low and hoping to exploit the poor (but improving) judicial cooperation between Croatia and Serbia. But more recently, he was allegedly back in Belgrade, in possession of false documents, and in charge of Alcatraz, including ordering the burning of the jeep I mentioned before. In addition to this, the *Blic* newspaper, one of the more reliable in Serbia, said he was running a profitable drug-dealing business from an anonymous tower block.

Why is this a fight for justice? Because lots of Partizan fans believe that the wrong people were convicted, and that the convictions for those who were sent down were overly harsh. Even within the ranks of those who are 'fighting for justice', there are different varieties of the 'truth' that needs to come out, but there are two common themes that run through all of their accounts.

The first is that it wasn't a fair trial. The government, under pressure from France and the wider European Union, and keen to repair the damage to its reputation, told the police to make sure they convicted someone soon. The evidence gathered was flimsy, and the defendants weren't given enough time to prepare a defence. Then, conditions for the trial itself were influenced by a long phase of 'preparing the ground', as one Grobar, calling himself Sentinel on the forums, put it. The media were heavily involved in creating a case against the men eventually convicted. The second thread is that the sentences were too harsh – over 30 years for people not directly proven to have hit Brice Taton, and therefore surely not guilty of murder, in the eyes of the convicted men's supporters. The principle of collective guilt applied by the trial judge adds to the fury of those involved in the borba, another demonstration that the judgement was written before the trial began.

Had a miscarriage of justice taken place? My sympathy for the convicted was limited by the differing stories I had heard about 'the truth'. The truth ranged from none of the convicted being guilty ('our brothers aren't killers') and the real perpetrators supporting another club, to the French fans having started the fight, to the trial having only caught some of the real perpetrators and then gathered up a few Partizan 'undesirables' to make up the numbers, and get people disliked by the police off the streets.

Another reason for not wholeheartedly joining the campaign was the nationalist overtone that part of the campaign had taken on. It took less than a few minutes of searching online for material relating to the case to find some grotesque examples of moral relativism and claims of bias against Serbs – the apex of which was one forum poster (who got plenty of support from his mates) comparing the number of years in prison received by Brice's attackers to the number of years that Croats had received at the International Criminal Tribunal for war crimes against ethnic Serbs during the 1992–95 war.

Serbia's judicial system was in the middle of some major reforms, some of which had gone well, others which hadn't. Outside observers said that overall, the country's justice system was improving. I couldn't do much else but to hope that this would rub off on the appeal hearings and that there could be some genuine closure to the case, enabling Brice's family to move on with their lives as far as possible, and for Partizan fans to accept that justice had been served, even if that meant swallowing the fact that some of their fellow 'fans' were in fact criminals.

It was easy to forget that, on the pitch, a football match was trying to break through the sporting torpor and draw the crowd's attention from the political protest. On the stroke of half-time, third-choice right-bank Miljković overcame his fear of attacking and crossed the ball in. Four players from each side had a go at either clearing or scoring, and it bobbled to Marković, who poked in from about six yards. It was a fitting Sunday league goal for the Sunday league surroundings.

In the second half, Javor had a bit more of the ball but they weren't ever really threatening, and Partizan scored another goal.

Babović, who had had an anonymous if inoffensive game, played a through-ball which was diverted into the path of Vukić, who had been playing similarly inconspicuously. His first touch wasn't great, and his shot hit the keeper but skidded under him and bounced up into the net. Two goals as far from the definition of classic as possible. Dušan, via text, was appalled at those two players continuing to justify their existence in the starting line-up by doing something as underhand and sneaky as combining for a goal.

We got a three-minute treat at the end of the match when David Manga made his league debut. He looked like a good enough player, if slightly baffled at his surroundings. Ivanjica is a long way from the Paris Saint-Germain youth academy. We didn't get to see Eduardo, who stayed on the bench. His pre-match preparations had been interrupted by a story carried widely in the media of his wife being attacked by stray dogs while out jogging. This isn't funny, obviously, and luckily she wasn't seriously injured. But it was strange to see the story carried by practically every news website as if it was major news.

As soon as the final whistle went, I legged it back to the car. I didn't want to get held up while the police mounted a major security operation to get the bulk of the Partizan fans back on to their buses. And it was freezing. So I was pleased to get back into the car for the journey back, where it was warm. It smelled strongly of gherkins though.

League table after the ninth round:
1. Partizan 24 (+16)
2. Red Star 22 (+14)
3. Sloboda 18 (+4)

Ivan Perović

THE build-up to the derby with Red Star went astonishingly well on the pitch. Partizan saw off Metalac in the cup, earning the right the play the quarter-final away at OFK. Vukić's great run of form continued with two goals that virtually ended the game after just nine minutes. Partizan's mostly sub-and-reserve line-up saw the rest of the game out in comfort, conceding a goal but sealing the victory with a late effort from substitute Babović for 3-1.

Stanojević used the opportunity to try out a few players – with Manga getting his first start (he had a brilliant opening 15 minutes and then faded) and Brazilian defender Anderson Marques making his first competitive appearance for the club. Marques had been brought in from the Brazilian Second Division over the summer, arrived in Belgrade and got immediately injured. An abortive 'comeback' was prevented by another injury, but this time he did actually play. Metalac were so poor that it wasn't really a test if he was any good. But he played 90 minutes and only fell over once, to a pre-emptive wince from Goran, who was sure that Marques's glass ankles/knees/hips (delete as applicable) wouldn't withstand the impact.

In the league, Partizan extended their lead over Red Star (who drew at Sloboda) to four points with another 3-1 home win, this time against Smederevo. Claire was in Belgrade and came to watch again, noting that this wouldn't have been the case had I not pleaded the match's importance for this book.

This time the game itself was impressive, with Partizan creating a series of chances, and looking dangerous every time they went forward. Smederevo contributed too by actually trying, unlike the majority of teams who had played against Partizan so far this season. I don't mean to overstate it, but it was actually an enjoyable, high-tempo game that neutrals would have wanted to watch. That could only have been said for one or two games so far this season.

Vukić (who else?) scored first with a curler through a crowd of players, and Claire (in full knowledge that it would wind Dušan up) praised his contribution to the team. 'He's playing really well, isn't he? So how come you don't like him?' Dušan made to speak, then thought better of it. Composing himself once more, he said that many of the reasons were unrepeatable in front of a lady, even one from Bradford. 'But mostly I don't like his fat arse.' It was an irrational argument, but he had a point – it looked like the slim Vukić had half a pumpkin jammed down the back of his shorts.

Šćepović doubled the lead with his best moment of the season, running 30 yards, beating two players and firing in a low diagonal shot. After Partizan had conceded a sloppy goal to make the second half more interesting, they cut Smederevo open with a slick four-player move before Ilić rounded the goalkeeper. Going the wrong way, his pass to Marković left the young striker wide of the goal and allowed two defenders to get back. No matter. Marković lobbed them and the goalkeeper for a fantastic third. We even got to see David Manga again, to the delight of Miša Tumbas, who yelled at 'Mangica' [the little mango] hoarsely for a full ten minutes. Manga looked utterly bewildered.

BSK provided minimal meaningful threat but plenty of stubbornness, limiting Partizan to a 1-0 win in what was the worst game of the season so far. Šćepović grabbed his second goal in as many games, bursting through the middle and finishing neatly. Jovančić came on as a sub and got into one-on-one positions twice, only to mess them both up, but overall it was a thoroughly laboured performance. Although not many of them, Marković and the full-backs excepted, were trying to run that often, it was as if the team were being controlled by someone with a PlayStation controller who had jammed the sprint button down – every pass was straight forward with no thought or vision, and every dribble straight into a BSK tackle. Tomić looked pallid and sweaty on a mild day for early November, like he was ill, or hung over. Stanojević's substitutions were increasingly regressive, turning a team that initially carried a decent attacking threat into one that was slow, lacking dynamism, and unable to turn possession into chances. By the end of the match, the midfield five of Medo, Babović, Vukić, Ilić and Smiljanić, the latter looking like he was filling his shirt more capaciously than earlier in the season, was a ponderous bunch.

Vukić summed up just how terrible the game was when the ball scuffed its way towards him on the edge of the area. As the crowd urged him to shoot, he lined himself up for a curler towards the far post, and caught it clean in the middle of his shin, sending it out for a throw-in on the far side. The cliché of 'a win is a win' was never truer, but it was hard to believe that the performance against Smederevo and this one were both worthy of three points.

Against Borac, from the central Serbian city of Čačak, Partizan were on fire, burning through the thick fog to notch up a 5-1 win, their 11th consecutive victory in all competitions. Nemanja Tomić, looking much healthier than he did against BSK, opened the scoring in the 17th minute with a free kick over the wall that I could barely see, given how impenetrable the fog was from 80 yards. I charitably assumed that the goalkeeper's vision was similarly impaired. Marković scored a second goal that emphasised his pricelessness to the team, creating a chance from nothing by scorching clear of the defence and jabbing the ball under the goalkeeper. Dušan fretted that Partizan might not be able to keep him beyond the January transfer window, such was his form.

After Borac scored a good goal on the counter-attack, Partizan stretched their legs in the second half and added three more goals. Firstly, Vukić (having just been bumped off the top scorer's slot by Tomić) cut through the middle of the Borac defence and scuffed a shot over the keeper diving at his feet. Then Tomić put himself back at the top of the charts, scoring his tenth and best goal of the season so far. Receiving the ball on the edge of the area after a sweeping Partizan move that left the Borac defence stretched, he bent a shot into a postage stamp of space in the top corner, beating both the keeper's dive and a defender's despairing jump on the line. 'Prodaj ga odmah!' [Sell him immediately!] urged Dušan to the total bemusement of everyone around him. Borac completed the rout themselves, when one of their defenders' motor skills deserted him and his left leg beat his brain to the ball and sent it skidding past his own keeper.

Red Star had won every game since their draw against Sloboda, so we would go into the derby four points clear. A few of our group muttered darkly that the gap 'should be bigger' but for soft penalties and surprising late turnarounds. But the gap meant that they were under more severe pressure than us for the big one. The teams fighting for third had taken turns to drop more points, making it more and more obvious that this was really only going to be a two-horse race. Incumbents Radnički were now nine points behind us, and five behind Red Star.

Partizan made it 13 wins in a row in domestic competitions with a straightforward 2-0 success away at OFK in the cup, a game I couldn't make because it was at 1pm and I was on a work trip in the south of the country. Diarra, allowed a rare start, got the first, and Lazar Marković scored two minutes after coming on as a sub (his legs being saved for the derby at the weekend). So Partizan were through to next year's semis, where they would face one of Red Star, Vojvodina or bottom-of-the-table Borac. Borac please!

Off the pitch, it was a whole lot more unsavoury. Where even to start? Best to start with the light misdemeanours and move from there. The players' commitment to the club wasn't looking too wholesome. Lazar Marković was in the papers before the match with Metalac declaring his wish to play for Chelsea. The story had made it back to Serbia via the BBC's gossip column and a website entirely dedicated to rumour-mongering. But the message was the same no matter what language or what site the story was on 'Chelsea's the club that I love the most, after Partizan of course. I'd like to play there. I believe that the best football is played in England, that league would suit me.' There was also interest from Fiorentina, who wanted to take 'the new Stevan Jovetić' to add to, well, Stevan Jovetić, the Montenegrin striker who had left Partizan at 18 to become a huge success in Florence. Chairman Đurić and sporting director Krstajić said that they had no intention of selling their young star, but neither the player nor his agent denied that the story was true.

Nemanja Tomić went a bit further, giving an interview to the daily sports paper *Sportski Žurnal* in which he openly said that the coming January transfer window should mean his departure from Partizan. Tomić had been subject to a bid from OGC Nice in the summer, of about €1.5m, but this hadn't been enough for the board, so he had stayed. There had been talk of those fervent Partizanophiles Fiorentina making a bid in January, something Dušan was constantly and publicly hoping for. Even after ten goals in less than half a season, he still wasn't convinced that Partizan were improved by keeping him. He only really tolerated Tomić's presence in the side and the goals he scored on the grounds that it would accelerate his exit from the club. Pearlers like the one he got against Borac were appreciated for their market value rather than their technical excellence.

Tomić's interview melded an inflated belief in his own talent and a recognition that his partying habits and constant appearance in the gossip columns might have worn a bit thin. 'To be honest, I think that it's time for me to leave Partizan in the winter transfer window. The people in charge haven't said whether I'm on sale in January, however, if a suitable offer arrives, I believe that they won't stand in my way. I've helped Partizan a lot in the last two years, and also, probably being honest, I recognise that I have, at some moments, been a significant burden to the club. That's in relation to activities that haven't pleased either the fans or the coaching staff, and which I alone initiated. When you look at it realistically, I've been through a lot in Serbia and it's logical that I would continue my career overseas.' Maybe if the club you moved to was in a country with no bars and no women, eh, Nemanja?

If Marković's link to Chelsea had irritated the board a bit, then Tomić's naked manoeuvring for a transfer really hit a nerve. Krstajić, having to deny an impending transfer for the second time in less than a week, said that Tomić should shut up and concentrate on recapturing his early-season form.

Even players who weren't angling to leave weren't exactly behaving themselves. In Vladimir Volkov's case, he denied any wrongdoing, but his name was plastered all over the tabloids for allegedly stalking Serbian 'starlet' and *Playboy* playmate Stanija Dobrojević. Stanija had gone public with a series of lovelorn text messages, said to be from Volkov, and was now saying that an angered Volkov was threatening her, again by SMS. It looked more like the girl was trying to get her winsome picture in the papers. Either that or one of Smiljanić or Tomić had been borrowing Volkov's phone …

Marko Šćepović had managed to upset most of the fans too. Straight after scoring his fantastic goal against Smederevo, he had sprinted to the touchline nearest the Istok and raised a lone index finger to his lips to silence a fan who had been giving him all sorts of stick during the warm-up. The trouble was, it looked like he was actually trying to silence the whole Istok. Given that most of his touches in the previous three or four games had been met with a mixture of scepticism and hostility, that was a fair assumption.

Šćepović's great goal, which had initially been met warmly by the crowd, suddenly counted for nothing. This lazy good for nothing was giving us stick? Well, screw him. Maybe there were only 800 people in the whole of the stand, but half of them were on their feet, booing, whistling and otherwise making clear to Šćepović that one goal didn't make up for half a season of inactivity. Stanojević had the right idea and took him off at half-time to avoid any more misunderstandings, and then shoved him out of the dressing room after the game to a waiting pack of journalists to say a half-hearted sorry to the fans. When he scored the following week against BSK, he had the good sense to just be happy. It didn't stop 300 people standing up to shush him in mock retaliation, and some wag shouting, 'Shut up and score more goals!', but at least one incident had been put to bed.

All the good football Partizan were playing mattered little, because no one was coming to watch it. Against Metalac, there were maybe 2,000 in the ground, and against Smederevo fewer than 1,500. Away at BSK, there were only about 200 hardcore Grobari when there was space for more like 800 – and at a ground only six miles from Partizan's own. The fatal shooting of Ivan Perović had been a step too far in the battle for supremacy of the Jug. Lots of fans decided that enough was enough, and that they weren't going to come to the stadium anymore if they were going to have to share it with a group that had murdered one of its rivals. To fight for control of the south stand, even using physical violence, most people could cope with, but guns were another thing.

Dušan and Igor both told me that several of their friends, who had been coming to Partizan for decades, just couldn't justify it anymore. In most cases, it wasn't a fear thing – the Alcatraz hoods or any of the main rival groups weren't going to target anyone not in a direct rival gang, but more a protest that the club was still semi-officially endorsing Alcatraz as the dominant group. Dušan hoped out loud that something good would come out of Perović's death, and that the club would realise that their divide-and-rule policy wasn't working.

Between the Metalac and Smederevo games, Ivan Perović's funeral had been held. Over a thousand people had attended, according to the media, and the cortege had been accompanied by 600 Grobari as it passed through the city. The scene around the grave looked and sounded like a scene from the curve of the Jug, mourners decked out in black and white, flares lit, Perović's favourite Partizan songs sung mournfully by the Grobari choir. The boundary between football and religion was truly blurred. Perović's father wore a Partizan shirt as he paid his last respects to his 21-year-old son. Theirs was a family that lived for Partizan, but wasn't prepared for anyone to die for Partizan.

Of more concern to the authorities, and to the club, was the threat of repercussions. Vengeful posts had begun to appear on the internet in the immediate aftermath of the killing, and more sprung up following the funeral. Members of the Zabranjeni wanted to end their mourning period and concentrate on avenging Perović's murder. The police took the threat of violence seriously enough for police sources to leak to the press the threat of a thousand-plus fan fight between the Zabranjeni and Alcatraz being organised somewhere in the city. On the day of the game against Smederevo, you could have been forgiven for thinking that Barack Obama was in Belgrade, there were that many police on the streets across the whole city. The largest concentration was outside the Saint Sava church, Belgrade's biggest, just a few hundred metres from the stadium and a known meeting point. On this day, the police outnumbered Saturday afternoon tourists and worshippers by four to one, saturating the area to dissuade Alcatraz and the Zabranjeni from facing off on the church's plaza (a holy but conveniently sized expanse of concrete).

Đurić and the club took the extraordinary measure of banning all ticket sales for the match, restricting the game to season ticket holders only (meaning that Claire had to come to the game pretending to be called Martin). In purely security terms, this was probably a sensible thing to do. It prevented a thousand people from coming to the ground, or having a pretext to come

The atmosphere inside the stadium suffered for their decision. Numbers were low, but the real reason was that the core Alcatraz followers took up their regular places behind the goal in the Jug and behaved at best like nothing had happened and at worst with a degree of pride. Against Metalac and Smederevo, the two games immediately following Perović's death, the main banners behind the goal (which change from match to match, displaying a variety of messages, either pro-Partizan, anti-opposition, something nationalistic or, on occasion, the name of a prominent group) gave a stark message. The only two banners visible at the start of each match read GROBARI – ALCATRAZ. They may as well have said F*** YOU. WE RUN THIS JOINT. Serbia doesn't have as solid a tradition of minutes' silences as in England, but there was no commemoration for Perović, nor any official expression of condolence or remorse at his death.

Our regular group was only at half-strength against Smederevo, a couple unable to buy tickets, the others not willing to come to the stadium. Our group was not alone. Throughout the games with low attendances, the guys who did turn up were constantly receiving texts from people still too scared or too angry to come. Of those who did, their disgust for the bullish attitude for those self-congratulating Alcatraz members singing behind the goal was palpable. Also their fear. Before they would let me note down anything, they insisted that I didn't name names when I quoted them in the book. They said it was touch and go whether I should really write about it in terms of my own safety, given Alcatraz's intolerance for criticism and competition. This felt like a bit of an exaggeration, and in any case the still hypothetical book wouldn't be published, if at all, until well into the following year. So I quote a couple of things that were said, 'It's like nothing has happened. As long as they're in place, and they're still in control, they don't f***ing care.'

And, 'I wonder why the club is putting up with it. The club can't make any money if there aren't any fans. Even the TV money and selling all the best players won't cover it. It doesn't work as a business model.'

Plus, 'So what do these guys have on the management? They've all been up to some dodgy sh**, the management must know that the Alcatraz guys will take them down with them if they're cut loose. You're not writing that down, are you?'

The Zabranjeni decided to go guerrilla with their protests, seeing as the stadium and city centre were out of bounds. Partizan's women's basketball team played to a bigger crowd than the men's football team had against Smederevo, after 600 Zabranjeni turned up, frightening the life out of the Czech opposition. The Zabranjeni decided they liked it, and came to the next two games in even bigger numbers. The coach of the women's basketball team was delighted, if bemused, by the vocal support for her team, though conscious that it wasn't totally in the spirit of the game to scare the sh** out of your opponents with a thousand unfulfilled baying football fans.

Away at BSK, enterprising Zabranjeni had decorated the entire route between the main road and stadium with pro-Zabranjeni graffiti. To be honest, it blended in to the scruffy neighbourhood of Borča, where BSK play. More cheekily, they had spray-painted 'ZABRANJENI' on a row of seats that they knew the Alcatraz boys would be using for the match. It was funny, in a puerile way, but it wasn't really advancing their cause – the club was making no overtures towards their rehabilitation, nor efforts to rein in Alcatraz. But the club had to do something before the derby.

At this rate, the Partizan end of the stadium wasn't going to be full, with so many regular but vaguely sensible Partizan fans refusing to share space with the Alcatraz mob. That would be bad publicity, bad for the bragging rights of best-supported club in Belgrade, and bad for bolstering the team at (statistically) the hardest game of the season. A 'mole' within the club, well, a mate of Dušan's with connections to the marketing department, said that the club was going to do something before then. But it wasn't clear what.

Before the game against Borac, Dušan had also heard that the Zabranjeni were going to try and get into the stadium. Not into the Jug, and not in formation, but into either the Zapad or Sever. The tactics had not been discussed on their web forums, where the invitations to the female basketball had originated. This was all being done under the radar on text messages and BlackBerry Messenger. Partizan's efforts to keep its own fans out had gone far enough to include surveillance outside the stadium, but I doubted that they had the capability to start eavesdropping on fans' communications.

When we arrived, the fog was so dense that frankly we couldn't see anyone in the other stands, let alone identify them as Zabranjeni. But about ten minutes into the game, they started their own chanting, pitting their volume against the 300 or so in the Jug. So they definitely were here. Peering through the murk, it was just about possible to distinguish the grey shapes of maybe a hundred fans gathered in the Zapad, towards the back and just to the north of the halfway line. Their position was close enough that the board members, whose box is directly above the halfway line in that stand, could definitely hear them. I am sure that wasn't an accident.

Maybe this was a time for reconciliation, for the two sides to bury the hatchet and unite in support of the crno-beli? Well, frankly, no. I am so naïve sometimes. The Alcatraz reaction was to boo a bit, then turn up their leader's loudhailer to try and drown out the rival group. The Zabranjeni (having got in, they might need a new nickname, because they didn't seem too 'banned' anymore) sang some of the usual numbers, but also repeatedly chorused the name of their fallen member, Ivan Perović, cheekily asked the Jug to 'make itself heard', and pointedly sought the involvement of us in the Istok in some of their songs. I knew by now that there were plenty of people in the Istok who enjoy a bit of provocation, but I was taken aback by just how many people joined in around me. There was no torn allegiance here – this was a strong display of support from the Istok to the Zabranjeni. It didn't seem to bother the guys in the Jug – they just kept on with their routine of songs like nothing had happened. So I joined in too. But only because I support the idea of pluralism, not because I was taking sides. Honest.

Sensibly, though possibly with encouragement from the club, the Zabranjeni shuffled out of the ground with ten minutes to go. Sympathy for their 'plight' couldn't be sustained if they got into a physical fight with the Alcatraz boys straight after the game. And in any case, they had made their point – enough of them could get in to make some noise and show that the group lived on. They were either too smart for the club to stop them, or the club was relenting in its prejudice against them. Within and without the ground, the usual police 'spotters' and 'liaison officers' were in attendance, and club stewards had registered the presence of the group by moving some of their number round the ground to keep an eye on them. But they'd been allowed in, and allowed to stay. Whichever way you looked at it, the Zabranjeni had taken the points this time.

League table after the 12th round:
1. Partizan 33 (+23)
2. Red Star 29 (+18)
3. Radnički 24 (+11)

The Eternal Derby

THE practice of peace and reconciliation is one of the most vital and artistic of human actions. So said the Vietnamese Buddhist monk and peace activist Nhat Hanh. Unfortunately, he wasn't in charge of the arrangements for the 141st derby between Red Star and Partizan. Nhat Hanh's musings on football security, and the results of his many hours of meditation on segregating fans, are sadly unrecorded, but, and I am taking a bit of a punt here, he probably wouldn't have counselled in favour of jabbing the Zabranjeni with a stick.

No statement or other communication emanated from the club in the build-up to the match to try and heal the divisions, or even freeze them in the name of unity before the biggest game of the season so far. Dušan's mole had been burrowing in the wrong direction. Instead, official efforts to keep the Zabranjeni away from Partizan's games were stepped up.

The authorities seemed to have a mole with sharper claws and a better nose for whatever it is that moles sniff out. They had got wind that the Zabranjeni were planning to avoid sharing the south stand at the Marakana with their Alcatraz foes, but were going to pull a similar trick as they had against Borac, and filter into the east stand incognito, before forming up as a group inside the ground. The neutral/family east and west stands are supposed to be out of bounds for the ultras, and Red Star would not fancy the prospect of a thousand wronged Grobari in among their fans, and the accompanying risk of something big kicking off inside the ground. So they reacted.

Their security manager publicly asked fans not to form into big groups in those stands, and said that anyone doing so would immediately be escorted to either the north (Red Star) or south (Partizan).

An adroit plan, with just two minor flaws. Firstly, dragging a couple of Zabranjeni out of the east or west stand, if that's what transpired, was likely to be pretty messy for those at the group's periphery, and the people sitting near them. Secondly, having extracted them and wound them up a bit, transferring them to the south? Putting one group of fans in the Marakana's famous away fan 'cage' with the group that's their sworn enemy? That sounded like a recipe for some serious bother, not unlike the build-up to a cock fight or some other illegal animal pugilism in an East End drinking den.

Maybe I was being overly cynical. Then the ticket website we had planned to use put a notice up on their front page that the Ministry of Interior (Serbia's Home Office, so the police's bosses) had banned them from selling tickets for the east stand. Not the other stands, but just the east, where the Zabranjeni were most likely to congregate. So they had two choices if they wanted to see the game – pay for the most expensive tickets in the west and risk being chucked out, or go to the south and risk being involved in a fight.

In this battle of wills, the authorities seemed determined not to be outsmarted by the Zabranjeni again. It seemed like they were trying to do one of two things: stop the Zabranjeni from coming altogether – the safest option all round for this game – or force them into the south, where there would undoubtedly be trouble. If it did kick off, there would be strong legal grounds for banning (really banning) anyone involved, and indeed imprisoning anyone caught committing a violent act within the stadium – like our moustachioed friend from the Jagodina game. Was this what they wanted – a showdown that ended with an artificially-created judicial chance to silence the rebels? Equally likely was that this was just a cack-handed security response, but I had a nagging doubt, encouraged by Dušan, chock-full of conspiracy theories, that the force of the law was being used as a selective threat to advance the interests of a small group.

We got our tickets easily enough, two days before the game. We took a taxi to Red Star's ground, which Dušan refused to name, referring only to 'the ticket office on Ljutica Bogdana Street', walked up to the counter and bought tickets for the east (the exact same ones being banned from online sale). We weren't asked for ID, which is standard practice, and there was no obvious 'spotter' monitoring the sales, just a bored-looking sales clerk. We could easily have been a couple of Zabranjeni. Well, Dušan could. I look like the least convincing hooligan ever.

Friday and Saturday morning came and went without any additional layers of intrigue being added to the match. Five of us met up in a bar about a kilometre from the ground, comfortably outside the alcohol exclusion zone. Along with me were Dušan, Milovan, Uroš, and his mate Igor, who Dušan assured me was the mild-mannered humanoid who played the online role of Tommy Johnson. Uroš asked me if I had a black coat. I did. 'Good, that's how we're going to tell who are the Partizan fans in the east stand.' This wasn't the result of inside knowledge or clever planning on my part, I just have one warm coat. And it's black.

As we walked up to the ground, two things struck me. Hardly anyone was openly wearing any colours. In a 15-minute walk among the throng, I spotted one Red Star scarf, and an unmarked red bobble hat. Uroš noticed the same phenomenon. 'Sad, isn't it, that you can't show which club you support for fear of being beaten up.' There were a lot of black coats, though. Surely all of them couldn't be as coincidental as mine.

Police lines, grey and straight like Armco barriers, bordered the stadium-side of the road leading up to the ground, the other side a mess of hurriedly parked cars, reflecting the national importance of the game and its meaning for Serb communities in neighbouring countries – there were cars from the far corners of Serbia, as well as Kosovo, Croatia, a lot from Bosnia, and one from Romania too. All of these were minimum four-hour drives. For a home game. This was the heaviest police presence I had seen since Shkendia, and the police were alert and in defensive formation, not standing around looking bored like they do for most matches. Before now, I hadn't realised that human beings could tessellate, but the lines looked impenetrable.

We had missed quite a bit of action though by having that last drink. There had already been a couple of intra-Partizan scuffles before the police had started their shifts inside the stadium, daring Zabranjeni launching solo raids across the no-man's-land between east and south to stick one on an Alcatraz and getting roundly clobbered, before retreating. As the players' warm-up had finished, the Red Star fans had waited patiently for Stojković (who, remember, they hate even more than we do) to make his way back to the changing room. Stojković ambled disinterestedly to within 20 metres of the tunnel, checked that his personal line of riot police was in place, and then hared for safety, arms above his head for protection. The police shields kept the flares and bits of ripped-up plastic seats away, but they were no match for the hail of firecrackers, one of which deflected off a poorly-angled piece of Perspex and caught him on the leg as it exploded. It wasn't a mortal blow, but the Delije reacted like they had just scored an injury-time winner.

It was quickly apparent that everyone had been seriously underestimating how many Grobari would turn up. The south stand was three-quarters full, several thousand fans already in place and running through the Partizan repertoire at high tempo and higher volume. The east stand was full too, with black coats in abundance at the southern end, covering two-thirds of the entire stand. The cavernous north end was rammed with Delije, barely a seat visible, and the remainder of the east and three-quarters of the west were mostly Red Star fans. Nevertheless, despite the infighting and the bureaucratic obstacles, the away side had brought 30 per cent of the fans.

It was clear too that we had overestimated the unpopularity of Alcatraz – they had plenty of people prepared to be around them for this game. For the derby, it's easier to forget one's principled position. The desire to boycott and just watch the game on TV is simply not as strong as it would be against Smederevo in the freezing cold. Finances might have played a part, too. Tickets for the east were 1,000 dinars each (about £9). For the average Belgrader, that was just short of a day's net wages. Tickets for the south were half that price.

The Zabranjeni had, if anything, been a bit too successful in infiltrating the east stand. There were clearly too many people for the police to try and move everyone into the south stand, or into 'the cage', a rusty metal frame covering a space for around 1,000 people in the south-east corner of the ground, only ever used for small away groups in European games. At the same time, it was going to be tough to pretend that this wasn't a 'formed group' and that we weren't breaking the rules, and therefore risking arrest. I had started mentally preparing my defence, when the order Chinese-whispered its way up from the front rows for everyone to sit down. We were going to behave ourselves, and trick the police that way. Genius.

Unfortunately for Goran, the order didn't make his ears in time before he was nabbed by a plain-clothes policeman and lifted out of the stand, for the heinous crime of standing on a seat. He was probably one of 5,000 people doing it, but he was within easy reach. Through a clever combination of feigned ignorance of the Zabranjeni, and a solemn promise not to get his dirty trainers on Red Star's far-from-pristine seats, he managed to avoid the fate that had befallen our moustache-bearing chum at Jagodina.

A couple of minutes before the players came out, the Delije in the north stirred into life. The acoustics of the Marakana are good – it is built into a depression in the ground and hence referred to by Partizan fans as 'rupa' (the hole), so they are able to create an echo that reverberates around the ground. Dušan pointed to several loudspeakers positioned around the outside of the pitch, which he alleged were used to amplify the sound of the north. Whether a cappella or post-production, the swirling noise of their opening salvo filled the stadium with a deep bass rumble. Eleven flags, meticulously spaced out across the front rows of the stand, which spelled out DELIJE SEVER [Heroes North], were raised simultaneously, their heavy cloth swaying in a rhythmic but stately way. The choreography reflected Red Star's self-belief: we are a serious club, and we take ourselves seriously. We have won the European Cup. You away fans must look at, and listen to us with the reverence we deserve. Not that they were getting much reverence. The Grobari in the south were busy pogoing their way through a chant, deliberately blind and deaf to the audiovisual self-importance at the other end, as if they were wearing headphones and listening to the Sex Pistols at a gala performance of Holst's *The Planets*.

The Delije must have been in the middle of either Mars or Jupiter when Partizan's substitutes came out of the tunnel, welcoming them with a ferocious battle cry and a handful of firecrackers, one of which forced Diarra into a hasty jig to avoid one exploding at his feet. They dug further into their arsenal as the players lined up to kick off, lighting hundreds of flares, and simultaneously launching dozens of fireworks from within the ground. Not a few village green Catherine wheels, either. Real fireworks. Dušan, registering my furrowed brow, asked why I was surprised. 'Well, didn't "we" kill one of "them'" doing precisely this a few years ago?' 'Yep, but it still happens at every derby.'

The stadium was briefly ablaze in red light, but the glow was quickly masked by a dense cloud of white smoke, which hung over the whole stadium and reduced visibility to virtually zero. While we all waited for the smoke to clear sufficiently for the match to start, a couple of dim-witted Red Star fans in the east, who had not noticed the preponderance of black coats around them, lit flares in time with the Delije's choreography. They were swiftly frogmarched down to the front of the stand to be pushed around a bit by the group 'leaders' and given a Hobson's choice of quickly leaving the black end of the east stand, or not leaving and facing uncertain consequences.

The game kicked off while I could still only see the players on our side of the pitch, that is to say right-back Miljković, and Babović, lining up on the right-hand side of the midfield diamond. Stanojević had gone for what he would describe as a 'solid' line-up, but which we bemoaned as unadventurous and unnecessarily defensive. The two attacking full-backs, Volkov and Aksentijević, had been replaced by Lazevski and Miljković, the latter known, with no affection at all, as 'Miljkon', the Serbian Maicon, by those around me – in reference to his complete lack of any resemblance to the muscular, attacking, skilful Brazilian full-back. In midfield, Medo, Vukić, Babović and Tomić was a decent foursome (unless you were Dušan, for whom only Medo was worth picking), but not the most dynamic – they needed Volkov and Aksentijević to do their running for them. Šćepović, not renowned for his sterling work ethic, was played as a more withdrawn striker to help boost the midfield, leaving little Lazar to forage up front on his own. But still there was too much else going on around the ground to be able to focus on the football.

The smoke finally cleared. The Grobari in the south lit their own flares and threw their own firecrackers. What the display lacked in majesty and symmetry compared to Red Star's performance was made up for in 'accuracy'. A couple of flares, discarded before they were fully spent, landed on some advertising hoardings on the running track behind the pitch. In extinguishing one, the team of firemen, on hand for just such an eventuality, ended up bursting through the back of the canvas, like a firefighting version of the Keystone Kops. Their colleagues a few feet away, not to be outdone, dithered for a full minute while the hoarding started to combust and an orange flame rose up a couple of feet. Having dug out their hose and worked out how to turn the taps on, they discovered that the hose had a hole in it. Not a problem – they've got another one, which works. But they couldn't aim it. Finally they got it under control, with half the ground laughing at them. Under a further barrage of firecrackers from the fans in the south stand, they finally started to get the fire under control. Most people around me were still laughing, though I wasn't. 'We have a word for people who attack firemen while they're trying to do their job,' I ventured to Dušan. 'Yeah?' 'Yeah. We call them scum.'

The black column rising from the burning hoarding mixed with the white smoke from the flares and firecrackers, forming a nebulous badger over Stojković's goal. Half of the players were watching it, rather than the game in which they were supposed to be protagonists, which partly explained why the quality was so bad. Partizan had come out with a clear plan to 'keep it tight' for the first half, and were trying to disrupt Red Star's limited game without daring to venture over the halfway line themselves.

After 20 minutes of relative quiescence in our part of the ground, there was some commotion down at the front, and we were all shoved up a few rows. As the stadium clock struck 20 we were ordered to our feet. The Zabranjeni were announcing their arrival. I'm going to keep using 'we' from this point, because although I was trying hard not to get too involved (for reputational reasons as a British diplomat as much as trying to provide a dispassionate record of the events), I was right in the middle of it.

We had about three flares for 4,000 fans, which was pretty pathetic. Even the Red Star fans who ended up in the wrong bits of the stadium had more than that. What we did have was a simple, powerful chant to get everything going. Something to inspire the Partizan players, and intimidate those dirty Red Star b*****ds. Well, not really. It was another tribute to Ivan Perović, one half of the group chanting his surname, then the others following up with 'Ivan'. The second chant went 'Mi smo zabranjeni, svi to dobro znate, Alcatrazu svakom, jebaćemo mater' [We are the Banned, everybody knows it, we'll f*** every Alcatraz's mum].

Not many of the people around me were watching the game at all, they were too busy with this civil war, directing their ire at their fellow Grobari in the south. The Red Star fans probably felt a bit left out. Alcatraz had their answer though. Not with a witty verbal retort, but a 30-foot banner, proclaiming the loyalty of Alcatraz to Partizan, and the treacherousness of those who were not – implying indeed that the Zabranjeni were fifth columnists for Red Star. It was good that we were presenting such a common front against our worst enemy. Dušan mournfully admitted, 'You know, only Partizan can be like this. I hate Red Star, but they'd never turn on each other like this – at least they've got some discipline.'

At this point in the match, the good news was that in spite of all the threats before the game, the police didn't come to get us or march us to the cage. The bad news was that the game was awful. Partizan were stultifying and Red Star incompetent. It had been more visually entertaining when the pitch was shrouded in smoke. Without the attacking full-backs, Partizan's paceless midfield was going nowhere. Medo would mop up attack after Red Star attack, give it to one of his supposedly creative colleagues, who would then mess about and give it away. Little Lazar was totally isolated up front, while Šćepović wandered about aimlessly like the smoke had permanently damaged his vision.

The referee spent the first half an hour looking intimidated by the noise, and fearful of offending the beast that lay behind the sound, giving a succession of free kicks to Red Star and dishing out two harsh yellow cards to Partizan, without reciprocating for similar fouls by the team in red and white. Normal home ground stuff, but against Red Star, even Grobari who acknowledge that their side get a lot of soft decisions swear blind that the Establishment is out to get them. At the point where it seemed like he had recovered his composure sufficiently to officiate impartially, Vukić committed a needless foul about 35 yards out, and the referee gave a free kick. Those fans who weren't still taunting their intra-club rivals and were actually watching the game muttered a bit but it wasn't a controversial decision. The free kick, from our side-on angle, clattered into the edge of the wall and went out for a corner.

But the ref's hand was pointing down, not away. Penalty. How? Why? From where we were, no one had seen anything at all that suggested a penalty, not even a raised appealing hand from a Red Star player. Partizan's players really believed it wasn't a penalty, nine of them chasing the ref 20 yards across the pitch, bumping into him repeatedly without ever pushing him with a hand. It was as bad as the infamous Jaap Stam, Roy Keane et al pursuit of Andy D'Urso, who had the temerity to award a penalty against Manchester United at home. Aided by his two assistants, the ref just about restored order, choosing not to book anyone for fear of being hounded round the other half of the pitch. In the stands, we had made a clear decision that it wasn't a penalty, and so turned our backs to the pitch to register our disgust. Everyone except me. I was getting a bit fed up with all this choreography and wanted to see what was going on.

Eventually everyone else turned to join me. Brazilian midfielder Evandro stepped up and waited for the ref to get all of the players out of the area. Partizan defenders played cat and mouse for a few more seconds, entering, waiting for the referee to look like he was about to order them out or show a yellow card, then stepping back just as a Red Star player protested. Evandro stood there impassively while Stojković jumped up and down and limbered up. Evandro probably wasn't intimidated knowing that Stojković could touch the bar. He wasn't going to try and chip him. While this played out, Dušan received a couple of texts. It was a penalty, according to his correspondents. And they weren't antagonising him on purpose: 'they're from good people, you know, Partizan fans'. But for the tenth time today, he told me that this was now Partizan's 42nd derby since they last had a penalty (in the 99th), while Red Star had been awarded 'dozens'. So the very concept of a penalty award in the derby simply had to be the result of cheating.

Evandro had been waiting nearly a minute by the ball, and it must have been at least two and a half minutes since the penalty was awarded. The referee finally signalled his assent and blew the whistle. Evandro ran up at pace, and with confidence, striking the ball cleanly. Stojković gambled on the ball going to his right and hurled himself across the goal, angling forwards to give himself a greater chance of making the save. Without even needing to look at the ball, I could tell he had gone the wrong way – his neck was twisting counter to his body, and as he fell to the ground, he could see the ball making stately progress towards the other corner of the goal. Luckily for us, it made too much lateral progress, glanced the outside of the post and bobbled ignominiously out for a goal kick. Vukić jumped, his entire body clenched, in celebration. Stojković high-fived Rnić. Babović, who hadn't even been defending on the edge of the area, ran back 30 yards to abuse Evandro to his face. Evandro didn't even look up.

In the stands, the celebration around me lasted just a couple of seconds before a good third of those present started to lay into the seats, kicking and kicking until they shattered, then kicking the shards about. I was simultaneously perturbed but glad that Evandro hadn't scored – people would surely have been chucking them perilously close to my head if that had happened. In among the anarchy, a curious etiquette existed – you only kicked your own seat, instead of attacking the one in front of you, which someone else was standing on. This was meticulously well observed, leaving our group's row of five as probably the largest contiguous intact zone in our end.

At least it would calm down at half-time. In the stands, anyway. On the pitch, Stanojević went to confront the referee as he made his way towards the tunnel. Prosinečki weighed in and verbally sparred with Stanojević. Substitutes and a suspiciously large number of burly men in puffer jackets, one openly wearing a Red Star scarf, lent their bulk to proceedings.

As the round of handbags settled, the players made their way to the tunnel. The Red Star players got there first. The Partizan players never did. The fans in the north had kept back a third tonne of fireworks, saving them for this moment. Babović and Miljković, heading the group, took one look at the barrage and deserted. Šćepović got closer to enemy lines but was forced back by a couple of shells that got a bit too close. After a short negotiation among themselves, the whole team declared themselves conscientious objectors and refused to fight. Stanojević arrived, still het up from his clash with Prosinečki, jabbed his finger in the chest of another member of the Red Star authorities, and then decided to conduct his team talk on the benches, his players beating an undignified retreat from the mortar fire.

I exhaled. Milovan, chuckling next to me, compared the last 45 minutes to my experiences back home. 'It's not like this in England, even at a derby, is it?' Reflecting on his question, the worst thing I had ever seen at a north London derby was Jermaine Jenas. And I was once shoved in the back and called a c*** by a Chelsea fan outside Fulham Broadway tube despite having covered up my red shirt and not uttered a word between stadium and station, but no, it wasn't like this. 'If even a tenth of those fireworks had been thrown at players or firemen in England, neither team would get to play at home for a year.'

While I resolved to be marginally less po-faced in the second half, the Red Star players emerged from the tunnel to a powerful roar from the home fans. Trotting out behind them was the lonely figure of Medo, who had somehow made it to the Partizan changing room despite the incendiary carnage around the tunnel entrance. And then sat there for ten minutes with none of his team-mates. While the Red Star fans missed a chance to bombard Medo as he emerged, they missed no such opportunity to lob a few pyrotechnics at Stojković as he took up position in the northern goal for the second half. It was not a coincidence that he played more as a sweeper with gloves than a recognisable goalkeeper in the second period, so keen was he to be out of artillery range.

Two shady-looking guys materialised behind me as the second half kicked off. Sensing my unease, one guy said, 'We always do this – it's lucky if we change our places in the second half.' Everyone else seemed to buy this. Fair enough.

Partizan were marginally better than they had been in the opening exchanges of the second half. But it was still a dire game. Marković, starved of service, and perhaps dwarfed by the occasion, finally sparked into life, plucking a high ball out of the air, pirouetting before he had fully landed and then sliding the ball deftly into Šćepović's stride. His strike partner showed his gratitude with a heavy first touch, and allowed the keeper to claim. Stanojević still seemed to want to play it safe, and Marković's newly-rediscovered flair represented a threat to stifling the life out of the match. So he was subbed, replaced by Diarra. Finally, in homage to our Senegalese striker's successes against the old enemy there was a chant that the Zabranjeni and Alcatraz could agree on. For a minute, anyway, until the leaders in front of us realised the coincidence and hurriedly swapped songs.

Twenty minutes were left, and I was getting nervous. Ordinarily I would have backed Partizan to beat a team as inferior to them as this one, and especially to be able to ramp up the pressure in the last part of the game, when the lesser team usually tires. But 'obvious' supremacy counts for nothing if your team doesn't try to win, and especially not in derbies. The whole team had been guilty of playing economically at best, expending minimal effort and using as little mental energy and creativity as possible. Vukić, his pale complexion exacerbated by the smoky stadium and the multiple lux of the floodlights, was borderline translucent tonight, his appearance combining with his lethargic movement making him the first footballer to do a passable impression of a zombie on the field of play.

In the 72nd minute, Babović received the ball from Medo on the halfway line. Looking up, he pinged a ball over the top to Šćepović, who touched the ball three times on the outside of his right foot. Once to control in mid-air, once to stop and turn 180 degrees, dumping his marker on his backside, and once more to lay the ball off into the path of Vukić, who stole in from beyond the grave to reach the edge of the area and, on his left foot, glide past one defender, switching imperceptibly on to his right to slip past a second. A single stride later, another dab with the left boot sent the remaining Red Star defender the wrong way, before he passed the ball to the left of Red Star's goalkeeper and into the corner of the net.

I was prepared for the surge of noise that followed. The surge of people was harder to deal with as suddenly there were people jumping at me from all sides. Fortunately (in this instance, anyway), I am short and stocky, so it's hard to knock me off my feet. Uroš, standing next to me, is a much slighter built lad, and the first wave of shoving knocked him off his perch, then tumbling through a gap in front of us where a seat had been until after the Red Star penalty.

By the time he got back up to us, the celebrating had finished and the gloating had started. 'Zašto ćutite, zašto ćutite, pičke ciganske?' [Why are you so quiet, why are you so quiet, gypsy c***s?], enquired the Grobari with operatic glee, again briefly finding some unity. Uroš, dusting himself down, climbed back up and joined in as if nothing had happened. It was too early for me to sing along. Pre-emptive hubris usually gets its comeuppance, and surely Red Star were going to launch a proper attack now.

Seven minutes later, Medo, a warrior hero in this match, as he had been in so many others, gathered the ball, and spread it left to Tomić. Šumadinho's first-time chipped through-ball was OK, but a bit overhit, and should have been an easy claim for Red Star's keeper. But he hesitated, stopping in no-man's-land when he should have carried on advancing. His defender, expecting his keeper to come out, had slowed down too. Šćepović, who had not really registered the chance, let alone made much of an effort towards the ball, exploited the inertia and broke into a canter. The keeper, horror slowly dawning on him, made a belated attempt to come forward, but Šćepović, still not really sprinting, got there first, and poked the ball underneath him. The ball trickled forward. Dušan looked round at me in disbelief. I tensed my neck muscles to start the process of a nod. Yes, I also think it's going in. The ball rolled on. It was going to beat the defender chasing back, but was it going to squeeze in at the near post? Dušan looked at me again for guidance. I moved my shoulders upwards a bit. I don't know either.

This isn't a description of imperceptible movements and sub-conscious interpretation. The ball was going so slowly that we genuinely had time for this full and frank exchange of gestures. Eventually, it made it over the line. Dušan kept on staring at me, afraid to commit to the celebration. I persuaded him, helped by 5,000 around me cheering themselves hoarse. Having been so bewildered by the build-up to the goal and mentally off-balance, perhaps it wasn't much of a surprise that this time it was Dušan's turn to get knocked off his seat by the seething mass behind him. Dušan is much bigger than Uroš, and also disappeared through a seat. Genuinely through it, the back splintering into a hundred white pieces as Dušan took three other fans down with him. None seemed to mind; the morphine of a 2-0 lead was enough to dull any physical pain.

Red Star's players reassembled quickly and were in position long before the Partizan players had stopped celebrating and lined up for kick-off, or before Dušan had hauled himself back up to us, glancingly guiltily at the scattered plastic debris that he had created with his act of inadvertent criminal damage. They kicked off and attacked with purpose, breaking down the left and a forward striking a clean shot towards goal. Stojković, the least popular man in the ground, held firm, making a regulation save to his right and holding on to the ball. And that was it. Shoulders in red and white sank in unison, and the north end of the stadium tangibly deflated. They knew it wasn't going to be their day.

This mattered little where we were. The gloating began in earnest. Red Star fans were invited variously to suck our c**ks, allow us to manipulate their sisters, and to continue being quiet. Partizan were hailed as the greatest team the world has ever seen, the object of all our devotion, and the reason our hearts continue to beat. Ten minutes of rapture were spoiled a bit by one of the Zabranjeni leaders trying to stir up a chorus of 'Kosovo is the heart of Serbia', but no one wanted to sing. We were going to win the derby away. So not even the more nationalist types among us cared about Kosovo right now.

At the final whistle, with the Red Star players already off the pitch, our players wandered over to bask in the praise of the south stand. They were there a few minutes, while a swell of 'dodjite ovamo' [come here] emanated from our part of the ground. A few, Diarra, Medo, and Ivanov, started to stroll across the pitch towards us. I felt good about the world.

We had won the derby, and both sides of the Partizan divide were going to go home happy, and feeling equally loved. No better salve could be applied to the internal wounds than a chance to share in a victory over the old enemy. The club management though appeared to be in no mood to play doctors and nurses. The errant players (all foreign, it occurred to me) were quickly scooped back up by black-tracksuited hangers-on, and guided back towards the changing rooms. That was petty. But not even such a snub could spoil the mood.

We strode out purposefully onto the main road, heads held high. The Red Star fans, shoulders low and shuffling like sulky teenagers, were easy to spot. As we headed towards the city, an acquaintance of Dušan's (he couldn't be an actual friend, he supported Red Star) bumped into us. 'Primi moje saučešće,' said Dušan [accept my condolences]. The guy went to say something back but was talked over. He left it there. Much like the game, in that exchange Partizan had delivered two killer blows and Red Star had been lacking in imagination. Guaranteed to be leaders at Christmas, we were cock of the walk right now.

League table after the 13th round:
1. Partizan 36 (+25)
2. Red Star 29 (+16)
3. Radnički 25 (+11)

The Winter Break

SUSTAINING the post-derby euphoria was easy, without Partizan having to do anything on or off the pitch. Red Star's descent into navel-gazing and self-abuse provided enough joy of its own. It began before we had even left the stadium – the north end interrupting our seemingly interminable self-congratulation with a robust shout of 'uprava napolje!' That was three clubs I had now heard call for their own board to go, in less than half a season.

Initially, we joined in. Yeah, get rid of the board, you're rubbish. Hang on, said someone influential near the front. If they're rubbish, then surely we should try and maintain the status quo. 'Lukiću, ostani, Lukiću, ostani!' [Stay, Lukić, stay!] we trilled, our sincerest support for Red Star's beleaguered chairman echoing round the fast-emptying stadium.

Each day after the derby brought a new miniature piece of destructive joy, an early advent calendar that made our footballing rivals a bit worse with each door opened. On the first day of Christmas, some of the madder Red Star fans called for Prosinečki's head. Never really going to happen – a club legend, and on the kind of contract that made him too expensive to sack. Instead of turtle doves, Lukić called a board meeting to 'discuss recent poor performance', exactly what Đurić had done after the Shamrock defeat. How long ago that felt now. Fans argued that he should sacrifice himself for the club. He clucked a bit in the media about it, and then the story fell away. Why? Because Red Star were punished by the Serbian FA for the crowd trouble at the game. Their next home game, against Vojvodina, would have to be played behind closed doors. The one million dinar fine sounded like a lot, but that's about £9,000.

161

Partizan were also fined, 400,000 dinars, for their own fans' misbehaviour. Đurić went on TV to complain about the leniency of the punishment, piously fretting about the messages this sent to both hooligans and impressionable young kids. His piety didn't extend to much more than a derisory criticism of his own team's fans, and he was rounded upon by Red Star officials, and pro-Red Star critics, for his hypocrisy. How dare Partizan lecture Red Star on match safety, when someone had been killed in their stadium?

The next day, Red Star's debt was revealed to be worth more than five gold rings – more like €32m, enough to force a pre-emptive promise to sell at least seven million euros' worth of players in January, and a longer-term suspicion that this would keep them from mounting the kind of assault on the transfer market that could narrow the gap to Partizan. Prosinečki duly put 11 players on the transfer list and invited bidders.

All good things must come to an end. Like Partizan, Red Star ended their run of appalling news by winning a football match – a 2-1 win away at Rad, with the kind of 94th-minute winner that has Grobari foaming at the mouth. We would have to look to ourselves to preserve our happy bubble.

At home to Radnički 1923, from the central Serbian city of Kragujevac, in theory we would have our work cut out. Third in the league, and the only unbeaten team, they were a challenge on paper. But in practice, they weren't, on the only sunny day for a month in either direction.

Vukić scored a delightful goal from the edge of the area for a half-time lead. In the second half, Partizan were computer game unrealistic. First, glass-legs Anderson Marques leapt higher than everyone else at a corner to power in a ferocious header from 12 yards out. Loyal to his Brazilian roots, he celebrated with a lithe and sensuous mini-samba in the centre circle. Seeking a partner for his dance, he turned to Tomić, a man whose omnipresence at Belgrade's nightclubs made him the ideal target. But Nemanja looked lost without the arse of a TV starlet to grind up against, and shuffled like a dad at a wedding. Minutes later, Anderson's centre-back partner Ivanov thumped in his own header. Not wishing to be outdone, he launched into his own version of the Anderson samba. He looked very obviously like he was not from South America. The lambada-ing duo kept a clean sheet, though, maintaining Partizan's seven-point cushion, and extending the goal difference advantage to 11.

It (the result, not the dancing) was a fitting tribute to the old scoreboard, which announced its pensioning off after 54 years of service. 'As I go into retirement, you will stay with Partizan', it commanded, using a deliberately archaic form of Serbian to emphasise its age and wisdom. Since its debut as a young and virile piece of electrical equipment at the home game against FK Vardar (of Skopje, Macedonia), the lampaš had seen 21 title-winning teams and nine Partizan sides en route to domestic cup success. It had seen Partizan in the semi-finals of the European Cup and even seen Sebastien Squillaci score for Arsenal. Having wheezed its way through today's three scorers, it could look forward to a rest in the club museum before making its final journey to silicon heaven.

The last game before the winter break was away at Metalac, whom we had already beaten in the cup earlier in the season. FK Metalac began life as a company team, a group of metal-workers from the small town of Gornji Milanovac playing in the local leagues. They played in local and regional leagues like other company and social club teams until after the break-up of Yugoslavia, when Metalac (the company) decided to put more money into the club, using it as a marketing tool, and the club rose up to play in the lower national divisions for a few seasons, yo-yoing between the second and third tiers, before finally making it to the top flight in 2009.

Because Metalac's own stadium wasn't up to the SuperLiga's standards, since their promotion they had been forced to play their home games in the town of Lučani, at former SuperLiga side FK Mladost's ground. This was going to add nearly an hour to our journey to the ground, but we had something to look forward to – seats in the executive box. The brother of the owner of Dušan's gym was Metalac's left-back, so we would be able to save ourselves 400 dinars and occupy one of only 30 or so covered seats in the ground, among the great and good of Gornji Milanovac.

This was an example of something typically Serbian – the veza [connection]. Put simply, not much gets done without someone knowing someone, and therefore having a veza that can be exploited to grease the wheels. The link can be as tenuous as ours was, but it is a foot in the door. It can help access cheaper deals in shops, get priority on tickets, or get a plumber to fix your pipes a bit more quickly.

Sadly, the importance of the veza is just as acute, if not more so, in the public sector, where it borders on and sometimes is indistinguishable from actual corruption. Serbia's reputation for corruption, as measured by the respected NGO Transparency International's Corruption Perception Index, has been getting worse over the last few years. In some cases, a veza is needed to get you seen by a doctor this side of the next decade, to get into the good universities, and to get hold of ordinary documents provided by the State within a reasonable deadline. Sometimes it must still be accompanied by a financial incentive or a gift – the veza just gets you into the position where you can offer the bribe.

Before we had even got to Lučani, we had lost our comparative advantage. The full-back concerned was suspended and hadn't been required as part of the travelling squad. Without our veza, we were going to be one of the plebs, as usual.

Some of said plebs were still basking in the glow of the derby win, welcoming Partizan's manager to the bench underneath them with a jaunty rendition of 'Silovao si Zvezdu Stanoje!' [You raped (Red) Star, Stanoje]. Stanojević, impassive in the face of this sexually-charged praise, had picked what Dušan called a 'shop window squad' for the game, including Lazevski and Miljković, whose agents fancied their chances of securing a lucrative January move. Ranković, another fringe player linked with a move, was on the bench.

Players not actively seeking a move seemed to be unwilling to tax themselves too much in the opening phase of the game. Medo, admittedly on a terrible pitch, appeared to have forgotten how to trap a football, to the point where it seemed like he may have been trying to sabotage a move away from the club that he didn't fancy. Vukić only ran once someone had given him the ball to feet, and Ilić was an ambassador for the team's overall lethargy, displaying deft touches of class interspersed with long periods of inactivity. Someone behind me offered him an inhaler, so anaerobic was his play. I laughed at this until Dušan told me that Ilić actually was asthmatic, and that perhaps I should be more considerate towards the differently able. Eduardo played similarly, his personal footballing volcano erupting in the ninth minute with a superb curled shot from the edge of the area that squeezed into the top right corner and then embarking on an extended period of quiescence just as soon as he had finished celebrating.

Metalac, possibly the worst team that I've ever seen play professional football, flurried briefly after Eduardo's goal, creating a one-on-one chance that was well saved by a star-jumping Stojković, but their hearts weren't really in this game, except for their massive No. 21, whose one-man game plan was to throw his weight around, shoving, elbowing and otherwise nibbling at Partizan players until one of them reacted.

Dušan called the left-back's brother to see who this guy was, and was handed over to Dejan Stamenković himself. Dejan was unperturbed to hear that his employers were 1-0 down to the team he supported, and much more interested in getting Dušan's tips on whether to back Wrexham against Hinckley in the FA Trophy. Serbian bookmakers offer odds on the top five tiers of the English leagues, plus all four Scottish leagues, League of Wales, Northern Irish Premier League and all cups, including the FA Trophy, which has led to some people I met having an incredibly deep knowledge of British football that I have never attained. One MP, while Dušan was trying to organise a meeting between the two of us, asked for my tip on the likelihood of Crawley v Oxford producing a home win with more than three goals in the match while he was deciding whether or not to meet me. I tipped Crawley, they won 4-1, and I got the meeting.

The No. 21 was called Zivković. Apparently, he was a very angry man. His inner rage was getting the better of him in this game, and Partizan's players weren't rising to the bait. Metalac couldn't cope even with Partizan's reduced movement, and kept giving away frustrated fouls. He was guilty of one such foul on a dawdling Eduardo about 25 yards out just before half-time. 'Babović should really score from this,' said Dušan as the long-haired Afghan hound of a winger stepped up. Dušan had shown precisely zero faith in Babović until this point in the season, and was rewarded for his trust with an absolute peach of a free kick, which skimmed the hair of the players in the wall and bent away from the keeper into the far corner.

The second half had an end-of-term feeling about it. I don't mean that the players were allowed to come out in casual clothes and bring in board games, more that the pace of the game slowed to a gentle stroll, neither team keen to exert themselves at all. No point getting any injuries in a game that was already finished. Lazevski, still needing something to convince those agents and scouts in the crowd, hadn't got the memo on relaxing, tore down the left wing and crossed low for Vukić, whose thoughts were already on the beach somewhere in Egypt, to skid in a volley for his eighth goal in eight league games.

And that was it. Tomić and Smiljanić, excused from the starting line-up to give them more time to digest their Friday night kebabs, came on for their own last chance at self-promotion before the transfer window. Immediately, Tomić got on the end of Partizan's best move of the season, a beautifully lazy sequence of 20 passes that burst into life with a couple of quick one-twos, leaving Tomić one-on-one, his shot sticking in between the keeper's legs. Smiljanić struck a clean volley from the edge of the area which was well saved, before retreating to his comfort zone of sideways passes, a modern-day Serbian version of Ray Wilkins, with more hair.

There was nothing else to report on the pitch. Off it, texts and phone calls were coming in from Belgrade, to the joy of everyone whose heart beat black and white, which was to say everyone in the ground except the Metalac playing staff. And probably only half of them. Red Star were losing. Forced to play behind closed doors, and playing on live TV at the request of their opposition, who were keen to minimise the likelihood of dodgy decisions by increasing the available scrutiny, Red Star had fallen a goal behind against Vojvodina. 'Who scored?' asked one guy near me, craning his neck to address someone with a contact on the outside. 'Who f***ing cares?' answered half a dozen people around him. As our game entered injury time, the same wave went round the ground. 2-0. They weren't coming back from that.

Our game finished, and so did theirs, with no further changes. The applause that saw Partizan off the pitch was warm and heartfelt, and we fairly bounced our way back to the car, high on the drug of optimism and everything being right with the world. Like high-purity heroin, the effect soon wore off. Despite our great result, and the even better result coming from the silent Marakana, I felt empty in the car on the way back. The buzz of the victory and the schadenfreude from Red Star's loss couldn't fill the void. That was it. No football until March. Nearly four months until a ball was going to be kicked again in anger. What was I going to do until then?

Substitute it with a different kind of football, for a start. The first thing I did was to see whether I could do Stanojević's job any better than him, by buying Football Manager 2012, the methadone of football fans around the world, and installing myself as the new Partizan boss. I'm not going to write much about this, I promise. Just one paragraph of utter self-indulgence.

Here goes. I was about as good as Stanojević. It's been a while since I played FM, and the game has got a lot more detailed while I was away. Whoever was providing the background for research for Partizan had done a stunning job. My two favourite examples: Lazar Marković including Chelsea among his favourite clubs, though in my virtual world he didn't angle for a move there, and Smiljanić having persistent problems with his match fitness and never listening to my team talks.

I developed a bit more sympathy for chairman Đurić – he gave me €2m to spend but I couldn't persuade anyone that good to come. Fortunately there were plenty of ex-pat Serbs available to pick up cheaply to strengthen the team a bit – an education in itself to see how huge the footballing Serb diaspora is below international level. I beat Stanoje in Europe – my Partizan got to the Champions League group stages, but no further. But in the league, we were a few points short of the real Partizan's tally, and trailing Vojvodina by a point. The virtual Robert Prosinečki kept trying to draw me into a battle of mind games but I wasn't having any of it. We won the away derby 3-1, and Red Star slumped to seventh by Christmas. Dušan used this as yet more 'proof' that without the help of real-world referees, Red Star were a much more limited side than the non-virtual league table suggested.

Back in the real world, we were ten points clear. Presuming Red Star won all 15 of their games in the second half of the season, we could still get away with losing two more (in addition to the derby) and winning the rest. With a 14-0-1 record so far, it was easy to think that the second half of the season would be a cakewalk. Dušan was worried that the margin of our advantage would lead to complacency at board level. With the title seemingly in the bag, there was a risk that too many, rather than just some, players would be sold in the transfer window, and the rump squad, backed up by promoted youngsters and maybe one or two low-cost signings in January, wouldn't be able to hold off the chasing pack.

If the rumour mill was an accurate harbinger of what was to come, then this was a real risk. By the time the game against Metalac kicked off, half of the first team had been linked in the domestic press with moves overseas: Marković, Tomić, Medo, Ivanov, Diarra and Šćepović. In the latter's case, Fiorentina were reportedly ready to bid €3.5m for him. If this seemed like a lot, it should be put in the context of Fiorentina's predilection for Partizan players. Šćepović's putative arrival would make him the fifth Partizan alumnus on the Viola's books, joining Stevan Jovetic, Adem Ljajić (who had previously signed a pre-contract with Manchester United, but Sir Alex never took up the option), Nikola Gulan and 17-year-old centre-half Matija Nastasić, who left Partizan for €2.5m before he'd even played a first-team game. So they had previous.

League table after the 15th round:
1. Partizan 42 (+28)
2. Red Star 32 (+15)
3. Vojvodina 30 (+21)

Happy F***ing Christmas

CHRISTMAS in Serbia falls on 7 January, in keeping with Orthodox traditions and calendar. But the 'holiday season' starts with 'Catholic' Christmas on 25 December, when everyone starts winding down towards New Year's Eve and extends through to mid-January, ending after Orthodox New Year (15 January) or Sveti Jovan [Saint John's Day] on 19 January, the most celebrated slava – a saint's day representing your whole family and ancestors.

Aside from the religious elements, it's celebrated similarly to in the UK. Conspicuous overconsumption of rich food, lots of family duties as city migrants head back to their villages of origin and realise how little they have in common with their rural cousins, and getting unashamedly drunk during daylight hours.

My Christmas had been a stressful one – Claire came down with pneumonia and was rushed to hospital in mid-December. She told me over the phone that she was about to be sedated while I was at the Embassy Christmas party, and I rushed back to the UK to see her in intensive care. For a couple of days, she was really very ill. But the doctors and nurses did a great job, she fought the illness, and recovered enough in time to be home with her family for Christmas. Our plan for her to move to Belgrade before the end of the month had to be put on hold while she got stronger, but she was given permission to fly just before Orthodox Christmas. It had been a tough few weeks, but it had ended well.

Peace on earth and goodwill to all men, as the saying goes. Unless you work for Partizan, that is. If the men at the top of the club were writing each other Christmas cards, they were using bile for ink.

169

Đurić, as the holiday season approached, sought to maximise his in defiance of his reputation for not saying much and for occasionally stuttering. The former habit had gained him the epithet 'the mute' among the fans, among dozens of other, less palatable nicknames. Unscripted and seemingly unbriefed before going in front of the camera, he shuffled nervously in his seat, visibly bridling at difficult questions, and fired a series of staccato but simultaneously winding answers, like a heavy machine gun with an intermittent fault. If he was trying to develop a character, it was the Serbian anti-Christmas, Ebeneezer Scroogović if you will.

Stanojević and Krstajić had been naughty boys all year, costing their indulgent uncle Ebeneezer lots of lovely Champions League money. A ten-point lead at Christmas wasn't going to buy Tiny Tim a goose for Christmas. Not even a spatchcock. No, the club was in trouble financially so wouldn't be making any serious moves into the transfer market to strengthen the squad. Selling the family silver was an option, though.

Old wounds reopened quickly. Krstajić called Đurić a dictator in his own hastily organised and equally unscripted press conference, during which the usually calm and debonair ex-centre-back's sangfroid deserted him, and he launched a spittle-flecked monologue lasting 40 minutes against the club's opaque financial management and Đurić in particular. 'He says there's no money from the Champions League. So where is the money? We earned €15 million last year. Now I'm asking, where's the money from Nastasić?'

Krstajić's thinly-veiled accusation was that club money, raised through the sales of promising young players against the sporting management's wishes, had gone to pay off directors' other business debts. Grudges were still being borne from the pre-season sale of Savić. And neither Krstajić nor Đurić could let it go.

Krstajić revealed just how bad relations were within the camp. 'I only talk with the president when he needs something. But Đurić and Stanojević don't talk to each other. They spoke at a cocktail reception recently, but that was just for show.' Personal disputes apart, Krstajić had a point about the opacity of Partizan's ownership and cash-flow.

A legacy of Tito's days, when Yugoslavia's governance model was Communism-lite, Partizan remained a state enterprise, effectively a nationalised industry.

Željko Pantić, a journalist and businessman who sorted out my tickets for the Serbia–Faroes game, eloquently made the case for the privatisation of Belgrade's top two clubs on his TV show – the lack of competition for ownership of the clubs made for a vicious circle, in which political influence and opportunities for patronage were exchanged in the guise of football club management, and there were no shareholders to hold the board or chairman to account, or scrutinise the finances.

There had been many accusations in the past that Partizan funds had made their way into the Socialist Party's coffers to fund campaigns or simply enrich the leaders. The Socialists, despite having been turfed from power when Slobodan Milošević was toppled by the October revolution, had held on to the controlling interest in Partizan. The party, meanwhile, had been sufficiently rehabilitated by changes in personnel and public apologies, that they were once again a party in the governing coalition. While Željko did not have a specific accusation against the party, he was able to ask pointedly what checks and balances were in place to ensure that funds weren't misused again. Even if Željko's arguments had a strong grounding in economics and transparency, they were tainted somewhat by his choice of solution.

Privatisation is a dirty word in Serbia. In two waves, first in the 1990s and then post-Milošević, privatisation was touted as the panacea to cure the country's financial woes, and in part forced on Serbia by international financial institutions, whose loans came conditional on the state divesting itself of loss-making communist-era relics, as well as some theoretically profitable companies burdened by state bureaucracy and unsustainable staffing levels. But the reality didn't match the theory.

Too many times a well-connected businessman or consortium was able to buy companies for a fraction of their real value, enabling them to rack up huge profits and make further acquisitions. Similarly, rules designed to prevent naked asset-stripping were not always properly, or even vaguely, enforced, leaving thousands without jobs and some towns without any source of revenue. So although the fans don't like the current model, none of them are crying out for the club to be privatised, even though legally speaking there is no obstacle to it happening.

Đurić wasn't ready to tolerate any arguments about the club's business model or his leadership. Krstajić was sacked on Boxing

Day. The town simply hadn't been big enough for him and Đurić, and the rest of the board hadn't felt able to defend him, given the level of insubordination.

Back home in England, I wasn't able to judge the mood on the ground in Belgrade. But friends in the city told me that the stadium was sprayed overnight with a coat of 'UPRAVA NAPOLJE' graffiti and other messages in support of Krstajić. The message boards promised a demonstration if Stanojević went too. The Serbian media sensed that this was a real possibility and, like their English counterparts, decided to stoke up the row as far as they could. Stanojević, on the beach somewhere in the Mediterranean, was roused from his slumbers and asked for a comment.

The media pincer movement was expertly executed – from one side, Stanojević was asked to dish the dirt on his now-unemployed former right-hand man, baited with an allegation that Krstajić had sought to have Stanojević sacked after the Shamrock game and replaced with one of Krstajić's mates. From the other, Stanojević was invited to criticise Đurić's judgement in replacing the sporting director and outline how he would respond.

Perhaps emboldened by a couple of poolside cocktails, Stanojević eschewed both a polite 'no comment' and the chance to delay his response until after he had finished his holiday. 'I am no longer the trainer of Partizan and, when I come back from holiday, I'll communicate my decision to people at the club.' The media trap had snared its man, and the next week's worth of headlines with him.

If he had left it at that, maybe he could have changed his mind in the morning, put it down to the ridiculous levels of rum in his mojito and a touch of sunstroke, and called the club to say he had been misquoted. But he kept on talking, and invited Đurić to leave the club with him. 'He's a president who promotes himself as a massive Partizan fan, and who thinks exclusively in the interests of the club, but reality shows that this simply isn't the case. Everyone is against him. Just look at people's comments in public, in the stadium, on internet forums. Đurić is the only president of a football club who doesn't go to matches, who isn't in the stands with the fans. It's totally logical that he leaves, no one is with him.' Bye bye, Aleksandar.

As we moved into January, Partizan's board had still not been able to meet to ratify the seemingly inevitable decision to relieve

Stanojević of his post, or accept his resignation (if the media reports based on a mobile phone conversation were true), such was its commitment to taking full advantage of the long holiday.

The pro-Stanojević, anti-Đurić lobby had one more trick up their sleeves. Thanks to its Communist-era composition, Partizan's governance structure includes a club parliament. As with most of Tito's creations, it was never really designed to be a chamber for frank debate and the democratic resolution of problems – its aim was to provide a veneer of popular involvement in a resolutely State-run institution. But in theory, Partizan's assembly was able to execute a vote of no confidence in the chairman and prevent him from formally dismissing Stanojević. Though the assembly would struggle to find a majority to reverse the decision to dismiss Krstajić, if a new chairman came in, perhaps he or she could reappoint him.

An appetite for a bottom-up putsch definitely existed. Elements of the club's own structures were in open insubordination against the senior management. The club's own website, falling under the jurisdiction of the pro-Stanojević marketing department, featured an article on the battles within the club, which struck a balance between the pros and cons of each protagonist, but featured detailed instructions on how the club could be rid of its troublesome chairman.

'The regular, yearly assembly is scheduled for February, but on request of a third of the total number of members (65), it can be called earlier. One of the possible scenarios is that the members of the assembly, who in this conflict support the sporting sector [ie Stanojević and Krstajić], will seek an urgent sitting, and try to annul the decisions of the board.

'Then, and they have a right to this, members of the assembly could seek a vote of confidence in Chairman Đurić and the members of the board.

'Unofficially, the staff of FK Partizan, in this turmoil, support Krstajić and Stanojević's side, and in the assembly they make up 29 members, which is nearly half. If there was a sitting, it's clear that every vote would count towards the eventual victory of one side or the other.'

Đurić did not get to where he was by giving in to the masses every time there was a hint of discontent. Dashes of populism must be mixed with being prepared to make unpopular decisions, and consultation with the proletariat used judiciously, reserving the right to act unilaterally when in the best interests of the organisation or oneself.

Evoking the spirit of Tito's early years, when little dissent was brooked, the club's senior management ensured that the assembly would not have the chance to threaten their tenure. Even if a third of the assembly could be rounded up to request an emergency session (and it was plainly obvious that it could), they would not get their wish. The oldest trick in the bureaucratic book, deferring to a higher authority, was played with breathtaking disdain. The club's official line was that the assembly would have to await the culmination of the Serbian Football Association's own assembly, conveniently not scheduled until the middle of February. That way, in the club's words, any changes to the club's statute could reflect any new rules that the FA agreed upon at their own meeting.

The fact that this contravened Partizan's existing internal statutes was brushed over with the grace of Bobby Charlton's haircut in his latter playing years. One board member said 'so what if we broke the rules?' and left it at that. But this was 2012, not the 1960s. Fans weren't prepared to swallow this disenfranchisement or accept being ridden roughshod over like their mothers and fathers had been in the early years of Yugoslav communism. All the club management succeeded in doing was unifying an ever-larger part of the club's support against them.

Posters began appearing all over Belgrade, with a ghostly Đurić appearing in a red circle, a red line bisecting his face in a manner which suggested Bill Murray would shortly be along to bust him, accompanied by the simple tagline 'UPRAVA NAPOLJE'. This wasn't some half-arsed initiative by a couple of the Zabranjeni. The level of coverage across the city, from the upmarket parts near the embassy, through the commercial centre to the rubbish-strewn Roma settlements across the river in New Belgrade, and the high quality of the posters and stickers suggested that some money and organisation was behind this.

Upravanapolje.com materialised at the same time, with similar production values – this wasn't just a couple of Word documents slapped on the net. It was well designed, and offered visitors the chance to buy anti-Đurić t-shirts and a flash game to throw boots at Đurić's head, called 'whack-a-mute'. I only connected twice, but

enough visitors had been before me for the webmasters to tell me
that the mute had been whacked over 20,000 times.

The protest had some strategy too. A poster campaign is one of
the basics in the advocacy 101 – it raises public awareness. But at
some point you need to engage the elites of a nation if you really
want transformational change. So a group of about 150 season
ticket holders, representing, in their words, a group of fans from
across the four quarters of Stadion Partizan, wrote an open letter to
Đurić, which was published by most of the daily papers and news
websites. Instead of their names, the authors signed the letter with
their season ticket numbers. They invited neither me (6124106755)
nor Dušan (6008100206) to join their endeavour. Dušan was
crosser about this than I was, viewing himself among the vanguard
of the anti-Đurić caucus that was growing by the minute.

The letter sought to expose the mismanagement at the club for
exactly what it was. I make no apologies for translating it in full
now.

Dear Sir,
FK Partizan finished the autumn part of the 2011/12 season in
1st place in the Jelen SuperLiga, with a 10-point advantage over
the nearest competitor, as well as a place in the semi-finals of the
Serbian Cup. Instead of all those who have Partizan in their hearts
enjoying the winter break, a huge crisis has developed in the club,
as a consequence of the new 'strike' upon the sporting sector of the
club, which you have personally provoked and initiated.

In the last four seasons (07/08, 08/09, 09/10, and 10/11), FK
Partizan has won four Serbian Championships and three Serbian
Cups. This reflects exceptional sporting results achieved in the
domestic sphere, and most deserved in fact by those people who
have worked or now work in the sporting sector of our club.

It is a striking-sounding fact that in this recent period, you have
in fact sacked, driven away or made redundant these people – those
most responsible for the above mentioned successes. You drove
away Slavisa Jokanović (you know well how), after two 'double
crowns', Ivan Tomić was ill-suited to you, before him Gordan
Petrić and Zoran Mirković, Almami Moreira was 'too expensive',
and recently you have also sacked Mladen Krstajić from his role as
sporting director, who had only been promoted to the position six
months previously!

The reason for your sacking of Krstajić was his response to your repetitive, bare-faced attack on the sporting sector of the club, after you had already carried out a similar media assault – at the end of August last year. You have been trying to sack our current manager Aleksandar Stanojević, up to now without success fortunately, since September 2010 and our defeat in Novi Sad. We wonder just what you would do with all these people if they hadn't had so much success?

All this has not prevented you, and does not prevent you from ceaselessly garlanding yourself with the results achieved by the club, that is that you personally take credit for this success. What have you done in the time of your tenure? On what grounds do you deserve credit for the sporting results achieved? What have you fulfilled among the mighty promises given? FK Partizan has for some years generated its income practically exclusively through the furious sale of players and from a 'sponsor' called UEFA (income from the Champions League and Europa League). These revenues really have nothing at all to do with your capabilities and achievements, rather with the knowledge and skill of the sporting sector of the club which, despite being mightily handicapped by the constant bleeding of the playing staff (due to the furious sale of players from one transfer window to the next), nevertheless succeeds in producing new players and delivering excellent results domestically and solid results in the international arena.

Mr Đurić, as far back as October 2008, you stated: 'In the club we will instil professionalism and everything will have to be public, from the purchase of coffee to players.' But even an item as big and important as the yearly budget of FK Partizan is not known! You and your associates 'cleanse' the numbers, from 8 to 23 million euros, when the yearly budget of the club is in question! It is an unbelievably 'expandable' budget of which kind no other club on the planet could be proud! Really 'professional', not at all. When do you think you and your associates will 'agree' on whether the budget is either 8 or 23 million euros per year? For fully two years, you have not been in a position to secure a general sponsor for the club. How is it possible that no one wants to advertise themselves on FK Partizan's shirts, comprehensively the most successful Serbian football club in this 21st century? In a shameful manner, you have pinned the blame for this on the sporting sector (because Partizan didn't qualify for the Europa League), but you 'forget' not only that

Partizan played the previous season in the Champions League, but also the fact that at the start of the season you sold the players who last season clinched the Double, among them Stefan Savić, who had spent just less than a year at Partizan and who had become the backbone of Partizan's defence.

Instead of you and the club management of which you are head securing a regular income for the club on the basis of your abilities, it is more important to you to advertise some kind of energy bracelets – a product which across the world and in courts have been labelled as a fraud! This isn't important to you. It's much more important to you that this product is distributed in Serbia by one of your work associates. You promised in 2008 the building of a new stadium. In the meantime, not only have you not started to build it, more strikingly you are more and more silent on this issue. In this period, around Serbia new stadiums are springing up – in Užice, Niš, Novi Pazar, Gornji Milanovac ... It is a paradoxical situation that Partizan, differently to all the other clubs who regularly play in Europe, won't have anywhere to play in a couple of years' time. Why are you silent on the new stadium project? Does it have something to do with the building of the Delta shopping mall at Autokomanda?

You said in December 2009 that you would, in 2010, start the construction of an academy for the club's young players. You haven't even laid a foundation stone, and now we're in 2012. Why have you misled the public and in particular Partizan fans? You also said in December 2009, immediately after your re-election as president of the club, that you and the other members of the FK Partizan board would give significant funds to the club, you as president 500,000 euros, and the other members 200,000 euros each. That money, in the words of your colleague and board member Ratomir Babić, you either don't give at all (he himself has said publicly that for years he hasn't given so much as a dinar), or that it is given as a loan (as board member Dragoljub Vukadinović said recently)! Since when were loans a business model for a club like Partizan? Do you at least give these loans without collecting interest, or do you behave like veritable banks who charge interest? What does that look like? Are you aware of the way in which you've misled the public, and particularly Partizan fans?

You will be remembered as the chairman who 'succeeded' in selling a young player (Matija Nastasić) who hadn't played even one second in the Partizan first team. That boy had been prepared to become one of the most important lynchpins of the professional squad, and he was sold in extremely murky circumstances, completely hidden from the public.

You will be remembered too as the chairman who cancelled the prestigious international youth tournament that Partizan had successfully organised for years, and which enjoyed a high reputation in Europe. In this tournament, teams like Real, Barcelona, Bayern, Marseille, Roma. Disgracefully, you cancelled this tournament because of the paltry 40–50 thousand euros (!?!) which this tournament cost to organise. You didn't hold a club assembly in 2011, and in so doing have broken the club's statute. Board member Ratomir Babić is already arrogantly telling the public: 'So what if we broke the statute?!' Are you aware of the shame that you and your board bring on our club with such gestures? It would be possible to spend hours listing all of your deceptions …

Our conclusion is that you long ago lost all credibility to lead FK Partizan because you are not serious, and are unprofessional. The club that we love is neither your private property, nor your toy, with which you can do what you like. You do not work in the interests of FK Partizan and therefore you must go from the post of club chairman. Nobody supports you. You may have been able to hear from the stands of our decrepit stadium, since the end of August 2011, after the return leg of the match against Shamrock, and many times since. You haven't heard the shouts from the stands directed against you? Well, how can you hear them when in recent months you don't even come to the stadium to cheer on the team? The calls for you to leave the club didn't finish at the end of the autumn season. No, these calls were heard even in these winter months, from the stands in the Pionir Hall and Hala Sportova, in which Partizan fans have been following the female basketballers, and male athletes (basketballers, handballers and volleyballers) from the other parts of our sports association.

Because of all of this, we, owners of season tickets and people who regularly watch Partizan, publicly invite you and your board to submit irrevocable resignations, and spare Partizan a new 'fracture' in the forthcoming assembly. At the same time, we invite all former Partizan staff to distance themselves from this board.

Behind this letter stand us, 107 fans, owners of season tickets for FK Partizan's 2011/12 season. We 107 responded to the initiative of this letter in just the first two days of our campaign. That incomparably more people support your immediate exit from Partizan is clear from a survey conducted on the forums of www.partizan.net, which is the most visited portal which gathers Partizan fans, with nearly 4,000 active members. In this survey, 98.77% of fans declared that they believe you personally to be most responsible for the unbearable state of our club, despite the brilliant results achieved by the sporting sector of the club.

Attached to this open letter, which we are sending to you, are the numbers of our season tickets. These numbers can be checked by the club at any time, and only then will you discover the names and surnames of all of us who support the content of this lesson.

LEAVE PARTIZAN – BOTH YOU AND THE WHOLE OF THE BOARD!

Đjurić did not budge. He was able to point to the club's unprecedented run of success under his stewardship, the support of the board, and of large sections of the supporters.

Two days later, the board met and sacked Stanojević anyway. They were unmoved by the presence of a thousand Partizan fans outside the ground, replete with UPRAVA NAPOLJE banners and signs asking 'GDE SU PARE?' [where's the money?], referring to an alleged €18m missing from Partizan's accounts. It had gone up from the €15m discrepancy in the open letter. The crowd that had gathered was an eclectic bunch – young and old, powerful and powerless (there were two MPs among the many unemployed fans who had little better to do), rich and poor, Alcatraz and Zabranjeni, men and women. But they defined themselves as having one thing in common – a love of the club and a firm belief that the club was being taken down the wrong path.

As a final act, Stanojević was to hold a press conference at the stadium about an hour after the board meeting. Except that the club locked him out, and all the staff evacuated the building, leaving Stanojević looking bemused and angry in the car park, surrounded by most of the thousand fans from earlier, who had hung around to show their support for their fallen hero. 'I don't want to start a revolt,' said Stanojević, to roars of revolutionary approval, 'but this is despicable.'

For someone who was stressing the peaceful nature of his protest, as Stanojević went on, he sounded more and more like

Robespierre. 'I don't want us to fall into becoming revolutionaries, some kind of frivolous rebels, but I cannot accept that I am not able to give information to Partizan's fans. And I have a lot to say.' Having worked up the crowd to the point where they were ready to storm the Bastille, the assembled masses jostling the journalists present and chanting 'Uprava Napolje!' in the deep, threatening timbre that only Slavic football fans possess, Stanojević backed off. This might get out of hand. Promising 'the truth' at a later date, he ended his speech abruptly, got into a waiting car and left the crowd wondering what to do next. With gentle encouragement from the sizeable police presence, they decided to let it go, and live to fight (peacefully) another day.

Across the other side of town, another press conference was just about to start. In front of a hand-picked audience of three tame journalists, Đurić had the perfect antidote to all the unrest. So what if Stanojević had gone? He had an international manager up his sleeve, with Champions League credentials, ready to come in and lead Partizan to success. Brilliant. Except that this man was Avram Grant.

Welcome Avram

THAT was a bit harsh. I have actually got a lot of respect for Avram Grant. He took on the thankless task of following Jose Mourinho and came within a whisker of winning Chelsea the Champions League. It was only the indefeasibly high standards of Roman Abramovich, and the big-name draw of other coaches, which stopped him from taking the job permanently. Portsmouth were in freefall when he was their manager, yet he conducted himself with great dignity. And from an outsider's perspective, there seemed to be extenuating circumstances at West Ham too, though a team with those players should still never have been relegated.

Grant wasn't welcome in Belgrade much, though. Most of this was down to being seen as Đurić's stooge. Another open letter to Đurić made clear that in the eyes of most of the fans, Aleksandar Stanojević was still the legitimate coach, and so no one else had a right to be there, 'No one other than Stanojević is welcome, even if it's Mourinho.' If Grant had seen the signs about him accompanying the protest over Stanojević's sacking, maybe he would have thought twice about signing his new contract. Not many managers arrive at their new club to be greeted by placards like 'GRANT GO HOME' and 'AVRAM F*** OFF. YOU ARE NOT WELCOME HERE'. In English, so he would definitely have understood.

The odds were being stacked against Grant from the outset. The Serbian media translated and reported part of Karren Brady's *Sun* column with glee, turning her throwaway comment that 'Avram Grant must have a good agent' to have got the Partizan job into a headline back-page issue. Grant saw his most unambitious and banal comments given huge prominence, and his more interesting words ignored. So we learned (and the forums ridiculed) that Grant's main target was to win the league, in other words not to throw away a ten-point lead in 15 games, but we heard little about his plans to strengthen the side and make Partizan regular Champions League group stage participants (he said both). His foolishly open question at the beginning of one answer, 'Why did I join Partizan?' was held against him too.

Grant may have tried in several ways to reinforce the team before the end of the transfer window, but the only bid which received any press attention was a request for the funds to sign Carlton Cole. This earned him the shortest of shrift from the board, who weren't ready to sanction that kind of spending, and from the fans, who saw it as proof that Grant hadn't done his homework on the Serbian SuperLiga and was just going to try to recreate some lower-echelon Premier League team in the Balkans. Grant did little better with a plan more suited to the global economic crisis when he brought in a trialist from Grays Athletic, Harry Agombar. Grant was mocked by the fans while board members leaked their complaints about Grant damaging the club's reputation to the press.

The good news on the transfer front was that the mooted exodus didn't take place. Jovančić went off to some South Korean side for an estimated one million euros, which seemed like good business, and the academy was raided again, with two more youngsters who had never played in the first team shipped overseas. Šćepović injured his knee and was out for the rest of the season, but the most promising academy player Nikola Ninković had recovered from his own illness, and was ready to step up to the first team.

In a series of close-season friendlies, Partizan under Grant were playing quite well, winning the bulk of their games, including against half-decent European opposition in the shape of Maccabi Haifa and Chernomorets Odessa, drawing with Dinamo Moscow and losing narrowly to Champions League regulars Shakhtar Donetsk. Grant's Israeli nationality got in the way of a planned training camp in Dubai, and had led to an Iranian team at one of the close-season tournaments forfeiting the match instead of contributing to the cause of global Zionism, but Partizan went to Israel on an additional tour and won all their games there.

Friendly successes hadn't convinced the bulk of the fans, who still had their hopes pinned on using the Club Assembly session on 20 February to boot out Đurić and reinstate Stanojević under a new chairman. In the days leading up to the Assembly, the press was full of praise for self-declared candidate for the chairmanship Miroslav Bogičević, a wealthy businessman who promised to run Partizan as successfully as he'd run his diverse portfolio of companies, from pharmaceuticals to dairy products. He had the backing of a number of prominent fans as well.

But when it came down to it, the Assembly proved to be as toothless as the club's management had always intended it to be. The Assembly delegates, whatever their personal beliefs and views on how to take the club forward, owe their places within the Assembly to the current board, so it should have come as no surprise when three-quarters of them turned out to back the current board and ratify the decisions taken by Đurić and co. Bogičević's backers could only persuade a quarter of the Assembly to boycott the session, but even their effort to deny the Assembly quorum was doomed to failure. Like it or not, we were going to start the spring season with Đurić and Grant at the helm.

I don't know about you, but by this point all I wanted was to watch the team play a real match, and get all the buzz round the club back to football, and the pursuit of wrapping up the league, embarrassing Red Star as much as possible along the way.

The schedule for the second half of the season matches the first exactly. Game 16 would be the same as game one – against Novi Pazar. A long road trip to Sandžak beckoned, but with the promise of a victory against the league's second-bottom team. Even though the home team had gone to the trouble of slaughtering a cow on the turf to consecrate their new west stand and bring good luck to the team for the second half of the season, the sheer lack of quality in the opposition should mean that Partizan picked up some routine points – even with Avram Grant in charge. As a bonus, this was one of only three away games likely to feature much in the way of real atmosphere – Novi Pazar had been the third-best-supported club in the first half of the season, with their average attendance behind only the two big Belgrade clubs.

As had been the case for our home game, the authorities had some concerns about security, specifically the potential for inter-ethnic violence between Novi Pazar's predominantly Bosniak fan base and the more extreme Serb Partizan fans. Partizan fans were warned not to travel down to Novi Pazar without a ticket, and only 400 were given tickets. The police promised a multi-layer cordon round Novi Pazar to stop ticketless fans making the trip down, including a checkpoint of all vehicles attempting to enter the town of Raška (the last one before Novi Pazar on the main road from the north). This was pretty normal procedure, if likely to be annoying for people like us driving down.

What was less normal was seeing a couple of e-mails from colleagues of mine in the American Embassy and the OSCE office in Novi Pazar, usually concerned with local politics and reconciliation projects, discussing the prospect of violence around the game. Specifically, the Americans had got wind of a plan by the Novi Pazar ultras to create some kind of 'spectacular', in protest at Avram Grant, a Jew, daring to set foot in (mostly Muslim) Sandžak. In foreign affairs security-speak, 'spectacular' refers to events like the Mumbai bombings and shootings and other tragic terrorist incidents. It seemed to me that something had probably got a bit lost in translation, and that this was more likely to be some pyrotechnics-plus-flags display within the stadium – possibly with a deeply intolerant or otherwise sectarian/racist element – rather than a genuine threat of an attack. I told my American colleague that I had tickets and would report back.

The police hadn't been lying about the scale of their security operation. They had gone so far as to apply a temporary black-and-white seal on the borders, with people suspected of being Partizan fans turned back at the frontiers with Bosnia and Montenegro. For those of us already inside Serbia's boundaries, about five kilometres short of Raška, we joined the back of a slow-moving queue, which turned out to be caused by checkpoint number one. Coaches and minibuses were parked up by the side of the road, while Partizan fans stood around and tried to negotiate quicker passage with the police or p***ed out litres of en route Jelen beer in the bushes.

Ordinary cars were waved through. The other side of Raška, on the road to Novi Pazar, we encountered the second one, in which a patch of wasteland had been converted into a mass holding area for the ticketed Partizan fans. One hundred and fifty gendarmes, in full Robocop gear as usual, backed up by a dozen police vans with grilles on their windscreens and a few dog handlers, had about 250 fans penned in. Most of the fans looked like they had been there a while, and were pretty bored, milling about on the grubby patch of gravel, chain-smoking and trying to stay warm. It looked like a temporary prison camp.

'No wonder we can't change the dynamic in Serbian football,' moaned Dušan. 'People take one look at this and they don't want to come. How many families would want to be treated like this?' He was right – this was overkill, and the only people who would tolerate being treated like this were the most devoted of fans with nothing better to do, or the kind of guys who ultimately wouldn't mind having a ruck. It was very rare to see parents and their children, let alone any women attending as away fans. Dušan explained that the police were proud of reducing football-related violence in recent years, and having implemented what they called 'the English model'.

But theirs was the 1980s English model of overwhelming force – the shock and awe of crowd control, and treating everyone as a problem, rather than the modern intelligence-led approach and evidence-based restrictions on match attendance for known hooligans.

Not for the first time, I was glad of having diplomatic plates. The police probably didn't even think that we were going to the game. Having parked up in the centre, we walked across the city to the stadium. Central Novi Pazar combines both the worst excesses of Communist architecture, dominated by a building that looks like Stalin has personally designed it, and a pleasant pedestrianised bit that features the same red-tiled roofs as Sarajevo and looks (if you squint hard enough) like a prosperous trading town in the Ottoman Empire, which is precisely what Novi Pazar was several centuries ago. That same Turkish influence was of immediate use to us, as we were short of time but needed something to eat, having been in the car for nearly five hours. Having inhaled a chicken doner the size of our heads, we strode across the park and followed the blue-and-white scarves down to the stadium.

Dušan had pre-arranged with a Partizan club contact for us to get directors' box seats. The away allocation was in the hands of the Alcatraz leaders, and in any case neither of us fancied being caged in the away enclosure. If anything was going to kick off, it would be worst in there. But when we arrived, the police had cut off all bar the entrance to the west stand. And they weren't in the mood for negotiation so we bought two regular tickets and made our way in.

Or we tried to. The stand was already some way past capacity, and all the access points in were jammed solid. As we started shoving our way through to the middle, or at least somewhere that gave us a decent vantage point, I wondered if maybe we'd made a bit of an error. Almost everyone was wearing a blue-and-white hat or scarf, and we looked conspicuously like out-of-towners. There is too much diversity to make it possible to say what a typical Bosniak resident of Novi Pazar looks like, but Dušan's close-shaven head, sticking up 20 centimetres above everyone else's, and my obviously northern European complexion, gave us away pretty easily. Heads turned as we shuffled along the front of the stand, giving me my first experience of what it would have felt like to burst open the swing doors of a saloon bar in a hostile wild west town.

Opposite us in the east stand were the main body of hardcore Novi Pazar fans – the Torcida/Ekstremi. Novi Pazar's fans have fought the same battles for supremacy as Partizan's and any other club's, but the Torcida (who modelled themselves on Hajduk Split's legendarily angry firm) have the longer history of making non-Bosniaks feel unwelcome in the city, and the Ekstremi [the Extremes] the more numerous support, as well as the most graffiti tags around the city. With one of the big boys in town, the two groups were putting on a united front and making sure that the whole stadium joined in.

'NOVI!' boomed the east stand. 'PAZAR!' replied the whole of the west stand, except me and Dušan. This went on for a full minute, the chanting getting more and more passionate with every cross-pitch volley. Dušan looked at his phone, buzzing with text messages from our contact worrying openly about the danger we were in. The colour drained from his cheeks, he wondered out loud if standing here was the cleverest idea we had ever had. I thought that it was a nice change to be at an away game with some atmosphere. And by now it had become apparent that the fans around us saw us as an oddity rather than a threat. So I reckoned we would be OK.

Avram Grant came out of the tunnel before the players in his usual uniform of suit, jumper and shirt, possibly the same one he wore last time out for West Ham. The boos and whistles that accompanied his entrance were loud, heartfelt, and accompanied by invitations to go f*** himself, but they hardly amounted to a 'spectacular'. And a minute later no one was concentrating on Grant, as the players came out.

Grant had picked a team that screamed neither revolution nor even evolution. In front of Stojković were Ivanov and Rnić, with unsold and uninspiring full-backs Lazevski and Miljković. Medo would protect the back four, with Tomić, Vukić and Babović in front of him, while Diarra made a rare league start alongside Marković. Medo had spent more time away from the club during the winter break than might have been considered ideal, and had allegedly been close to the exit door as clubs sniffed round him. Either way, he didn't look as fit and lean as usual. Tomić, less renowned for leanness and fitness, had eaten to type over the holiday and was carrying some timber round the hips. Babović had spent the close season at the beautician and was sporting immaculately trimmed stubble and increased volume to his hair. And young Lazar Marković, who had turned 18 over the break and been linked with Chelsea, Liverpool and Newcastle as well as various Spanish and Italian clubs, but decided that he wanted to win something with Partizan first, seemed to have had a final pubescent growth spurt, looking a good couple of inches taller and no longer really living up to the tag of 'little Lazar'.

Perhaps beneath the staid shell of the 4-4-2, we were bursting with tactical genius imparted by Grant, the kind that had got Chelsea to the Champions League Final. Dušan wasn't so sure. Sources at the club had said that the biggest surprise in the way Grant worked was that he had thus far changed nothing at all. All the training routines, all the exercises, all the drills, were all the same, even if Stanojević had taken most of the training staff with him. Grant was still relying on a translator/assistant to get his messages across to the players, so maybe it was too much to expect him to engender a new mentality while everything he said was being mangled into Serbian. What Dušan had been told was that the Grant regime had stamped its authority on pre-match rituals, with all players expected to shake the manager's hand on the way out of the changing rooms. If that wasn't going to fire them up, what would?

So, exactly 90 days, 23 hours and eight minutes after the autumn season had finished, we were off again. Partizan stroked the ball around while Novi Pazar hurriedly organised themselves into a 7-2-1 formation and bustled after the ball. Tomić, like Babović under instructions from Grant to dribble the ball more often (as if that were either possible or necessary), received the ball on the left, beat his man and promptly stumbled into touch.

I had missed this so much. The typical away game pattern became clear before even the first minute was up. Partizan would be allowed the ball unchallenged up to 40 yards from goal, where the two genuine midfielders would try to harass them. If they got past them, Novi Pazar's seven defenders stood in a resolute line, manhandling attackers to the edge of legality, and hoofing the ball as far as they could once they got it. If Novi Pazar had decided to make their groundsman part of their game plan, then they were geniuses. If not, then they just had a terrible pitch. The ball bobbled around incessantly, never able to travel in a straight line on the ground, and skidding routinely into Partizan players' shins as they tried to play their usual game, and failed.

Although palpably the more skilful team, Partizan were struggling to shake off the sluggishness of the close season, and between the uneven pitch and hassling from the Novi Pazar defence, weren't making any inroads. And every time the home team got over the halfway line, the home support cranked the sound up another notch. As well as exhorting their own team to keep up their stiff resistance, the home fans found time to tweak the tails of their guests from the capital city. 'Gej parada, gej parada, ponos Beograda!' [Gay parade, gay parade, pride of Belgrade] they taunted, oblivious to the fact that there hadn't been any such parade in Belgrade for nearly 18 months, thanks to local politicians being nearly as reactionary as the chumps singing the song here.

This was followed up with a more committed 'Ovo je Sandžak!' (This is Sandžak), the subtext being a none-too-subtle implication that, for the home crowd, Sandžak was not part of Serbia but its own region. This is a sensitive topic in Serbia, a country that had tended to see itself as one of the main players in a major European country (Yugoslavia as was), now shorn of the other five republics, and the former autonomous region of Kosovo as well – which many Serbs view as the spiritual heart of Serbia.

The idea propagated occasionally by ambitious or opportunistic politico-religious figures in Sandžak, that the region might gain greater autonomy or leave Serbia altogether, is therefore one which more nationalist-leaning Serbs find hard to swallow. If we Partizan fans, either the 400 in the cage or the few fools in among the home fans, were unsure if this was directed at us, the next chant left us in no doubt. 'Ubi ubi ubi Grobara!' [Kill, kill, kill the Grobar!] rang around us. I was still pretty sure they weren't going to kill us. But less sure than I had been when blithely reassuring Dušan ten minutes previously.

Dušan, though concerned by our poor start, was unperturbed in the greater scheme of things and sure that the quality of our team would come through. 'They'll quieten down when we score,' he assured. But Partizan didn't score. And after 24 minutes, a hoofed clearance was flicked on by Novi Pazar's spectacularly tall, ugly and long-haired centre-forward Admir Raščić (think former Croatian international Dado Prso with a more wrinkled face and split ends) taking Rnić out of the game. Suddenly it was four against four as Novi Pazar's midfielders joined the chase forward. In trying to cut out the threat of a cross, Ivanov covered right, only for the cross to loop up off him, stranding Stojković under the flight of the ball, and landing on the head of Raščić, whose giant strides had made up the ground following his flick-on. Lazevski and Miljković, jumping ineffectually beside him, couldn't stop him from bundling the ball into the net.

We certainly had some atmosphere now. Bodies pressed against me as the mass surged forward, pinning me against the metal railing at the front of the stadium for a couple of seconds, before the home fans turned to hug each other, disbelieving at the reality of their team – never in the Serbian top flight before this season – leading against the undisputed best team in the country. 'NOVI!' 'PAZAR!' 'NOVI!' 'PAZAR!' 'NOVI!' 'PAZAR!' The choral tennis reached a new high volume at advantage Pazar.

Back on the pitch, Partizan had been waiting a full minute for the celebrations to finish. But there was still no real spark, even if, finally, there was a real chance. Babović reacted fastest to a melee in the penalty area, but his poked shot caught the keeper as he flung himself forwards, diverting it wide while oblivious to whether he had made the save or not. Novi Pazar had achieved everything they wanted from the game, and had basically decided not to play any more, thumping the ball as far down the pitch as they could at every opportunity, time-wasting as much as the referee could tolerate, and dropping their adventurous 7-2-1 for the much safer 8-1-1 variant.

Partizan started the second half as they had played the bulk of the first, managing to combine technical superiority with minimal effort and imagination. Five minutes into the half, Tomić and Babović managed to commit a couple of defenders following a cleared corner, and Babović spread the ball to Miljković, on the edge of the penalty area. Miljković, as hesitant in coming forward as in his defensive duties, summoned up the courage to shoot, but dragged it off target, where it was met by Diarra's foot and steered into the net. While the home crowd bayed for offside, the goal was given. Dušan, mindful of his surroundings, permitted himself a quiet 'get in!' in English, and limited his celebrations to that. Away to our right in the cage, the relief from the travelling Grobari had manifested itself in an unusual way – they had actually celebrated the goal, rather than just seeing it as a minor interruption in their singing schedule.

The home crowd were quietened for a minute, before the 'spectacular' arrived over in the east stand. The Ekstremi and Torcida had clubbed together for a really big banner and a few firecrackers. On the banner was a giant depiction of Isa Beg Isaković, with the message 1461 – Teşekkür Ederiz [Thank you – in Turkish].

I will be honest, I've had to look up why this combination of man and date was significant. Isa Beg Isaković is one of the most prominent figures in early Bosniak history and the founder of Sarajevo, as well as Novi Pazar, in 1461. Isaković is just the kind of figure that I would use if I was trying to wind up my Serb guests in Sandžak. A Slavic convert to Islam, his father conducted Ottoman military operations in Serbia, while Isaković himself led the Turkish military conquest of most of Sandžak and Bosnia, while his Ottoman colleagues took Kosovo and most of the rest of Serbia, completing a humiliating end to Serb hegemony in the region.

In Serbia, where the sense of history has been heightened by the nationalism of the 1990s, characters like Isaković are often portrayed as the enemies encircling Serbia against which the narod [people/nation] must resist. The modern Serb mentality is defined to a degree by the five centuries of Ottoman rule and the process of awakening, uprising and independence that developed in the 19th and early 20th centuries, and the toughness which living under occupation, and then throwing off its shackles, required.

This was the cue for a sustained spell of ethnic and sectarian winding-up of the Serbs from the home fans. Dušan muttered caustically that this was what a decade of international NGO spending and workshops was supposed to have been countering. I saw that as all the more reason for activity to promote reconciliation and, to a degree, an unhelpful but understandable recompense for the Ratko Mladić and other anti-Bosniak chants that the Novi Pazar fans had had to endure back in August.

In asserting their non-Serbian identity, the home fans first chanted 'Pet sto godina' [five hundred years] repeatedly, waving Turkish flags in the faces of the Partizan crowd to remind their guests of the length of the period of Ottoman rule. Hundreds of the Novi Pazar fans were decked out today in Fenerbahçe shirts and scarves, celebrating a club 'twinning' that meant more to them than it did to their pals from Istanbul.

The day before, the club had welcomed a bus full of Fenerbahçe fans who had made an ambassadorial visit to today's game overland from Turkey. They had been welcomed at the stadium late in the evening by over a thousand fans. A thousand people just to say hello to some visitors. If revelling in Ottoman occupation hadn't been enough, the Novi Pazar faithful followed that up by promising that Islam would take over the world and a chorus of 'Allahu Akhbar' [God is great – in Arabic], a chant they had initially developed to combat Rad fans offering them a choice of Orthodox Christianity or death in one of their own songs, but found to be effective in antagonising all opponents. If the Grobari had been listening, maybe it could have been the spark for something nasty. But as it was, they were too busy with their own repertoire, though when they started to sing about Kosovo, their songs were drowned out by affirmations of Kosovo's independence from the home fans.

On the pitch, unfazed by the sectarian hatred and interminable geopolitics, Partizan were huffing and puffing but getting nowhere. Grant brought on Saša Ilić and Eduardo, the latter having been allowed back to Brazil for a mid-season break to get over some of his late-autumn tiredness. Judging by where his neck had disappeared to, Eduardo had spent more time in the churrasquerias of Minais Gerais than he had at the gym. Despite his frightening new corpulence, Eduardo's first touch was exquisite, and put him in a great position about 20 yards out, from where he shot agonisingly just over the bar.

The goal still would not come. For Novi Pazar and their fans, it was more a question of inching towards a historic point against the champions. The volume went up around the stadium, and the disapproval of any free kick being given to Partizan was made abundantly clear. If the assistant referee, just in front of us, had any doubt that the home support felt his colleague in the middle should be allowing this game to finish 1-1, then this would have evaporated when he was spat on by a furious Pazar fan, who barged into me to get a better vantage point for his phlegm-based assault. Not just a few droplets of angry spittle. This was a glutinous loogie that lumbered through the air like a viscous Airbus and struck him squarely on the nape of the neck.

In the fourth minute of injury time, Partizan got another free kick. Tomić, having had a half-decent sighter ten minutes before, was a decent bet to hit the target. Flying past my ears were furious promises to f*** the referee's wife, sunflower seeds aimed at his assistant, racist gibes at Medo, and other untranslatable noises of rage. I wanted Tomić to score, and for Partizan to win, but for my own safety, I sort of hoped that he and we didn't.

He didn't. As the Pazar fans celebrated their cup final moment, Dušan and I decided not to test our theory that we had been lucky to escape being kicked in, and made for the exit. On our way out, the Pazar fans turned their attention to Stojković, as he made his own hasty dash for the changing rooms. 'MUSTAFA! MUSTAFA! MUSTAFA!' they shouted at him. Stojković is used to this – he gets called Mustafa all the time. But he gets called that because he is a convert – from Red Star to Partizan, the same epithet dished out to Bosniaks by some Serbs who believe that Bosniaks are just Muslim Serbs.

The Pazar fans were enjoying turning the weapon back the other way so much that I wasn't sure if they actually knew what it meant. But I might have just been suffering from xeno-fatigue, and to be honest I was more annoyed that Red Star had won and cut the gap back to eight points. Across the other side of Belgrade, they were delighting in our discomfort. 'Avram Grant, Red Star legend' said one crveno-beli troller on our forums. Avram hadn't even begun yet.

League table after the 16th round:
1. Partizan 43 (+28)
2. Red Star 35 (+16)
3. Vojvodina 31 (+21)

Return of the Banned

POLITICS is a big part of daily life in Serbia. This is, after all, a country where they had an actual revolution in 2000 and its Prime Minister was assassinated in 2003. Many people who were involved in fomenting that revolution have retired from political life, disappointed with the lack of meaningful reform since then. The hope inspired by Slobodan Milošević's removal and the opening years of Zoran Đinđić's premiership, abruptly terminated by a sniper's bullet, had evaporated for many.

In such a young democracy, it is not a surprise that there are still so many competing political voices – forty-odd parties contesting parliamentary elections, and more than a dozen of them in the coalition government. At this point, Serbia was still wrestling with how much it was prepared to concede in its battle to keep a toehold in Kosovo in order to gain the benefits of becoming a member of the European Union, and clawing back lost ground compared to other central and eastern European countries in terms of economic development, living standards and the rule of law. This debate divides public opinion, so there is plenty of scope for regular, impassioned debate, which is more existential than ideological.

Another key feature of Serbian politics is that policies and issues, even the big ones, tend to be subordinate to personalities and personal ideology. Instead of the main parties arguing over the reasons why their health or education policy is better than the other party's, they concentrate on the general corruption and incompetence of the other side, and the various perceived 'unpatriotic' acts committed by their political rivals.

As part of the method of disguising the lack of real policies and political maturity, some politicians resort to the bread and circuses school of populism. Football is one such circus. New stadia in Užice and Novi Pazar in the season preceding presidential, parliamentary and local elections were seen as obvious gifts to the electorate. During a working visit to Sandžak immediately after our footballing trip, politicians from several parties (though not the one accused of such populism) and a couple of independent observers said they were sure that FC Novi Pazar would win a couple of games in the week immediately prior to the elections in May to create a local feelgood factor and increase the chances of the local ruling party getting back into power.

We had now played Novi Pazar home and away, so the local elections in Sandžak were not going to impact on us. National-level elections were. Even two months before these polls, which were scheduled to come after 27 or 28 league matches had been played, and when the cup finalists were already decided, the conspiracy theorists were out in force.

The basic premise was this: Red Star, much as we hate to say it, are the most popular club in Serbia, with probably half a million more sympathisers. When Red Star do well, the country as a whole is fundamentally a bit happier. Yes, Partizan fans are unhappier, but it's an electoral price worth paying. The government of the day was unpopular, and unsure that securing candidate status for membership of the EU and unveiling a few major foreign investments was going to be enough to turn around a chunky deficit in the opinion polls. So they would lean on football to make Red Star fans – effectively half the country – that bit happier.

Igor's version of the story was at the maximalist end of the scale – referees would be paid to ensure Red Star won every game for the rest of the season, with the involvement and approval of the highest state authorities. Dušan's was subtler, in keeping with the more Machiavellian nuances of the Serbian political scene. State money would be channelled, most likely via one of the State enterprises, to Red Star. The goals would be twofold – to prevent the club from going under in the run-up to the elections (their debt was estimated to have risen to €33m), and to give the players an additional financial inducement to ramp up their performance. The league might be too hard to fix, but he was adamant that Red Star would be shoehorned into the cup final via a couple of soft penalty awards in time for election day.

Dismissing these theories as the ramblings of paranoid fans would be easier if politicians spent less time and effort pandering to football (in fairness, to Partizan nearly as much as Red Star). The most chilling omen of future meddling came at the start of the season from Foreign Minister Vuk Jeremić, one of the senior figures in the ruling Democratic Party. Jeremić, calling in on a Red Star training camp in Austria, addressed the players and, noting his sadness at Red Star's recent trophyless spell, said that 'we will do everything to make sure that Red Star wins something this year'. On YouTube within the hour, Partizan fans of all persuasions saw this as a clear demonstration that the powers-that-be were ready to intervene in favour of their biggest rivals.

When I had put it to friends, particularly over the winter break, that Partizan's ten-point lead was, to a neutral's eye, a quite stern rebuff to the conspiracy theories, I was dismissed as naïve. As an outsider, whose home league wasn't plagued by political interference, I couldn't possibly understand. And more to the point, the league was never fixed in the first half of the season, but everyone had plenty of examples of when 'corrective measures' had been applied in the spring.

Dušan wistfully told the story of how his father had stopped coming to see Partizan when Red Star had been 'given' the cup in 1995, while others had their own examples of attempts, successful and unsuccessful, to rob Partizan of their rightful trophies. But no one had an example of when Partizan had been the beneficiaries, even when up against the smaller teams. I, on the other hand, had felt throughout most of the season that Partizan had received a number of favourable decisions against the little clubs. Not wishing to be stung with more 'outsider' criticism, I kept that mostly to myself.

As politics involves itself in football, football reflects the political scene too. Songs about Ratko Mladić had been sung at the matches just following his capture and extradition, but now that he wasn't big political news, no one seemed to really care at the football either. When Serbia had been denied candidate status for EU membership back in December, our travelling fans, groping for an external enemy to excoriate in the face of the snub and perceived humiliation of Serbia by the 'great powers', had brought out one of their less-regularly heard chants: in English, 'F***, f***, NATO pact.' No matter that NATO had had nothing to do with the EU's decision.

The bombing of Belgrade and other parts of Serbia in 1999, in response to Serbia's actions in Kosovo, is still relatively fresh in the minds of many Serbs, and NATO remains deeply unpopular. The pointed refusal of successive Serbian governments to demolish bombed-out buildings in the centre of Belgrade serves as a reminder of the bombardment, and helps perpetuate those attitudes.

Football had featured in the campaign already – but not in the way the Red Star-fearing conspiracy theorists had suggested. A media head of steam had been worked up against the nefarious characters running the hooligan firms and football-related violence in general. Headline news had been drip-fed over the last month, detailing what the Red Star and Partizan leaders got up to when they weren't pretending to watch football – organising mass brawls, dealing drugs, and stabbing their internal rivals, mostly. These were oft-repeated allegations, which had become accepted as the truth through their repetition rather than the presentation of any specific evidence.

The latest media campaign was different in that specific allegations were levelled at individual leaders, and the scale of the control wielded by the firm leaders was revealed to be greater than I had imagined. Yes, the firms were running rackets and dealing drugs. But the infrastructure they had in place to do so was sophisticated, and involved firms controlling the appointment of club security personnel to their end of the stadium and providing a delicate degree of cooperation with the police – enough discipline among the firm's members to prevent the kind of chaos that would necessitate a direct police intervention in the stadium, combined with an understanding that in the event of trouble, the firm would hand over to the police the occasional miscreant, usually those who lacked sufficient links to the firm's top brass, so that the police could viably claim to have arrested the trouble-makers.

Worse than that was the credible media claim that the criminal tail was wagging the football dog. Two of the main firm leaders, Aleksandar Vavić and Đorđe Prelić, had previously been fans of rival clubs, Red Star and OFK respectively. But, as we read in one newspaper, sensing the opportunities for more criminal gain through the medium of black-and-white, they had seized control of Alcatraz, backed up by some heavy muscle.

The goal of the politically-inspired media pressure was fairly simple. Create an impression that a group is causing a problem, show the strength of the government and State in dealing with it to prevent a repeat, receive the plaudits for a strong stance on law and order issues, and distract the electorate from the country's ongoing economic woes. Rank-and-file firm members, the grunts on the ground, lack the sophistication to realise when they're being played, and therefore when they need to keep their powder dry. They didn't so much walk into a trap, as pick the absolute worst time to have a couple of needless barneys.

A bunch of Partizan and Red Star fans, operating in parallel rather than unison, attacked Croatia fans at the Croatia–France Handball European Championship match in Novi Sad, leading to multiple arrests, a brief flicker of tension in bilateral relations with Croatia, and then an iron ring of security round the Serbia–Croatia semi-final match. Which worked, enabling all connected to the police and home affairs in general to pat themselves firmly on the back. A Red Star-on-Red Star clash around a basketball tournament in Nis was given the same spin too.

The police and Interior Minister Dačić had also been busy trumpeting the arrest of Miloš Radišavljević, better known by his nickname Kimi. Unlike his famous nicknamesake, this Kimi wasn't a taciturn Finn with awesome car control. This one was a former Alcatraz leader who had served time in the past, and had legged it from Serbia during a trial that interrupted an ongoing prison sentence. He had surfaced in Skopje, Macedonia, and had been arrested and extradited the same day. To go through the full list of Kimi's misdemeanours, proven and alleged, would take too long, but his most infamous deed was leading a chant in the stands that amounted to a death threat to a B92 journalist, Brankica Stanković.

As well as promising that Stanković would be killed, Kimi and his cohort mock-executed an effigy of Stanković in the stands. Stanković's crime, in the eyes of Alcatraz, had been to make their leadership public figures, broadcasting their names and photos on national TV as part of her *Insider* programme, and detailing the numerous crimes they were linked to, which in turn had not resulted in any prosecution. The powerlessness of the State to tackle these groups and their crimes was Stanković's wider point. But the threats from figures linked to Alcatraz and the main Red Star and Rad firms meant that the same State was now compelled to provide her with round-the-clock security.

More recently, Kimi had also been accused of arson, taking part in an attack on Belgrade's main Bajrakli mosque. The mosque's mufti, Muhammed Jusufspahić, had publicly declared that Kimi could not have been responsible, indeed that he had warned Jusufspahić that an attack might soon happen, enabling children to be evacuated from the attached madrassa, and for several priceless artefacts to be saved. The mufti, himself a huge sports fan (I met him once to talk about the very serious issue of unifying Serbia's Islamic community and preventing intra-sectarian violence, but he spent a good third of the meeting talking about basketball and how great a player he thought Scottie Pippen was), complained that the police weren't taking his evidence seriously. The wheels of justice would keep on turning.

Like Brankica Stanković had said, there was plenty of evidence to take down all the group leaders, not just certain mid-level commanders like Kimi. But thus far that hadn't translated into much.

Kimi was still in detention for the game against Sloboda – thus far the only team to have beaten Partizan in domestic competition all season. A banner at the front of the stand let him know that 'your Jug will wait for you'. Alcatraz, for all their faults, were faithful to their incarcerated lovers. In the meantime, Serbia had been granted candidate status to become an EU member. This had come as a great boost to President Tadić and his Democratic Party, with elections due to be called on 13 March, and to be held eight weeks later. The Democrats had seized the moment and flooded the city with posters promoting their great European achievement. Although most parties had been in solid pre-electoral mode for several months already, this signified the start of the full-on campaign.

But the promise of a utopian European future wasn't the cue for an outpouring of celebration in the stands. Not at all. Apart from a couple of refrains of the anti-Tadić chant I'd heard at the Serbia match back in October, Grobari politics remained a firmly internal affair. Having got used to there only being 2,000 people in the stadium, it was a bit of a shock to find the stadium three-quarters full. The Zabranjeni were back in full force and running the Istok as their own fiefdom. Their insistence on not singing the same songs at the same time as the Alcatraz-led crowd in the south, which had seemed funny against Red Star when it meant that the

Red Star fans were insulted twice as often, just seemed quite sad today. Instead of a single, throaty and intimidating roar, we had competing sounds and a total lack of rhythm. Never had I heard such a disjointed atmosphere at a ground, so it shouldn't have come as much of a surprise that the performance on the pitch from the players was just as mal-coordinated.

Of the four or five 'leaders' at the front of the Istok, one's job was to listen for the chanting in the Jug, to ensure that on no account was our sound to match theirs. And whenever there was a dip in the volume away to our left, it was the signal for an accusation of fratricide through another rendition of the Ivan Perović song, or a new one calling on the 'dealers' in the south to quit and once again allow the Jug to be a home to all Grobari. Thus they reflected the official Zabranjeni line that their grievances were over the misrule of the Jug, not because of a falling-out over who got which bit of the ill-gotten drug and racketeering money.

The game reached half-time scoreless, Grant's 4-5-1 formation leaving Partizan without the support Marković needed or the dynamism in midfield to make a run past him. Ilić and Smiljanić, the latter sporting a haircut that would make both Emmanuel Frimpong and Raul Meireles blush, had come into the side in place of Diarra and Medo, and added nothing. Grant, 135 minutes into his Partizan career, was booed off with a Zabranjeni-led plea to get rid of the 'mute c***' (as those around me were labelling Đurić) ringing in his ears.

In the second half, the Zabranjeni leadership struggled to motivate much singing at all, except for further eulogies to Ivan Perović. And when they tried the 'Kosovo is the heart of Serbia' chant, they basically got nothing, overestimating the obedience of their public. This was another example of football mirroring party politics. Few politicians really wanted to be seen as 'unpatriotic', allowing anyone to take a position to the nationalist side of them on the rights of Serbs in countries other than Serbia, and on Kosovo being, in their eyes, an integral part of Serbia. So, with a couple of honourable exceptions, parties considered moderate on almost every other issue felt they could not afford to be anything other than hardline on Kosovo.

Away from politics, even the most liberal people I met in Serbia, with very rational views on the need for a peaceful and negotiated solution on Kosovo, would struggle to express a belief that yes,

Kosovo should be an independent country if they were in front of other Serbs. Partizan is not even the second-most nationalist club in Belgrade, let alone Serbia. But the Alcatraz leaders don't feel that they can be seen as anything other than fiercely 'patriotic' if Red Star, Rad and OFK are going to behave that way, so the old songs about Kosovo get trotted out regularly, sung by those who still hanker unrealistically for its return to Serbia and those who just don't want to appear weak in front of their mates. The Zabranjeni, in trying to establish themselves as the voice of the 'real' Grobari, feel forced into the same corner. But the population of the Istok, as liberal and Europhile a bunch of football fans as you're likely to find in Serbia, weren't really buying it.

On and off the pitch, the discord continued into injury time, without a goal to paper over the cracks. Red Star had won earlier in the day at Javor, cutting the gap to a temporary five points, but another draw would only get us back to six in front. This wouldn't have happened if Stanojević had still been in charge. Instead of completing their own chant, the Zabranjeni (and I) addressed the south once more. 'UPRAVA!' we offered. Not much back. 'UPRAVA!' we ventured again. A few dozen, mostly those less Jug-indoctrinated next to the fence separating us, replied: 'NAPOLJE!' We tried again, and a few dozen became a couple of hundred. A fourth attempt brought over a thousand. And a fifth 'UPRAVA' was met by three-quarters of the stadium completing our sentence for us. It had taken 91 minutes, but finally we agreed on something. The only exception was a pocket of a thousand hardcore Alcatraz, demarcating themselves in the seething crowd by staying stock still and silent, a rectangle of obduracy, aloof to the consensus building around them.

Avram Grant walked alone to the tunnel looking pretty miffed at the anaemic performance from his team, into a hail of cigarette lighters launched by some around me. In an irony the subject failed to appreciate, one kid in a hoodie ten rows in front of me lobbed his lighter, missing Grant by several feet, only to get clonked in the back of the head by one which whistled over my head. His plaintive look back at the anonymous perpetrator behind him suggested he wasn't really cut out for a long-term career in hooliganism.

The players, unable to salute their victory for the first time in the league this season, dithered in front of the tunnel, unsure whether to go towards the Jug and risk a verbal lashing, or skulk back to the changing rooms and look ungrateful for the support. Eventually, Smiljanić seemed to persuade them that they should do it, a decision which his team-mates probably immediately regretted.

As they moved into position, black-clad and heavily built fans from the Jug scaled the perimeter fence and dropped down on to the athletics track to confront them until there was a group of 20 around the players, with all the luminous-vested 'security' staff looking on impotently. While the players too stood frozen, the Alcatraz mob started a shoving match among themselves as they competed for the right to bollock the players. Still the security staff did nothing. Then Marković, having said something out of turn, was struck, and the shoving match intensified.

Marković, probably wishing he had gone to Chelsea in the winter break, did the right thing and strode away, followed by a couple of the other players for whom this was well above their pay-grade. And the police, hitherto observers, decided that enough was enough and that this had to stop. Only then did the brawling Alcatraz, with the security staff looking on, leave their dispute for another day and haul themselves back over the fence. The media campaign against the fans' groups might have had a political motivation, but this demonstrated pretty clearly that they had a point – within the territory of the Jug there was only the law of the jungle.

Only after I had left, and read a couple of post-match reports at home, did it dawn on me that this was probably going to ensure that a couple of home games got played behind closed doors. So it was realistic to expect that the club would come down hard on those who had invaded the playing area and especially the guy who hit our best player in the face.

As I was coming to realise, expecting the logical from the club was a distinctly illogical act. In a statement released two days after the match, by which time the FA had already threatened a three-game ban, Partizan officially said sorry. Sort of. The club released a statement, a mealy-mouthed recognition that the public and authorities would judge the club harshly, but attributing that to Marković's fame and youth. Its wider attempt to minimise the incident and deflect the blame, backed up by a couple of interviews from the chairman, harked back to Soviet era propaganda. My favourite couple of sentences described the incident thus (I have inserted my own corrections in parentheses), 'As the players left the pitch, one fan (15 fans) jumped the fence in the east (south) stand and on the athletics track pushed (slapped) the player Lazar Marković. Although it was an individual (group) and an isolated incident, which was immediately (not) dealt with by the intervention of club security ...'

It begged the question of just how far the club would go to protect the group in the Jug. Such blatant lying just isn't possible in the age of YouTube – videos showing the size of the group that had approached the players from the Jug and the total inertia of the security personnel were up within minutes. Marković, in an official club interview, denied he had been slapped – it had been more of 'a shove in the face'. In the media, no one was buying it. Đurić was described in *Danas* as 'in his own style, [having] told a series of proven untruths and a load of contradictions'. A group of fans, identifying themselves through their linguistic register and vocabulary as the Zabranjeni's intellectual wing, asked the more worrying question – why had the police done nothing since the incident? With police spotters operating around the ground, how had it not been possible to identify even the person who had physically assaulted a football player next to the field of play? Their summary – there was no will to do so. 'In a normal country,' one journalist lamented, 'someone would go to prison for this.'

Away at OFK, the police moved the Zabranjeni from their sneaky hiding place in the home end into the neutral west stand, but let them stay and sing a slightly different set list again. Having been allowed in to all these games, their nickname wasn't really accurate anymore. But the 'occasionally permitted' or 'mostly marginalised' were less powerful monikers. At least Partizan won, 2-1, with a wonderful free kick from Tomić and a glancing header from Ivanov, either side of the shortest player on the pitch, OFK's Ecuadorian midfielder Batioha, rising above a flaccid, static Miljković to score a header past Stojković. Avram had won a game at last.

Three fans were arrested just after the OFK game, and were charged with illegal entry on to the playing area and other public order offences in relation to the post-Sloboda events, and faced either 45 days in prison or a fine of several thousand euros. Marković's assailant wasn't among them. But the police were able to show they had done something, and face down the criticism from many Partizan fans that surely, with multiple police spotters in the stadium, and CCTV and YouTube footage covering most of the angles, they could arrest the culprits with minimal effort. A few days later, a fourth invader was arrested, just leaving the remaining 11 unmolested. Between the arrests and the apology from the club, it was enough to get the ban down to just the one game – to be served immediately at home to Jagodina.

Freed from the shackles of having to listen to their own fans arguing among themselves, and able to hear Avram's instructions above the discord in the stands, the team played really well. I was forced to watch on TV, which usually makes me far more nervous and liable to bouts of unjustified swearing. But I had reason neither to sweat nor swear. Ilić scored within a minute with a long-range belter, and Diarra made it two before half-time.

Both players doubled their tallies in the second half, Ilić scoring an even better goal than he did in the first half. Jagodina did nothing all game, failing to live up to the promise of their larger-than-life Mayor Marković Palma that his boys would give ours one hell of a beating. This was the most impressive we had been under Grant, and Red Star's momentum in closing the gap had been checked. He wasn't exactly winning the fans over – the closed-door game against Jagodina had been the first time that Grant hadn't heard the fans chant 'Ti si prvi trener, Stanoje!' to his face, reminding him that their loyalties still lay squarely with his ousted predecessor. He would hear it again, for sure.

League table after the 19th round:
1. Partizan 50 (+36)
2. Red Star 44 (+25)
3. Vojvodina 38 (+24)

Red Star's Chetnik

LOTS of lessons had been learned for the second of this season's four derbies, the first leg of the Serbian Cup semi-final. Firstly, we got our act together and managed to get to the ground a full 15 minutes before kick-off, avoiding the last-minute scrum, providing Dušan with the opportunity to remind everyone this was now the 43rd derby since we had last been given a penalty, and giving us the chance to find somewhere decent to stand.

Or so we thought. The police too had done their homework and been much better prepared for the invasion of the east stand by the Zabranjeni. A couple of hundred seats had been removed to create an exclusion zone between the main Zabranjeni cohort, who had been scooped up on arrival and escorted skilfully into the cage, and the impressionable quasi-Zabranjeni. This greatly reduced the amount of space available to us, forcing us to shuffle into whatever spots we could find. But more importantly, it gave the police the vantage points and defensive lines they needed to prevent any of the intra-Partizan scuffling that had happened last time.

At the other end, the Red Star fans had understood the value of good behaviour as well. Needing as much home support as they could to sustain their hopes of a successful overhaul of Partizan in the league, they could ill afford another game behind closed doors. So they kept their pyrotechnic stash in the stands with them, not launching a single projectile at the Partizan subs as they walked out, despite having a clear shot. Red Star had done a better job at managing Partizan's fireworks too, placing all bar one of the advertising hoardings out of range, and when one did briefly ignite (it was a herculean throw to get it there), the firemen had a fully functioning hose ready to douse the flames in seconds. Everyone had clearly been responding constructively to customer feedback.

The competing sounds of Red Star and two sorts of Partizan chants, the thick smoke from the flares, the tension, the aggression and tribalism of those around me, the physicality of standing and being bumped from all sides, all of this was just as intense as it had been in the league derby in November. But now it just seemed normal to me – this was a regular theatre of operations. I was worried about what this meant for my future as a football fan in England – watching Arsenal would feel like going for afternoon tea at Fortnum and Mason's. But equally I was glad that I had adapted to my new environment pretty quickly.

On the pitch, Red Star continued the theme of learning and development – they had decided to play much smarter. They were content to let Partizan have a lot of the ball, relatively safe in the knowledge that they weren't going to have to deal with anyone running beyond Diarra. Grant's five-man midfield of Medo, Babović (now playing in the 'quarterback' deep-lying midfield position), Tomić, Vukić and Ilić wasn't going to surge past their striker very often. And neither Lazevski (in the side because Volkov was injured) and Miljković (for some unknown reason preferred to the vastly superior Aksentijević) had ever shown much propensity for overlapping. When Partizan eventually gave the ball away, Red Star would commit five or six immediately to the counter-attack. But they didn't seem to have much of a plan once they got into our half either and would then lose the ball cheaply. Both teams gave the ball away a lot in the first quarter of an hour.

Diarra had just scuffed a shot wide from about five yards out, and our howls of anguish at how big a miss it was were only just subsiding when Partizan gave the ball away again. Red Star surged forward to the edge of the area where Ivanov, keeping a cool head and standing his ground while others were tearing back chaotically, calmly took the ball off his opponent's toes. But he dithered in bringing the ball forward, losing the ball to a slide challenge. No worry, the ball was breaking for Ilić. But he was muscled off it with minimal resistance and suddenly Red Star were three on three, 20 yards out. Two passes later and Luka Milunović, one of Red Star's transfer window signings, had lifted the ball over the advancing Stojković and into the net. It was his third goal in three games since signing, but this was the one that made his name. The north stand, having been mostly dormant in the first derby, erupted. We might not like them, but they knew how to make a noise when they scored.

The pattern of the game stayed the same for the rest of the half. Partizan had no Plan B without an injection of pace. Miljkon made a rare foray forward just before half-time, and an even rarer cross of quality, which Diarra controlled and volleyed just over. But that was about as exciting as it got. As the players went off, Partizan showed that they had done some study too. Just because the north hadn't firebombed the subs, it didn't mean that they didn't still have a hefty arsenal cached ready to lob at the first team as they came off at half-time. So as soon as the whistle blew, they attached themselves like limpets to their Red Star counterparts. Throw what you like at us, we'll take your boys down with us. Whether because the Red Star fans feared this collateral damage or because they just weren't going to throw anything anyway, I don't know, but the Partizan players all got into the changing room unscathed.

During half-time, Dušan and Goran dissected the first half. Blame was laid squarely on one set of shoulders – Avram Grant's. Dušan was in the zone – in the kind of rant that could only be stopped by the players re-emerging. 'He's clueless. He knows nothing about Serbian football. I don't think the club has properly prepared him for all this, and they've given him some translator who happens to have been to Israel, but he's got no support. What the f*** is Babović doing as a defensive midfielder? He doesn't do enough work on the wing, let alone in the middle. How come Miljkon is in the team when that midfield's crying out for support? Why is Marković on the bench when what we really need is some pace? Why is our best player on the bench? Why?' A dozen similar conversations were taking place around me, split between disbelief at Marković's absence and criticism of Grant for not understanding the importance of the derby (though in the press conference before the game, he had actually made the case quite eloquently as to just how much he did understand – it just wasn't translating on to the pitch).

As the players kicked off again, we gave our lads something that they hadn't had in ages in a fresh effort to spur them on: one chant. The eastern and southern disciples joined together, and sang the same song for three whole minutes. Only a stubborn pocket in the western corner of the south, from its line-up of flags clearly a heavily Alcatraz-influenced group, refused to join in, staring steadfastly forward while everyone else bounced around them, caught up in the delight of a shared purpose and the intellectually-unchallenging 'Na na na na naaaa!' chorus.

As fans in both corners applauded each other's efforts, Diarra ran on to a long ball and guided the ball with a left-foot volley across the goal and on to the far post. It was agonisingly close, but by far the most meaningful action we had produced on the pitch for the whole game. It had taken the prospect of defeat in the derby to galvanise us, but perhaps we the supporters had learned that we were more likely to motivate the team if we concentrated on cheering for them rather than against each other.

Not completely. The Zabranjeni leaders, bolstered by the success in leading the chant that had unified us, instead of consolidating their advantage with a couple of other uncontroversial pro-Partizan songs that we could coalesce around, tried too hard to ram home their present superiority and started another round of Ivan Perović tributes. South and east went back to singing their own songs. But we did find some common ground a couple more times, each time coinciding with a better, more sustained spell of Partizan pressure.

Just before the hour mark, as Partizan started to ease off the gas, Red Star gave the ball away while in a promising position. Partizan swept forward on the counter, Medo launching the ball right to Vukić with space to run into. Knowing that he couldn't outpace the Red Star defenders in front of him, Vukić instead drew one of them in before passing inside to Diarra, sprinting forward. The ball was just too slow for Diarra to take it in his stride and beat the last man, so instead he pirouetted gracefully, leaving his defender flat-footed while he laid the ball off to the onrushing Ilić. Eight yards out, with no one near him, the ball was perfectly placed for Partizan's most experienced player to open his body and line up a pass into the net. His body shape was perfect. His eye was on the ball. His backlift was short and his follow-through clean. And then he shanked it four yards wide. Red Star jeers drowned out the remnants of our joint chanting, as the home fans gloried in their lucky escape.

Ten minutes later, Red Star scored again. Some central midfield dithering by Partizan was followed by some defensive dithering, and the ball broke for Kasalica, the former Sloboda forward who had scored a good opportunist goal against us in August, and was signed by Red Star in the transfer window, who poked it under Stojković for 2-0. Kasalica, having scored on his debut within 75 seconds of coming on, and now against us after only a few minutes on the pitch, was quickly becoming a Red Star hero. Everyone around me thought out loud that he was actually a massive d**k. He and most of his team-mates vaulted the perimeter advertising boards and celebrated in front of the north end for as long as they could get away with while we struggled to get our voices back and start encouraging the team to get a much-needed away goal.

Red Star showed that their lesson-learning hadn't just been about how to attack, but also how to defend, as they switched from counter-attack to Italian-style catenaccio, doing everything to spoil Partizan's rhythm and waste time from niggly fouls to falling over theatrically off the ball with fictitious injuries. I have never seen a club suck the life out of a match so effectively, testing the referee's patience and provoking a barrage of invective from the increasingly angry mob around me. I say club, not team, because the ball boys, hitherto just people who returned the ball to the players, became agents of procrastination, systematically delaying the ball's return to Partizan players, and then throwing on a second ball as the dead ball was struck, forcing the referee to stop the game. It was ugly, but effective.

When midfielder Milivojević, already on a yellow card, hacked down Marković as he burst through the middle, they took it further than even the most extreme advocates of catenaccio would usually dare. As the Red Star players surrounded the ref and tried to block off their opponents from demanding a red card, it became apparent that they were trying to pretend that someone else had committed the foul. The officials were not going to be swayed, so every time the ref tried to approach Milivojević to show the card, another off-the-ball incident miraculously happened, diverting the ref's attention and granting Milivojević a stay of execution. Three minutes after the foul happened, the ref eventually managed to get close enough to Milivojević to send him off.

The spoiling tactics were good enough to prevent Partizan from even coming close to getting a goal, and the game finished 2-0. We had been good enough and had enough of the ball to get a draw, or even a win, but had come away with a reasonably-sized hill to climb in the second leg. As we slunk out of the stadium, the home fans in the north, conducted by their players, led a rousing chorus of 'Jebi,

jebi, jebi Grobare!' With minimal resistance, we did as instructed and snuck out of there.

Two weeks passed. The disappointment of losing the first leg was slowly replaced by optimism that we could still win the tie. We had proved ourselves capable of beating them by two goals – enough at least to take the game into extra time. And then home advantage should be enough. There was no one among our group who didn't think we could still do the double. Even Dušan, secure in his belief that a 44th derby would pass without us getting a penalty, as he reminded me several times in the week leading up to the game, still thought we could win.

Wandering down the hill from the city centre towards the stadium before the return leg, I could hear the Jug, in full voice, wafting on the wind a full two kilometres away. It was enough to make me think I had got the kick-off time wrong. I had previous, after all. As usual, there were hundreds of police on the streets on each of the principal routes towards the ground, including a small detachment holding a jostling group of Zabranjeni back temporarily on the main road down from the city centre. As I nipped through the park opposite them, another group of police, as replete with body armour and truncheons as their colleagues over the road, was trying to enforce the alcohol-free zone, but was struggling to differentiate between who was having a pre-match livener and who was having a picnic in the evening sunshine, and being forced into contrite apologies, despite all their padding.

Dušan was in the UK and couldn't make the match, promising that he would be watching in one of the Serb-owned pubs in west London. Only Uroš had arrived before me, then Debeli and the younger Milovan showed up in quick succession. All three of them separately asked me where he was. This was my 23rd game of the season (and fourth without Dušan being there) and they were still surprised that I had come without him. There was still work to be done in persuading them that I was a genuine supporter.

As the first home derby, I was keen to see how intimidating the atmosphere would be. Like them or loathe them, Red Star had succeeded in making the stadium distinctly unwelcoming for both our games so far. There were some fireworks, a few of which landed on the pitch a few metres away from Red Star's staff as they walked out, but without the accuracy that had been shown by Red Star in the first derby.

Robert Prosinečki was roundly booed and called a series of anti-Croat names by groups within the south. But what the crowd lacked in intensity, it made up for with variety. The main chants, 'Jebi, jebi, jebi Cigane!' [f*** off, gypsies], and 'Sisaj, Zvezdo!' [suck it, Red Star] were not the most imaginative, but they were certainly loud. An enormous flag was unfurled in the south, an amalgamation of Red Star's and Olimpiacos's badges on a rainbow flag, implying none too subtly that Red Star and their red-and-white Greek partner club (ours, by the way, is the black-and-white PAOK Salonika) enjoyed homosexual relations. Having tried to offend today's opponents with ethnic and sexual obscenity, the last salvo was reserved for the political arena.

With a banner that stretched thirty metres around the curve of the Jug, Red Star were denounced as being unprincipled. 'When the DS (then President Tadić's party) pays, you can't muddy the President's name any more.' Red Star's supporters, usually the most overtly party political of any in the SuperLiga save for the nihilists at Rad, who hated everyone, had gone unusually easy on the President in recent weeks. Alcatraz and the Zabranjeni's shared interpretation of that was that Red Star needed some political favours – probably to shore up their parlous finances – and so the fans had been persuaded to lay off. It was a clever, and quite cutting observation, but it was hardly going to intimidate the Red Star players, was it? This had more place in the comment section of a broadsheet newspaper.

We grudgingly admitted upon seeing the line-ups that Avram had got it right for this game. Marković, whose pace would be crucial to unlocking a stubborn Red Star defence, was in the team, nominally as a right-winger in a five-man midfield, ready to spring forward in support of Diarra, who had yet to live up to his nickname and make any impact against Red Star this season.

Red Star had come with the same counter-attacking game-plan as had been so effective in the first leg, but with a bigger side serving of catenaccio, sitting even deeper than before and wasting time almost as soon as the first whistle was blown, with their strikers under clear instructions to sprint as hard as they could at our centre-backs (Ivanov and Rnić) whenever they had the chance to force a mistake or chase a long ball. Just one goal for them would see the tie almost certainly beyond us.

A pattern emerged. We would raise our hopes by coming close, then Red Star would show how fragile our defence was, and demonstrate by how thin a thread our hopes were dangling. Vukić hit the post in the fifth minute, the ball ricocheting back off the woodwork on to the disoriented keeper's back but somehow staying out. Five minutes later, Red Star were in our box, and one of their forwards hurled himself over Rnić's leg on to the floor. Half of us gasped in horror at the inevitability of the penalty award, the other half instinctively yelled for a dive. The ref sided with the second group and showed a yellow card to their player.

Another five minutes later, Vukić seized on a loose ball and fed Marković, who dashed past his man and into the right-hand side of the box. Such was his speed advantage that he didn't get forced wide, and turned towards the goal. Neither the keeper nor the centre-back came towards him, giving him time for one touch, then another touch, and a third, until he was just six yards from goal and had most of it to aim at. My knees were already aching from standing on the uneven surface of the seat, designed for an ergonomic fit to a bottom, not feet, but I went through the pain barrier to tiptoes, ready to launch myself upwards in celebration. And Marković put it over. Not by a little way, but by a mile.

Then Rnić had one of his daydreams in which he is a skilful winger, and got tackled by Lazović just inside Red Star's half, with no one behind him. Lazović left Rnić in his dust, and it was clear as soon as he crossed into our half that neither he nor Ivanov was going to catch him. Lazović pressed on towards the box while Ivanov got into his stride and started to narrow the gap a little. But Lazović was inside the area now, and while he could surely hear the thunder of Ivanov's hooves, he was going to have a free shot at goal. As Stojković came out, Ivanov launched himself in the direction where Lazović had to shoot. He got the tiniest of touches, enough to guide it within range of Stojković, arms spread like goalkeeping tentacles, who parried back into Lazović's path and then flung himself at the baffled striker's feet and seized the ball again.

We went straight down the other end and Diarra missed by inches. Then from another long ball Lazović outsprinted Ivanov off a three-yard handicap and chipped inches past Stojković's post with the goalkeeper in no-man's-land. At half-time, it was still 0-0. Red Star had tried to kill the game as much as they could, but in that respect they'd failed. It had been breathless. But they still hadn't conceded, and were very much in the pound seats.

Red Star would have been even more satisfied with the first 15 minutes of the second half, in which the game remained goalless and Partizan had just one real chance, when Babović got on the end of Volkov's cross and managed to head it over a hundred degrees in the wrong direction, leaping like a salmon but displaying similarly piscine skill in heading a football.

And two minutes later, it was all over. Another Partizan attack foundered on the rocks of Red Star's defence and, with too many men upfield, Red Star's Evandro was able to wander unchallenged for half the field, play in Lazović, and watch his team-mate nip past Rnić and poke the ball under Stojković with his studs. We now needed four, and Red Star knew it. Robert Prosinečki had mounted and was dry-humping one of his backroom staff in celebration, as Red Star fans streamed from the Sever (as well as northern corners of the Istok and Zapad, where they had achieved a similar level of occupation as we had at the away derbies) on to the athletics track to celebrate with Lazović.

Could we at least score before the inevitable defeat? Vukić pulled off an outrageous dummy to leave Diarra in the clear, but he made a hash of his finish. Then Red Star scored again. Rnić gave the ball away on the halfway line once more, allowing Red Star to release Borja, who bumped his way past Ivanov and scored with a weak shot that Stojković should really have saved. A few rows back from me, someone was still trying to calculate what we needed to win. Five goals in ten minutes, in theory. You had to admire the optimism and strength of character of a fan who would even open their mouth at that point in the death spiral of a tie like this, let alone believe we could do anything about it.

To our credit (the fans', not the team's), the noise level had not gone down at all from the start of the game until this moment. But even the combined but competing voices of the Jug and the Zabranjeni couldn't sustain themselves looking down the barrel of this defeat. It was Red Star who were making the most noise. Most of their invitations to go f*** ourselves, I had heard before. But they had a new one tonight:

'Ti si Zvezdin Četnik, Avrame, Avram-e-e-e!' [You're (Red) Star's Chetnik, Avram], they serenaded our manager. It was clever, because it was a variation of the chant Partizan usually use about Robert Prosinečki. In advance of the full explanation, the Chetniks had been the main enemy of the Partizans in the Yugoslav Resistance in the Second World War. Hence, in the most basic terms, why Prosinečki, out to beat Partizan, fitted the role well. Sadly for us, Avram fitted it even better, as in our joke Prosinečki only tries to beat Partizan, whereas Avram was succeeding.

The issue of who the Chetniks were, and what their role was, is still controversial today in Serbia and across the Balkans. The Chetniks defined themselves as the monarchist (as opposed to Tito's republican and communist Partizans) resistance to the Nazi occupiers during the Second World War. But although they definitely wanted the Nazis out, their resistance wasn't always so straightforward in terms of its actions. Members of the Chetnik movement seized the opportunity of 'resistance' to carry out atrocities against non-Serb populations, notably Bosniaks and Croats.

And where they thought it would advance their long-term goal of gaining post-war power in Yugoslavia, they were prepared to collaborate with the Nazis to the detriment of the Partizans. When the Allies started supplying Yugoslav resistance fighters from 1942, they initially couldn't decide who to back, and helped both the Chetniks and the Partizans. Over time it became clear that the Partizans were going to be more effective, and so the Allied effort, led by Fitzroy MacLean, as chronicled in *Eastern Approaches*, was concentrated on them. At the end of the war, with the tide having turned against them, many Chetniks fled, fearing reprisals under the new regime. Many others suffered those reprisals.

The term Chetnik therefore entered the post-war Yugoslav lexicon as a byword for a traitor – someone who had fought against the Partizan cause and was therefore a Nazi collaborator. It was never really that simple, as many British government papers from the time, since published, testify. But it was much more convenient for Tito to have all Chetniks come under a single label and add them to his list of enemies of the State.

Since the resurgence in Serb nationalism that began in the late 1980s, the word Chetnik had made a bit of a comeback. For royalists, it had never really gone away, but the term was appropriated by new groups of 'patriots' who wanted to fight for Serb rights in other parts of Yugoslavia, particularly in Croatia and Bosnia. One of the leaders of the neo-Chetnik movement, Vojislav Šešelj, is in The Hague right now because of his actions during those wars.

In 2011, Serbia developed new laws on restitution (the process of compensating people for property losses inflicted during wartime). So that their descendants might not be excluded from restitution, certain figures formerly considered traitors had to be officially rehabilitated. Under pressure from one of its minority partners, a party dedicated to the promotion of the version of history in which the Chetniks were equal resistors alongside the Partizans, the government had been forced to make a concession and extend the laws to include descendants of Chetniks. Thus, a process began to rehabilitate Draža Mihajlović, the wartime Chetnik leader - executed on Tito's orders after a show trial in 1946. This had gone down badly at home with descendants of Partizans and abroad, particularly in Croatia, where memories of Chetnik atrocities against Croats had endured.

Contemplating the ugly history behind the chant put into perspective how little our defeat really mattered in the grand scheme of things, even if this meant that Red Star would almost certainly win the competition – their opponents in the final would be bottom-of-the-table Borac – and would have something to crow about.

Avram Grant had probably focused less on the historical significance of the abuse being directed his way, but he must have realised that the pressure on him to deliver the league, and win the home league derby in April, had been made all the more intense.

Red Star Spring

IN between the semi-finals, we had four league games with which to try and create some momentum and halt the Red Star juggernaut in the league. Any more lost points would be punished by Red Star. The second half of the season in Serbia is often called Zvezdino Proleće [(Red) Star's Spring] because the crveno-beli appear never to lose a game in the second half of the season. Advocates for Red Star call it peaking at the right moment. Partizan fans see it as the inevitable consequence of the footballing Establishment being bought off by Red Star. Red Star's penalties get softer, their opponents try less hard, their confidence builds, they start playing well. A six-point lead, down from ten, wasn't enough – they had overhauled bigger in the past. So we had to forget about the cup and get on with the business of winning league games.

Eleven games were still left to go in the season. Dušan reckoned that Red Star only really had three places where they might drop points – away at Radnički Kragujevac, away at Novi Pazar, and in the derby against us. 'But I think they'll win every game between now and the derby. And then they'll get some dodgy penalty and beat us too.' If he was right, we could only get away with dropping two points before the derby.

First up, we were away at Kula, in the smallest town to have a SuperLiga team. Nick Hercules had warned me not to expect much. It was the only ground where urinating against its walls was not a punishable offence, because the stadium had no toilet (I did not conduct an exhaustive search to see if this was true). He also recalled that Kula had once qualified for Europe, but been forced to play their home leg at Partizan to satisfy UEFA

215

standards. None of their fans had attended what was their only ever European game. That couldn't possibly apply to any other club.

I took Claire, having felt guilty about my repeated absence at weekends. I promised a nice drive in the countryside, sunshine and a fun day out in Vojvodina. At least it was sunny. The drive, on bumpy roads across the flat brown plains of western Vojvodina, towards the least-signposted place in Serbia, was a precursor to a match of equal frustration.

Thank goodness we won, though. It finished 2-0 in one of the worst games of football I have ever had the misfortune to witness and, for Claire, comprehensively the worst, and she has seen Bradford City play a number of times. It would be a long time before I could be trusted again to suggest a 'fun day out'.

Our players looked tired, physically and mentally and, even against the ten men of the opposition, failed to find any space on the pitch. Our players resembled dumb electrons, buzzing about and consistently choosing the path of most resistance, eschewing the space on the wings for ploughing back into the congested midfield. Tomić, who spent the whole game getting hopelessly outpaced by Kula's full-back, scored a penalty in the first ten minutes and a half-decent finish from the same man a minute from the end gave us a result we barely deserved.

The most interesting aspect of being in Kula was the thick Montenegrin accents of those 'home' fans around us, which mostly involves adding a lot of extra j's to words where, two villages down the road, those j's just don't exist.

The second game away at Rad had the potential to be much more exciting. Throw in Serbia's best-organised hooligan firm to the mix of Partizan's own two factions, and a team which, despite a limited budget, often challenged for a top-four place (though currently ninth in the league), this was a match that could get tasty on a number of fronts. A couple of weeks previously, there had been open warfare in the stands between Rad's United Force mob and Novi Pazar's fans, with rocks, flares and punches thrown to the point where the game was suspended for a while.

As part of the punishment for that violence, Rad were forced to play their future 'high-risk' games, including ours, at a different stadium. Their own home ground has just the one stand, meaning little room for separating rival groups. Fortunately for Rad, a vacant stadium with two stands was available just up the road, the ground formerly occupied by FK Obilić.

FK Obilić had gone from champions of Yugoslavia in 1997/98 to playing in the seventh tier of Serbian football today, in the Danube section of the Second Belgrade League – akin in standard to the upper echelons of British Sunday league football. They didn't need their 5,000-seater stadium very often these days.

Obilić had never been a true footballing powerhouse until 1996, when the paramilitary and war criminal Željko Raznatović, better known as Arkan, took over the club. Arkan's activities are worthy of a book in their own right, but, in short, he went from being a career criminal across Europe in the 1970s and 1980s, to the head of Red Star's Delije in the late 1980s, to becoming one of the most feared characters in Belgrade's criminal underworld, before heading up his own paramilitary force that took part in some of the bloodiest battles of the wars in Croatia and Bosnia, committing many atrocities and making huge sums from looting, smuggling and sanctions-busting. He also married the popular turbo-folk singer of the 1990s, Svetlana Veličković, better known as Ceca, and enjoyed both celebrity status and the ear of many domestic politicians until he was assassinated in 2000.

Post-1995, Arkan's Tigers were forced to disband, and he looked for other means of translating his financial means into power and influence.

Not unlike other 'businessmen', he invested in football, taking second division Obilić into the top flight, and then on to the title in 1997/98. As well as pumping money into the club to bring in better players, Arkan spent heavily on buying off Obilić's opposition, and where that didn't work, threatening individual opposition players. One famous example was Red Star's captain of the time being asked if he wanted to continue playing enthusiastically if the price for his enthusiasm was some knee surgery using a Heckler & Koch. Obilić's home crowd, often made up of a baying mob of ex-Tigers and other nationalist nutters, sometimes allowed to bring in weapons to the stadium, added to the reason not to beat Obilić.

If the threats didn't work, Ceca's occasional appearance behind the goal, cheerleading via the medium of her capacious bosom rising and falling in time with the fans' chanting, was a distraction in itself. In 1997/98, it all came together. Obilić only lost one game, pipped Red Star to the championship by two points, and reached the cup final, where they lost to Partizan.

UEFA worried publicly about what it meant for European football if a team belonging to someone like Arkan was allowed to participate in the Champions League. So before Obilić started their campaign, eventually losing in the second qualifying round to Bayern Munich, Arkan stepped back, still controlling the club from the shadows with Ceca as the club president. Between Ceca and another president, Obilić continued to feature in the top four for a few more years yet, but after Arkan was killed, the team's fortunes plunged, suffering consecutive relegations to the point where their former stadium, proudly proclaiming their championship success of 1997/98, was already a historical relic.

United Force had declared themselves against the stadium move, and the day before the match had declared that they would boycott the game. Neither we, nor the police, were sure whether to believe them. Wandering down to our pre-match meeting point, I passed by the stadium to buy tickets in advance, and saw the police had taken no chances and had flooded the streets round the ground with men.

The away game at Obilić being 'old school', Dušan and the boys decided to go for an old school pre-match warm-up, with drinks in a small park a kilometre away from the ground. As I arrived, this had the makings of yet another situation where I either had to drink beer and feel ill, or explain for the umpteenth time why I don't like it, and earn the undying enmity of everyone in my vicinity. But I was saved in the unlikeliest way. Dušan, 6ft 3in and skinheaded, was busy topping up a plastic cup of white wine with fizzy water. 'Dušan, are you having a spritzer?' I asked. He was, the massive class traitor. So was Uroš, protesting that he needed to go easy because he had been up until five drinking vinjak, a vile-tasting spirit that could only mean that he had run out of other booze. No one else batted an eyelid at these two indulging in such a delicate and feminine beverage. Hmm. Don't mind if I do.

Refreshed and recharged by our aperitifs, we nipped on a trolleybus back up the hill to the ground. As we arrived, it was clear that United Force weren't showing up, but nevertheless, the police were probably right to saturate the area. Dušan noted the presence of several Partizan hotheads who elected not to attend most games, and I saw plenty of people who, without wishing to 'profile' them too much, looked like they were up for a ruck. The sense of potential aggro spooked the lines of police next to the stadium, who squeezed us towards the entrances, nudging us forward with riot shields no matter how much we protested that we were waiting for someone and that we had his ticket (this was true – the Engleski Grobar was running late). Eventually, they decided they had got us in a manageable enough coop, so we weren't quite 'kettled', but we might have been if Nick had been five minutes later.

United Force's trick, when boycotting other relocated games, had been to sabotage the pitch the night before with a mixture of rubbish, broken glass, and human excrement. But this time they hadn't bothered. The pitch, despite never being used, was immaculately maintained, which meant that Avram Grant's widely publicised excuse for Partizan's recent poor performances – that even Manchester United couldn't have won on Novi Pazar's pitch – wasn't going to work today.

In the end, we needed no excuses. Partizan were brilliant. Ivanov scored a thumping left-footed shot after a one-two with Eduardo after just six minutes. Ivanov had already gone up in the fans' estimation the previous week for playing just days after his mother had died and, as he scored, he pulled up his shirt to reveal a picture of his mum. Alcatraz and Zabranjeni, at either end of the west stand, briefly joined in the warm reception for Ivanov's gesture, before going their separate ways again.

Five minutes later, we were two up, Diarra sprinting on to Ilić's long through-ball before rounding the keeper. 'He's missed it. He's f***ed it up,' said Nick, before quickly retracting his statement as Diarra found the net. Babović scored a sumptuous volley after half an hour. The ten of us in our group turned round to bait Dušan (still actively campaigning against Babović's inclusion in the side), but he drowned us, and indeed most of our section of the ground, out, leaving 400 people turning round in bafflement to see why this hugely loud man was demanding Babović's immediate termination despite such a great goal. Rad got one back before Diarra nodded in Aksentijević's super-accurate cross for 4-1 at half-time.

The second half, dull on the pitch, was just a sing-song in the sun, enlivened by the younger of the two Milovans stealing a ball that got kicked out of the ground over our heads, nearly clouting a woman walking in the street, before being returned to us by another passer-by. The game even got interrupted by the fun, with the Zabranjeni hardcore causing a minute-long delay to the game by throwing all their t-shirts on to the pitch.

Next up, we were at home to Vojvodina. On paper, this was one of our hardest games. But we were boosted just before kick-off by news that Red Star had drawn a blank away at Radnički. From seeing our league crown slipping inevitably off our heads a fortnight ago, Dušan was convinced that the trophy was almost certainly ours. 'If we win today, and then away at Spartak, there's not enough games for us to slip up in.' Mathematically, it was fanciful, but the run-in, and the low standard of most opposing teams in the SuperLiga, meant that there were only really four chances for us to drop points after today, even with Avram at the helm.

Vojvodina came to Belgrade with two interesting players in their line-up. The first was Stephen Appiah, a free transfer Partizan hero in my private world of Football Manager but only really of interest to me and Dušan. The second, who everyone was talking about, was Almami Moreira. After a year in China following his Đurić-inspired exit from Partizan, Moreira had been tempted back to Serbia by Vojvodina, though Dušan questioned their motives in buying him. 'They've only done it to p*** us off, probably,' he said, ignoring the previous five minutes where he had explained why Moreira had been such a great player for Partizan and had been one of the best-adapting foreign imports into the SuperLiga. I ventured that Vojvodina might have just wanted to use his skills to, you know, improve their team. But this only triggered a further mini-rant about why Vojvodina were just a Red Star feeder club and therefore a bunch of fifth columnists.

The fans, Alcatraz and Zabranjeni and all others in between, hadn't forgotten what a good servant Moreira had been, and gave him a welcome of genuine warmth. Moreira looked a bit conflicted as he walked out on to the pitch, before eventually deciding to recognise the chants of his name by applauding us and then joining his team-mates in acknowledging his own fans, who were just being allowed into the stadium. Bringing nearly 400, they were the second most populous group we had seen in the JNA this year, after Novi Pazar, though Red Star would obviously bring more.

Before kick-off, the crowd was invited to join a minute's silence for six young people killed in a nightclub fire in Novi Sad, where Vojvodina play their home games. I'd been warned in advance to expect some sick chants by the Jug in response, but the silence was observed impeccably. Uroš and Dušan, both late arrivals, were visibly surprised when I told them. 'You mean the guys in the Jug didn't say something really offensive?' 'No, nothing. They were really good.'

For 20 minutes, we followed the usual pattern of Partizan possession and lack of penetration, while Vojvodina toiled in the unseasonal spring evening heat to stifle the match and launch counter-attacks, including forcing one great save from Stojković before quarter of an hour was up. I noted contrarily to myself that Appiah was doing an excellent job at breaking up the Partizan attacks, just like Medo does for us week in, week out, and congratulated myself on having signed him on Football Manager. Dušan caught my inadvertent grinning at my own prescience as a virtual manager and reminded me of where my allegiances really lay.

Despite the lack of a goal, Partizan were pretty good. Dušan was still excitably explaining to everyone around us about how these next two games, if won, would give us a 99 per cent chance of winning the league, when the entire Zabranjeni troop upped sticks and shuffled across to the far north of the Istok. A brief debate among the more senior members of our group, conducted via the medium of nods and shrugs of the shoulders, determined that we wouldn't be leaving our space. Sympathisers to the Zabranjeni cause, advocates of a post-Alcatraz world and occasional mourners of Ivan Perović we may have been, but we always stand where we stand, a few rows above the tunnel entrance. So we stayed put. So did lots of others, many of whom spent the rest of the game joining in with the Jug's chanting instead. The Zabranjeni might have carved themselves a new geographical niche, but they'd not secured any of the floating voters beforehand.

Vojvodina got a corner with their second meaningful attack, and scored from it. The ball wasn't properly cleared twice before their big striker Skuletić slammed it into the roof of the net from five yards. From looking at going back to eight points clear, suddenly it was looking like the lead was being cut to five. Before half-time, Eduardo and Ilić contrived not to score with the ball practically on the goal-line, Eduardo hit the post, and Tomić grazed the bar. It wasn't our day so far. No matter that the team had attacked from the start and dominated the game, there was no charity for Avram as he walked off at half-time, greeted by deafening boos interspersed with the odd pička here and there.

One fan, concerned that Avram's Serbian was not yet up to scratch, and that he was unable to understand the sentiment directed at him from the stands, made his way down a few rows to translate, though I fear he was enjoying his linguistic role a bit too much, because he was embellishing the simple translation of *pička*, adding descriptors like 'massive' and 'useless'.

As big drops of rain started to fall on us at the start of the second half, the spring warmth giving way to a late-August thunderstorm, my decision to only wear a t-shirt to the game looked only to be matched by Partizan's erroneous shooting as Babović weaved his way into a good position and then scuffed wide. But as the storm clouds veered left to soak central Belgrade instead, Diarra outsprinted his marker on to a long ball, and crossed into the middle. Vojvodina's goalkeeper got underneath the ball and could only palm it on its way to Tomić at the far post, whose shot hit the ground less than a metre from his foot but looped up in a lazy trajectory and in before the keeper could recover his ground.

Tomić, who had done absolutely nothing in the game up to this point, and had been lucky not to be substituted at half-time (instead Ilić had gone off for Vukić), celebrated in front of us like he had capped off a masterful performance with a finish of sublime beauty, instead of fluking a bobbly one during a personal shocker. In among the backdrop of loud and relieved cheers, he may also have heard an anonymous man not far from me describe him as an illiterate peasant.

For a team that Dušan alleged to be under the influence of Red Star, Vojvodina did their best to help us out for the rest of the game. Their centre-back Mojsov, a good player who had looked solid all game, committed a stupid foul and got his second yellow card. On came Milovan Milović, a robust-looking bloke with Dušan's build and shiny head. As an ex-Partizan man, Dušan's affinity with Milović didn't end at physical resemblance. 'He's a good bloke, Milovan, and a decent player. Not like the rest of these Red Star rejects.'

Milovan turned out to be one of two things: either nowhere near as good as Dušan said, or a Partizan saboteur working behind enemy lines. His first act was to shin a clearance straight back to Partizan from the first free kick he had to deal with, and his second was to haul down Tomić in the area 30 seconds later and give us a penalty. He should have been given a red card, as Tomić was just about to shoot from seven yards, but the referee took pity on Milovan's crestfallen face and only gave a yellow. Nevertheless, it had been a terrible 90 seconds for the lad, but enormous fun for us.

'It's definitely sabotage. We've got Milovan on the inside,' said Uroš. Dušan thought it would be good if we thanked him for his efforts. From a humble beginning, our chant of 'Bravo Milovane, Bravo Milovane, Bravo Milovane-e-e-e-e!' managed to get around two hundred followers singing along, enough for Milovan to hear it, before Vukić scored the penalty and everyone forgot about our little joke.

Five minutes later, another one of Vojvodina's players got themselves sent off, managing to combine a foul, dissent and handbags in a breathtaking 60 seconds that brought two yellow cards just for him. But it took another 20 minutes before Volkov sealed the win with a deflected shot and we could really relax.

Sadly, the relaxation meant the trotting out of a chant I hadn't heard before, which plumbed new depths of inaccuracy, unacceptability, and xenophobia. The chant goes: 'Uz Partizan odrasto k'o ja, za Vojvodinu sada navija, pička najveća, duša prodana, pola madjar, pola ustaša' [He grew up with Partizan like me, but supports Vojvodina now, the biggest c***, sold his soul, half-Hungarian, half-Ustasha]. The first two-thirds of the chant is harmless enough – aimed at those fans who changed their allegiance, that most heinous of footballing crimes.

It is the second bit that's the problem. Vojvodina, though less than it used to be, is a multi-ethnic area of Serbia with substantial communities of ethnic Hungarians, Croats, Slovaks, Romanians and others. It was part of the Austro-Hungarian Empire rather than Ottoman for much of its pre-Yugoslav history, and occupied by Germany (with Hungarian help) during the Second World War. So it's easy to label people from there as not being 'proper Serbs', even if virtually no one in Serbia can really prove a 'pure' blood line because the area has been under so many different rulers in its history.

The Ustasha part refers to the Ustaše Croatian fascist movement which, among other things, was responsible for some of the worst atrocities against Serbs during the Second World War. The Ustaše started out in the 1930s as a nationalist organisation and with a stated aim of establishing a greater Croatia, which included all of modern-day Croatia, along with parts of Bosnia, Montenegro and Serbia – in the latter case all the way up to the Sava river (which would include half of today's Belgrade).

During the Second World War, when Yugoslavia was occupied by Italy and Germany, the Ustaše (who had been given refuge in fascist Italy) were put in nominal charge of the puppet Independent State of Croatia. They went on a merciless killing spree of non-Croats, including hundreds of thousands of Serbs. So awful were their crimes that even the Nazis thought that they were unnecessarily brutal. They also collaborated with the Axis against Tito's Partizans, the Yugoslav Resistance. As the tide turned against the Axis, and first the Italians capitulated and the Germans withdrew, the Ustaše were either killed in fighting, fled the advance of then Partizans and went into exile, or stayed put and pretended it never happened.

Memories are long in the Balkans, and the resurgence of nationalism in the 1990s saw Croatia being rebranded as the heirs of the Ustaše in many Serb eyes. Even today, many Serbs are unable to separate the state and people of Croatia from the crimes of the Ustaše and the horrors of the war in the 1990s. Croatia's choice of post-independence national symbols (including their famous chequered football shirt) are too close to Ustaše symbols for the taste of many a Serb. Ustasha gets trotted out quite regularly as a derogatory term for Croats, even in conversation among ordinarily moderate people, whenever Croatia or a Croat does something that Serbia or Serbs don't like. Robert Prosinečki was called an Ustasha by Partizan fans, as an example of this deliberate misuse.

Many people in Vojvodina are proud of their province's ethnic diversity, so take umbrage at the kind of simple racism and crass stereotyping that this song perpetuates. Vojvodina Football Club had previously complained to the Serbian FA about the song being sung by Partizan fans, most notably after the 2011 Serbian Cup Final, when they accused Partizan's players and staff of leading the rendition.

They were particularly sore because they had just lost the cup final in acrimonious circumstances. During a tense game, which had been delayed by half an hour to allow Vojvodina's fans time to get into the ground, Partizan were leading 2-1 through a soft-ish Vukić penalty when Vojvodina had what they felt was a perfectly good goal disallowed. Their coach led his players off the pitch, argued with the referee and Partizan officials for ten minutes over whether the team was going to return or not, and then decided that they wouldn't. Match officials awarded the match, and the cup, to Partizan, who received the trophy in front of a half-empty stadium with no runners-up. Compounding the embarrassment for Serbian football, the Grobari who remained had saved the more offensive parts of their repertoire for the post-presentation.

Back in the present, Vukić somehow outjumped the luckless Milovan and headed in a Volkov cross in injury time to complete an amazing turnaround and provoke another round of the same chant. It is hard for an English football fan to relate to, but there was a genuine combination of a racist party atmosphere. For some fans in Serbia, a decent win and a chance to sing some xenophobic songs is a great day out, so going eight points clear and having an excuse to bash the Hungarians and Croats was sadly hog's heaven for a few thousand of those around me.

As the Vojvodina players trudged off, our new best friend Milovan was probably hoping he could slink off the pitch unnoticed after a toxic half an hour on the pitch, but he was about to be disappointed. Dušan started another round of 'Bravo Milovane!' timing the loudest point of the chant to perfection as Milovan got to within five metres of the sanctuary of the tunnel. Shame etched across his features, Milovan's attempt to scowl and cow us into quiescence was as ineffective as he had been on the pitch. He just looked quite sad. Glowing from the contentment that only a good-natured round of bullying a stranger can produce, we left the stadium happy as Larry.

We completed four out of four with a hard-earned victory in a testy match away at Spartak in Subotica. Claire and I were in Albania for the weekend, marvelling at former Communist architecture, so I couldn't make the match, and I was punished for my lack of commitment to the crno-beli cause by missing the best goal of the season so far. Already a goal up from a poacher's finish by Eduardo, Vukić seized on the goalkeeper's fumble in trying to claw the ball off Diarra's toes, span through 400 degrees to beat one man, and then lifted the ball over three players between him and the goal, dipping it just below the bar. Spartak pulled a goal back, and pressed hard in the final minutes while Partizan resorted to a series of rhythm-spoiling fouls, but the boys hung on for a massive win.

So, yes, we were out of the cup, but the league was looking more and more likely. Such is the two-horse nature of the league, combined with a mid-season collapse from Vojvodina (entirely unrelated to their signing of Stephen Appiah), we had already reached the point where we could finish no lower than second.

More importantly, with seven games to go, Red Star could only get a maximum of 21 more points, taking them to 75. On 62, we needed 14 points to guarantee the championship. Four wins, two draws and a loss. Brandishing a printout of the fixture list, Dušan went through what we had left: 'Javor at home – definite win. Smederevo away – should be a win.' That was six already, especially as even Dušan recognised that Smederevo, who benefit from a player loaning agreement with Partizan, were unlikely to try too hard to upset their benefactors.

'BSK at home. Sure win. Borac away, they're rubbish this season but the atmosphere can be a bit tasty. Call it a draw.' Ten down, four to go. What of the season's fourth derby? 'If the gap's down to six points by then, they'll find a way to engineer a Red Star win. A soft penalty probably. You do know it's 53 derbies since we had one in the league against them, don't you?' I had heard it before, funnily enough, and I was sure it was actually only 45.

'Radnički at home, same as Borac but with a better team, so another draw.' Eleven. 'Metalac at home to finish, terrible team, even Red Star can't fix it so we don't beat them.' Fourteen. As Dušan put it, only Partizan could be eight points clear with seven games to go and still think the league was in the balance. But even he, the biggest conspiracy theorist and believer in Partizan's own capacity to shoot themselves in the foot, believed that we could actually do it.

League table after the 23rd round:
1. Partizan 62 (+45)
2. Red Star 54 (+35)
3. Vojvodina 39 (+18)

Dragan Mance Street

TO add insult to the injury of our abject exit from the cup, the fireworks launched from the Jug and Istok, combined with the club's failure to stop Red Star's fans from scampering on to the athletics track to cavort with their players, meant that we were forced to play another game behind closed doors. There had been three or four fireworks that had made it on to the pitch or got close to detonating near Red Star staff, compared to the 50 or 60 in the first derby of the season, but the Serbian FA had to be seen to be 'even-handed' in punishing both the big clubs for their derby transgressions, so we were punished exactly the same as them for a smaller, though equally unacceptable, crime.

This meant that we wouldn't be able to see the boys in action against Javor. As it was, it was probably good for those of us who stand near Dušan that we didn't go to the game. His blood pressure would never have been able to cope with the fact that yet again, his arch-enemies Vukić (a penalty) and Tomić scored, taking their combined tally to 31 for the season – nearly half the club's total goals. In between their goals, Javor managed to equalise, which would also have given Dušan cause to launch into a violent diatribe against Avram Grant, the club's management, and anyone not actively promoting urgent regime change within the club. But we did win, and with Red Star held 0-0 away at Novi Pazar, we were back to being ten points clear.

For our away game against Smederevo, I cut short our holiday in Macedonia by a day and subjected Claire to a four-hour sprint from Skopje to Smederevo. How many English girls could claim that they had watched Smederevo home and away in the same season? I was excited at the prospect of watching the team again, and at a ground which the Engleski Grobar had said was his favourite away game of the year.

It wasn't difficult to see why. Although the outskirts of Smederevo, ringed by steelworks in varying degrees of dilapidation and functionality, are caked in metallic dust, the centre, with its 15th-century castle, bearing the scars of sieges by Serbs and Ottomans, and Second World War bombing and jutting into the Danube, is actually quite pleasant. As Claire and I wandered along the riverfront to meet Dušan, Uroš and Gule in a splav – as frequented in Belgrade by Tomić, Smiljanić and thousands of others – I could feel the warm spring sunshine adding some much-needed colour to my cheeks. I had a good feeling about the game.

Gule and Uroš were already comprehensively sh**faced, necking Viljamovka [pear brandy] shots having only eaten a few chips all day. When I mentioned the Chetnik chant about Avram Grant, it was a cue for Gule, in broken English, to try and give Claire a history lesson. 'What you must understand,' he slurred, 'is that we are communists. Well, we're not communists, but we were communists, and we were good fighters. The Chetniks, they are fascists, and bad fighters. This is Serbian history.'

He was definitely more succinct than I had been in explaining it. Dušan ventured that there was evidence that suggested the Chetniks weren't as bad as made out. 'No!' bellowed Gule. 'Claire, don't listen to him. You need to understand. What you must understand is that we are communists. We are good fighters. Don't listen to Dušan. He is a Mihajilović. He has a fascist name. My name is Milatović. It is a communist name. We are good fighters.'

Enriched by our lecture on history, we strolled up the riverside to the stadium. 'You're not the first Brits to come here,' Dušan told us. 'Ipswich Town played here in 2002 in the UEFA Cup, so the Tractor Boys beat you to it. The home fans were complete d**ks and racially abused Darren Bent the whole way through.'

Having taken our seats in what was probably the most impressive stadium outside the big two – two-tiered with seats on all four sides and the fans close to the pitch without a running track, in the English style – we were joined by the Engleski Grobar. 'You know Ipswich played here in the UEFA Cup in 2002?' 'Yes.' 'Oh. Terrible racial abuse against Marcus Bent.' The internet was called upon to adjudicate which of the Bents had been abused. The answer was that both Bents had played, and that racial abuse had been a salient feature of the whole match. Dušan and Nick both settled back satisfied that they were right.

No longer as good as the team who had finished third and gone on to face Ipswich (then as FK Sartid, in deference to the club's steelworking owners), this was on paper simultaneously a tough and an easy fixture. Tough because Smederevo had many ex-Partizan players and trainees and a high level of skill. Easy because of the regular player-loaning relationship between the two clubs and Smederevo's unofficial 'feeder club' status.

Dušan came down on the hard side of the fence because of the team that Avram had put out. The midfield of Smiljanić, Babović, Tomić and Vukić was, in his eyes, 'the slowest midfield ever assembled in the history of midfields'. At the mention of Tomić and Vukić, Claire looked Dušan in the eye and declared herself glad that 'her favourites' were playing. Dušan glowered while Nick and I smirked at how easy it was for him to be wound up. I wondered out loud if it was possible that Dušan actually hated over half of our starting line-up.

We worked it out. Stojković – hate. Red Star past. Volkov, Aksentijević. Like. Ivanov. OK. I guessed that Rnić would be a hate character. 'He would be, based on incompetence, but he's not playing. We've got some Academy kid called Ostojić. So he's a like.' 4-1 to the good guys. Smiljanić. No. Vukić. No. Babović. No. Tomić. Definitely no. 5-4 to the dark side. Diarra. Yes. Marković. Yes. The good guys won out 6-5. Dušan was allowed to support Partizan today.

The home fans, noisy despite their limited numbers, had gone to the trouble of preparing a bit of banter for our arrival. Calling us 'Grobarske pičke' [gravedigging c***s] hadn't taken much imagination, but they had a good banner urging an end to cult movements. Alongside Marxism (a hammer and sickle) and fascism (swastika), they had Partizanism (and our badge) listed in the same bracket. The club-authorised Partizan away following responded with a banner of their own, proclaiming the Smederevo fans as lunatics, indistinguishable from the inmates of the nearby Kovin asylum. It was unusual to see some proper p***-taking of each other between the teams' fans rather than the same old repertoire and internecine wrangling. Behind us, the Zabranjeni, increasingly a single-issue party, had brought with them a ten-foot-tall banner with Ivan Perović's face made up like an Orthodox icon. No tribute could ever be enough to compensate for the tragedy of his death at such a young age, but this picture was just plain creepy.

Basking in the sun, my forehead lightly toasting as the bits of scalp that used to have hair on them last year adjusted to their new-found freedom, and with the Zabranjeni belting out Depeche Mode's 'Just Can't Get Enough' (crno-beli remix), it was too nice a day out to really care that much about the football. This was fortunate, as Partizan were even more frustrating than normal, veering between sublimely picking Smederevo's defence apart only to fluff the chances, and leaving a similarly porous membrane through their own midfield, relying on a solid debut from young Ostojić and a typically stoic display from Ivanov to keep it scoreless.

With 15 minutes to go, Avram brought on Saša Ilić for Babović. The ponderous midfield had just lost another yard. While Dušan and I shook our heads and Uroš bemoaned just how clueless Grant was, Nick was sure this was the right move. 'Ilić is a legend. He will make things happen.'

Ilić really is a club legend. By coming on in this game, he moved up to become the second-highest Partizan appearance-maker of all time, with 568. In his first spell at the club, he moved from the youth team to professional, winning six league titles as Partizan established themselves as the best team in post-break-up Yugoslavia. His finesse and vision in midfield set him apart from his peers, as did his loyalty to Partizan. He had given his all for the club under three different managers, including under the high-performing but turbulent reign of Lothar Matthaus, who reinvented Ilić as a defensive midfielder in the quarterback mould.

At a time when footballers were leaving the league in droves, Ilić gave his best years to Partizan, before he did try his hand elsewhere after turning 29, taking in Celta Vigo, Galatasaray and Red Bull Salzburg. On his return he had slotted back in like he had never left, a yard shorter on pace (though that had never been his strong point) but still possessing an eye for a pass that left his much-hyped colleagues looking inferior. And Partizan were on the verge of taking their second consecutive title under his captaincy.

Present-day Ilić's first touch sent Marković clear but, having gone round the keeper, his shot was blocked. Grant was forced to roll the dice again. Off came Diarra, and on came David Manga, to our considerable joy. Manga had been out of the team since Grant arrived, and this was his comeback. A few weeks before, while he was still stuck in the reserves, Manga had given an interview where he had confessed that he had been forced to work in McDonald's in the evenings in Paris after his first foray into football outside France with the Austrian side Eisenstadt had ended in disappointment.

He had done so to support his young family – even at 18, he had a young son, but the rumour was that his current team-mates had ignored the human interest part of the story and had taken to calling him the 'Royale with Cheese' in training. His first couple of touches were appalling, leading to a series of naff jokes about fat having dripped off the grills on to his boots or him using filets-o-fish instead of shin pads.

With four minutes to go, Manga shrugged off our fast food gags and two defenders before rolling the ball into Marković. The striker's back-heel, intentionally or not, looped up in to Ilić's path. One touch to control, and a second to lash it left-footed into the corner. The legend had spoken. Nick, rising in applause and puffing up his chest with pride at his proto-punditry, surveyed us and said simply, 'I told you.'

Avram immediately took off Marković, our remaining striker, bringing on his namesake Saša, a defensive midfielder. We were now playing a 4-6-0 formation. Nothing like a bit of confidence in the team to see this one out. Dušan was still shaking his head over the manager's negativity when, in injury time, Manga received the ball from Ilić and drove forward. 'Big Mac! Big Mac! Big Mac!' urged Uroš in encouragement. Still Manga drove on, into the area, still accelerating away from the weary Smederevo defenders. His touch might not be great, but he's certainly quick. To our utter astonishment, from eight yards out, he scored, sliding the ball under the keeper like a processed cheese slice under a beef patty.

'Manga! I'm lovin' it!' I exclaimed. It was only half a joke. It is one of the best feelings as a football fan when a perennial underachiever comes good. I remember at Arsenal that the whole crowd loved Glenn Helder despite the fact he couldn't cross (a bit of an issue for a winger) because he tried hard and his gaffes reminded us of how we played ourselves on Sunday mornings.

No one got the McJoke anyway, or maybe they were too busy celebrating the fact that we privileged few had actually seen David Manga score. T-shirts would have to be made to commemorate the occasion. I could visualise it already. 'BIO SAM TAMO KADA JE

MANGA DAO GOL' [I was there when Manga scored]. It would mark me out among my peers as a real fan.

Lots of t-shirts, none about Manga, had been made up by the club before our next game against BSK Borča, the Beton [Concrete] Boys, so-called because the majority of the suburb around their home ground is scruffy, unplanned, and made mostly of said material. The club put on a big pre-match presentation for Ilić on becoming the club's all-time second-highest appearance-maker. The t-shirts, worn by the presentation party of Partizan's various youth teams, summed up his achievements well: 568 matches, seven titles, four cups, 213 goals, 68 European games, and still he goes on … Ilić had even been given a couple of advertising hoardings. Instead of plugging the club magazine, they simply read: 'Jedan je Ilić kapiten' [There's only one captain Ilić].

At the head of the presentation party was Momcilo 'Moca' Vukotić. Vukotić is the all-time leader for Partizan games, with 752. Ilić was never going to catch him. Was Vukotić the best ever Partizan player, though? He couldn't be faulted for loyalty, playing for the first team from 1968 to 1984, with a solitary and quite successful season at Bordeaux in 1978/79. And, for an attacking midfielder, his 306 goals was a decent return.

Vili added, on the back of Vukotić's goal tally, 'this wasn't just against the rubbish we play these days'. It was a good point. Vukotić's goals and the three titles he won through scoring them came in the days of the Yugoslav First League, pre-war and pre-break-up of the footballing infrastructure. Vukotić had had to play against Dinamo Zagreb, Hajduk Split, Železnicar Sarajevo, Velež Mostar, Olimpija Ljubljana and Budućnost Titograd (now Podgorica), and had far fewer games against the likes of Javor, Metalac and Kula, teams who would barely been good enough to stay in the old Second Division, let alone the top flight.

So he was definitely a contender. But although I got the feeling of a lot of respect for Vukotić from the lads, he wasn't viewed as definitively the greatest.

Many of the true greats were from before all of our times. Each member of our group had their favourite historical player, about whom their fathers and grandfathers had told tales of heroism and triumph. Croat Stjepan Bobek was remembered as one of the stars of Partizan's formative years, and to this day holds the record as all-time top goalscorer, with 425 at a ratio of just under a goal a game.

He was voted Partizan's all-time top player back in 1995 when the club celebrated 50 years of existence.

Partizan's European Cup Final team of 1966, which had beaten Nantes, Werder Bremen, Sparta Prague and Manchester United (replete with Stiles, Law, Best and Charlton) en route to a narrow 2-1 loss to Real Madrid, and secured bragging rights for us in terms of European achievement in Yugoslavia until Red Star won in 1991, provided a few more names, and four of the starting 11 for the 1995 Magnificent 11.

Velibor Vasović had captained that side and scored the goal that had Partizan on course to win the European Cup until 20 minutes from time. For that, he would always be remembered. But he had tarnished his legacy for ever by having a season-long dalliance with Red Star in between his two stints at Partizan. Vladica Kovacević, Milan Galić, Radoslav 'Zaza' Bečejac and goalkeeper Milutin Šoškić were others from the generation known as the 'Partizan Babies', a group of youngsters who had surged through the youth system at more or less the same time and taken Partizan from a mid-table Yugoslav team to one of Europe's best, known in Yugoslavia as the Parni Valjak [the steamroller], so successful they were. Sadly for Partizan, the European Cup proved to be too effective a shop window, and half of the team was snapped up by western European teams before the 1966/67 season had started, heralding one of Partizan's longer barren patches.

That same phenomenon acted much more quickly these days. Stevan Jovetić, Stefan Savić and Zoran Tosić had all had the potential to become Partizan greats, but the globalisation of the football industry had made the rest of the world aware of their talents much more quickly. And although as 1966 proved, Yugoslav football had its limitations as to how high wages it could pay, the differential between salaries in Belgrade and salaries in the big European leagues had been magnified many times since. Even allowing for the cash, Jovetić and Savić would have had many more years at Partizan if their only exposure to foreign scouts had been at the sharp end of a run in a European competition.

This fact was noted with a degree of sadness, but also pride. Jovetic and Savić were good ambassadors for the club, and it showed that the youth system was capable of producing world-class players. Sadder still was the case of someone like Smiljanić, who had been club captain at 19, and looked to be on course for world stardom and a place in the pantheon of Partizan greats, only for the wheels to come off, whether caused by injury, bad management or his own indiscretions. Now he was lucky if he was a sub in today's Partizan, a side that everyone agreed was thoroughly average.

We could have used the assistance of two of the other contenders for all-time great, such was their finishing. Diarra had got us off to a great start, scoring after ten minutes with a low left-footed drive that had everyone muttering about how he should score more goals from outside the area. But then first Tomić (off the line), Marković (wide), Medo (over) and Vukić (off the bar from five yards) contrived to miss chances that seemed easier to convert. At half-time, our discussion moved on to those two players.

Premier League aficionados may be surprised by the identity of both these players. Mateja Kežman didn't set the world on fire at Chelsea, and indeed he only had two seasons at Partizan before he was snapped up by PSV Eindhoven, so he was never really in the running for best player of all time. But in those two seasons he was brilliant, scoring 33 goals and almost single-handedly shooting Partizan to the title in 1999. Rumours of his comeback had been a season-on-season occurrence after he had gone to Chelsea, but had never come true. It was a sign of how much affection he was held in at the club that even after he had officially retired, Partizan fans still wanted him back. Five goals in five Belgrade derbies had a lot to do with that.

Savo Milošević, especially for Aston Villa fans, will come as even more of a surprise. But with 191 goals, putting him ninth on the top scorers' list despite leaving the club aged 22, he is a significant figure in the club's history. His goals powered Partizan to two league titles in 1993 and 1994, which marked the first seasons in which Partizan played in the new post-break-up Yugoslav league, and set the tone for the club's dominance of most of the next two decades. Milošević was still popular to this day, not least because he had maintained links with the club despite being abroad, and after his retirement he made an unsuccessful bid to become club chairman in 2009, defeated by Dragan Đurić.

In the second half, the ghosts of Kežman and Milošević haunted us again briefly, as Diarra got clean through only to hit the post. Vukić, the phantoms of his (not actually dead) former club-mates swirling around him, managed to get the ball stuck under his feet as he found himself on the end of the rebound, poking the ball against a defender before it bounced back to him. Taking a supernatural amount of time to sort out his legs, he prodded the ball into the corner, exorcising the goalscoring demons in the most inelegant manner possible.

The game was cruising towards a comfortable 2-0 win for us, and the football was taking a back seat to our attempts to wind up either Tomić, or Dušan, or both. Tomić had started a trend in the team of wearing the latest adidas boots, which were a hideous shade of day-glo orange. Now there were five of the team in them. Dušan, not ordinarily the most reactionary of people, was resolutely insistent that football boots should be black. These orange boots were spreading like the plague and affecting the players' consciences. Every time Tomić came near our part of the ground, Dušan exhorted him to change his boots, 'Menjaj Kopačke!' By the fourth time, he had about 500 followers in the chant. But still Tomić wouldn't turn round. Had he been able to hear us, he would have permitted himself a chuckle when Ilić was substituted and Tomić got the captain's armband. 'Jedan je Tomić Kapiten!' we taunted Dušan, who looked aghast at the prospect of his least favourite player leading his club, and told us firmly where to put our chant.

With our interest in today's game petering out, we were able to get back to the matter at hand. Who was the greatest player? Among our group, there was near unanimity that the answer to the question was Dragan Mance. With 262 appearances and 145 goals, Mance's numbers are respectable but not troubling the top tens in either chart. Nor does his list of honours with the club, a single Yugoslav championship in 1983, come close to the silverware accumulated by other Partizan greats. But Mance, as well as being a fantastic footballer, captured the imagination for three main reasons.

Firstly, he was a local lad, born in Belgrade, and lived all his life with his family in Zemun, just a few kilometres from the centre of Belgrade. Secondly, how much he loved playing for Partizan. A smile was permanently etched on his face whenever he played, and his goal celebrations were always the same, and always joyous – arms outstretched, mouth wide open as he roared with delight, finding an extra yard of pace after he had scored, his hair blown back as he sprinted to the crowd. Thirdly, and most tragically, because we will never know exactly how good Mance could have been.

Less than a month short of his 23rd birthday, after having made a promising start to the 1985/86 season, his fifth as a professional for Partizan, Mance was killed in a car crash on the main highway between Novi Sad and Belgrade. He had already been Yugoslav League top scorer once, and scored Partizan's 'goal of the century', a thumping volley against Queens Park Rangers that formed part of the amazing 6-6 away goals win. He had made four appearances for Yugoslavia, and was, as everyone said to me, on the verge of absolute greatness when he lost his life.

His image as Partizan's James Dean had captured the imagination of the generation that followed too, which had never even seen him play. Uroš rattled off stats about how many goals Mance had scored in derbies, and how crucial they had been. Dušan, for at least the tenth time that season, got his Mance tattoo out for everyone to marvel at. Today's Partizan fans occasionally award the Dragan Mance trophy to players of outstanding commitment and contribution to the Partizan cause – criteria they felt had only been met three times since the trophy's inception, with Saša Ilić the most recent winner. Thousands of younger fans had signed a petition for one of the streets next to the stadium to be renamed 'Dragan Mance Street', and succeeded in persuading the Belgrade authorities to make the change – something which required a degree of cross-party consensus sometimes lacking in local politics.

Dragan Mance didn't live to see Partizan's tenth league title, which the team captured in his honour in 1986. But he would have been proud to see Partizan taking their 24th, for which the calculation was now very simple. Red Star were now 12 points behind with 12 points available. We needed one more point from four games, including matches against bottom-of-the-table Borac and second-bottom Metalac. Indeed, it was still also mathematically possible to lose all four games and still win the title on goal difference.

This was finally enough to convince the group that we were definitely going to win the league. No combination of conspiracy theories and inability could stretch that far. 'Put it this way,' said Uroš, switching into fluent English, 'even with Avram in charge, we can't f*** this up.'

League table after the 26th round:
1. Partizan 71 (+50)
2. Red Star 59 (+36)
3. Radnički 46 (+14)

Robert Prosinečki: A Grade-A Hipster

PARTIZAN'S away game at Borac Čačak was on Sunday afternoon. Red Star had ground out a 1-0 win on the Saturday to ensure that the equation remained the same as we had expected. Avoid defeat, and the title was ours.

Having had to make a short, urgent, but thoroughly administrative dash to the UK over that weekend, I was the only person at the stadium who had started their journey to the ground in Brighton, and made my way to Čačak via Luton and Belgrade. But all the connections, with my car cleverly pre-positioned at the airport, had worked, and I took up my place ten minutes before kick-off.

Dušan had been talking to his father, a Partizan fan but too disillusioned with the corruption within football to want to come to matches anymore, and was armed with the latest story as to why today's game would not go as smoothly as it should on paper. Borac, needing points desperately to give themselves a chance of hauling themselves past 14th-placed Novi Pazar and not be one of the two relegated teams, were prepared to offer us their defender Maslac at a knock-down rate in return for three points today. It was far-fetched in its own right, but mildly believable in the context of the bigger, electoral conspiracy theory that said that the league would be left undecided until after election day on 6 May – the day after the season's final derby.

Happier Red Star fans, who still sensed a chance of league glory, would be more likely to turn out on polling day and cast a vote for the ruling parties. To the Serbian mind, this made perfect sense. To mine, the two consecutive defeats seemed very difficult to contrive, and the almost insurmountable 12-point lead, even if reduced to six after the derby, was so big that I didn't think any Red Star fans would be fooled so easily into changing their political preferences.

David Manga's first start of the season might have been interpreted by some as another indication that Partizan were not going to try as hard as they might. But in reality it reflected a situation in which Avram Grant had just one recognised striker available for selection (Diarra), and was experimenting a little with a new five-man midfield during this pre-pre-season period of almost certain league success.

Any worries that the main body of Partizan fans may have had about the league being stolen from them, or at least temporarily denied them, lasted about ten minutes, when one of Avram's experimental picks, Saša Marković, slalomed past a couple of challenges like a Slavic Alberto Tomba and slammed in a low left-footed shot from the edge of the area.

The shirtless mass behind the away goal, having stuck to a generic mix for those 11 minutes, broke out into a booming rendition of 'PARTIZAN ŠAMPION!' In fairness, I had heard this chant at every game so far this season, but its accompaniment by mass toplessness, white and black t-shirts being waved like pom-poms, and concerted pogoing, which threatened the very foundations of the crumbling away end, implied quite strongly that this was a renewal of the chant: the 2012 version being sung for the first time rather than the continuation of the identical 2011 ditty.

Still Dušan did not look relaxed. No logical argument: that only three teams had scored twice against Partizan over 90 minutes all season (and one of them was Belgian); that Partizan had put five past Borac earlier in the year and had already created enough chances in this game to suggest a repeat; that Red Star would probably win the cup and satisfy the masses that way; or that Borac were just rubbish, would wash with him. There was still a chance that something fishy might occur.

When Stojković jarred his knee on the post and had to be taken off, Dušan could still smell something piscine in the air. Perhaps it wouldn't actually affect the league, but an unclean, pre-arranged draw would be an ugly memory to associate with the capturing of Partizan's 24th league title.

In the second half, Partizan doubled their lead through an Ivanov header. The big Bulgarian had been one of our best, if not the best player since the winter break, and had outscored wunderkind Marković three to none since then. At this point, Dušan conceded that yes, it would be very hard to fix a result other than a Partizan victory from this position.

The police agreed that we were definitely going to win the league, deploying massive resources within the ground – yet another poky two-sided 'stadium' that would look sub-par in the Blue Square Premier, and which outdid some of the other 'stadia' for kitsch charm by being the only ground so far in which a wooden dining room chair had had to be brought out by hand during the match to supplement the insufficient seating in the visitors' dugout. In front of us, there was a thinnish blue line of regular cops. In front of the hardcore Grobari, two lines of armour-plated gendarmes reinforced a thicker blue line of regular police. Any pitch invasion was going to be treated as a full-on declaration of war.

Grant took off Ilić and brought on Ninković, a young player he had mostly ignored during his tenure so far, but one who evoked the most excitement among our fans. Ninković was a real star for the future, an attacking midfielder with two feet, a great range of passing and a cocksure manner beyond his years. Because of his injury, which had kept him out before the winter break, he wasn't attracting the covetous looks that had put Marković off his stride since March, so we might also be able to keep him next season.

Ninković took ten minutes to play his way into the game, but marked himself out as head and shoulders above his more experienced team-mates, demanding the ball and constantly looking for team-mates in space, while also showing a selfish streak and holding on to the ball if he sensed glory. The trouble is, reflected Dušan, that all the players start off like him, keen, energetic, hard-working and full of promise. Then they either go abroad, start believing their own hype, or get sucked into a party lifestyle (or indeed any combination of the three) and their ability collapses in on itself like some dying star.

Ninković hadn't yet gone supernova, but he temporarily exploded into life with ten minutes left. He sold three Čačak defenders with an outrageous step-over, limbs extending theatrically beyond the ball in a manner that would have made even Cristiano Ronaldo yearn for someone to boot him into row Z, and squared for Diarra to tap in. Two minutes later, as Partizan counter-attacked, he nonchalantly flicked a 30-yard through-ball off the outside of his right foot into the path of Partizan's two African attackers as they charged forward. Diarra outsprinted a tired Manga, unused to the rigours of 90 minutes, feigned a shot to dump the keeper on his backside, and dinked it into the corner for 4-0.

As Grant decided that he could afford to blood another youngster, Dejan Babić, Ilić rose from the dugout to let his young team-mate exit, revealing a 'Mi smo Šampioni' [We Are The Champions] t-shirt.

I wanted to disapprove – we hadn't won anything yet, and the club had risked jinxing us by printing such shirts in advance, but the 12-point lead had probably led them to believe it would be a safe investment.

With the league in the bag, we could afford to dispense some generosity to our hosts. Not on the pitch, mind, but by offering our support to Borac in an important endeavour a few weeks hence. 'Kup je vaš, Kup je vaš' [the cup is yours] we willed, not out of any great love for them, but because of their opponents. The home ultras, a group of 30 teenagers fenced off in the far corner, responded with 'Jebi Cigane' [f*** the gypsies] to warm applause all around us, the reverie not disturbed by the fact that Borac stood virtually zero chance of achieving any kind of result in the cup final against Red Star.

Amid this brief moment of community, the referee blew the final whistle. We were champions. I had never seen Arsenal capture the title live (rather than on TV) on any of the four occasions they have done so in my lifetime, so this was a first for me. But there was little ceremony, just the players donning the t-shirts Ilić had modelled earlier, and squirting a bit of water at each other. On the bench, Avram Grant looked more relieved than happy, like a man who has found out that his illness isn't terminal, and apart from a couple of slaps on the shoulder, neither he nor any of his backroom staff really showed much emotion.

So it was hard to get really excited about our success. Partly because it had been coming for a while, but also because this half-empty little park didn't really capture the magnitude of what we had just achieved – a fifth consecutive league title, a run that had taken us from trailing far behind in Red Star's wake to within one more trophy of equalling their record.

The players eventually wandered over to the main Grobari corner to share in the celebrations. But they still seemed more focused on chatting among themselves and generally messing about than on the solemnity of the occasion, and in fairness couldn't get within 20 metres of the fans, such was the security presence designed to separate them. The booming salutes of 'Partizan Šampion!' seemed a bit lost on most of the players, and the festivities, such as they were, had finished almost as soon as they had started.

Despite it all feeling a bit flat in the immediate aftermath of our victory, we had something big to look forward to. Tradition in Serbia is that the championship trophy, if captured before the last game of the season, is presented to the winning team at their next home game. For us, this was against Red Star. What better way to toast your championship success than to do so in front of your near and dear neighbours?

Except that, for 'crowd safety reasons', the presentation was prohibited from taking place against Red Star. I could see their point – trouble would be less likely against any other opponent. But it was the euphemistic use of 'crowd safety' that I objected to, when really they meant 'to stop Red Star fans from rioting'. It was as if winning the league had been somehow a deliberately provocative action on Partizan's behalf.

My friend Paul, who for reasons that have been explained to me several times but have never really registered is called 'Bish' by a very small number of people including me, came out to Belgrade for the weekend and came with us to the game. Bish had seen my pictures and heard a few snippets about what derby games were like. Initially he sounded less than enthusiastic when I told him he had a ticket. It was the flares that scared him most. 'Will I die, though, Jim?' he asked. 'I really don't want to die.' I reassured him that, despite it being one too many, only one person had died at a derby in the last 15 years. Those odds seemed enough to placate him.

En route to the game, we stopped at a bar to pick up Dušan and a couple of others, to find several other Englishmen were present and intending to come to the game. They were nice lads, who knew a lot about Partizan for non-residents, and watched a lot of live football, from the nonnest- of English non-league to World Cups.

But I was instinctively defensive: they were here on a sunny afternoon in May for a dead rubber Belgrade derby? Where were they when I was cold and wet away at Ivanjica in November? Dušan quickly disabused me of my false notion that they were in any way tourists – a couple of these lads were on their tenth or 12th visit to Belgrade, and not just for derbies. And unlike me, they had to fly here for every game. I climbed back into my box.

Despite being an end-of-season game with no official prize to play for, there was plenty still at stake. We hadn't scored in 180 minutes against Red Star, and Avram badly needed a first derby win if he was ever going to win over the crowd. Secondly, if we avoided defeat, we would nigh-on seal the 'spring league' title as well, denying Red Star any bragging rights about having the most points over the half-season. And thirdly, we were champions, and had to defend our honour. It was all very well waving white bits of card and having 'Partizan: Champions' written on the big screen, but if we lost today, Red Star would have a 3-1 derby tally for the season and would almost certainly invent some nonsense about being 'Unofficial Champions' like Scotland did after beating England in 1967.

Although we had been denied the trophy presentation today, the club indulged in some ceremony before kick-off, in fact about as much as they could probably get away with before it openly held the league's decision in contempt. The centre circle was covered in a 'Partizan Champions' tarpaulin, all the electronic advertising boards displayed black-and-white 'Partizan Champions' graphics, and there were five flag bearers, each representing the years the club had won the league consecutively.

Mr 2009, who in theory had a heavier flag with embroidered league and cup trophies on it, was really struggling, having warmed up too thoroughly before the players were even close to exiting the tunnel. The players finally came out with him visibly buckling under the weight of the ten-foot flag and 15-foot pole. While the four flags around him stood proud and rippled majestically under the locomotion of their bearers, his was a limp cloth that threatened to smother him. Finally, heroically, as the players shook hands and the stadium announcer incited us to salute the players one more time, he found his last ounces of strength and delivered a magnificent full wave so that the key photo, the money shot if you will, shows how proud we are of all five titles.

Red Star's fans had come well prepared to show as much disdain as they could muster for our achievement. As the pre-match pleasantries finished, they unveiled their own banner, covering the whole of the front of the Sever, reading 'Cigani pozdravljaju svoje šampione' [The Gypsies salute their champions]. Their champions were 12 points behind ours, but I grudgingly admired the lengths they had gone to in order to pretend they didn't care.

With the shackles of needing a result cast off, it was quite an open game. Not necessarily good, but it wasn't boring, which was more than could be said for several games this season. Young Ostojić was getting some more playing time, and dealing with Red Star's attacks well. Youth keeper Petrović was getting some big-game practice too, having made a couple of other appearances and leapfrogged Radiša Ilić to become the obvious second in command to Stojković. Both sides had a few shots, and Babović and Volkov could have both scored before half-time, but didn't. It was now over 230 minutes since we had last scored in a derby.

To pass half-time, Bish and I played a game in which we talked to each other quietly about penalties and timed how long it would take Dušan to trot out his stat about the number of games since Partizan last got a derby penalty. The game was over in under 30 seconds, Dušan's injustice radar picking up our conversation and firing the stat at us. Forty-five.

I asked Bish what he thought of the game and the experience. 'Well, I think I was prepared for everything. Lots of angry Serbian men shouting at each other, people chucking flares, firemen rushing around to put them out. Terrible, terrible standard of football. But the big surprise is Robert Prosinečki. I mean look at him, the man's a Grade-A hipster.'

Not for Prosinečki any of the familiar managerial looks: the suit, the puffer jacket, the tracksuit, Cloughie's green jumper, the Owen Coyle sweater and shorts, or the traditionally Balkan leather jacket. No. He was sporting a black jacket with brown elbow pads, stylish jeans and Converse trainers. Sometimes it takes an outsider to appreciate the uniqueness and beauty of something you've otherwise become accustomed to.

What about the players? Had anyone caught his eye? I had taken care not to try and pollute Bish's mind with any of my own opinions about the squad, and had certainly kept Dušan's jaundiced views well away from him. 'Who's the number 25?' Babović. 'Yeah, he's the kind of long-haired midfield jinker I really can't stand. He keeps holding on to the ball for too long. He should probably be the best player on the pitch, but he isn't. The central midfielders aren't working well together. You've got a lazy one, with the stupid hair [Smiljanić] who's never in position, and then number four [Medo] is having to work too hard. And the right-back [Mijkovic] is sh**. Other than that, no comments.'

I praised him for his highly perceptive analysis, and Dušan, overhearing us, clarified that Miljković wasn't sh**, he was just scared. On the training pitch, he was regarded as an excellent player. 'In Serbian, we'd call him a Zec [rabbit].'

The second half started slowly, enlivened only by the battle for intellectual supremacy, fought between Grobari and Delije via the medium of more banners. We invoked the spirit of Shelley's Ozymandias, 'Sve je postalo pepeo i dim, 5 godina za redom, najbolji si tim' [All has turned to ash and smoke, five years in a row, you're the greatest] to strike at the crumbling façade of Red Star's pre-eminence, while Red Star's reply relied more heavily on the playground musings of the outwitted bully, using as it did the 'and your mum' school of repartee. 'Ja imam tugu 5 godina dugu, ali brzo mi prodje kad vidim vas na jugu' [I have a sadness five years long, but it passes quickly when I look at you in the south].

The game eventually reheated itself to be as exciting as the first half had been. Tomić missed a good chance, then so did Ostojić and Ivanov from the same corner, and Diarra slipped when he could have scored. Still the goal wouldn't come, as we moved past four hours without a derby goal. With ten minutes left, Avram brought on Marković, but he was clearly not fully fit and the players on both sides looked to have settled for the draw.

As we went into injury time, there were already some rumblings of discontent on our three sides of the ground. It had been getting on for four hours of playing time since Šćepović had scored our last derby goal, the worst run for years. All bar 13 of those minutes had come since Stanojević had been sacked, a fact which was still hanging over Avram Grant even though he had delivered the league title as promised and had even extended our lead over Red Star from ten to 12 points.

The rumblings got deeper as Partizan refused to push forward in search of a winner. Red Star got hold of the ball in midfield and moved forward towards the right-hand corner. They would either find time-wasting safety or a chance to cross there. They found the latter, and then Borja, our scourge from the semi-final second leg, laid off to Kadu on the edge of the area. From the exact same angle as I had been forced to watch Shamrock's Sullivan score his wonder volley, I could see the direct line between Kadu's right boot and the ball-sized part of the goal not blocked by one of the crowd of players on the edge of the box. Kadu hit the ball cleanly enough, if not that hard, and Petrović in goal did not have the benefit of my vantage point, seeing it only as it nestled in the corner while he stood flat-footed in the middle of the goal. Red Star had the lead with 15 seconds left of injury time.

The chants of 'Uprava Napolje' broke out even quicker than Dušan trotting out his penalties stat, before the net had stopped rippling. It was hard to quantify exactly why, but it felt like the target of the Napolje wasn't just Đurić and the rest of the board. Dušan felt it too. 'Even objectively, I can't see Avram keeping his job after this,' he said. 'We never lose three derbies in a row.' His sources on the inside of the club told him that the board was of the same view as him and the howling masses, and that they too wanted to end the experiment, but they were tied into a contract until the end of the following season. To get rid of Avram pre-term would be very expensive unless he left of his own accord.

At the start of his time with us, he had appeared a bit uncommitted in that he had openly said he wanted to return to England at some point, but he had learned to keep that a private dream since. Dušan had calculated that a relegated Bolton or Blackburn might be a suitable destination and was heartily backing their opponents every week.

Despite winning the league so convincingly (and remember, we were still nine points clear and likely to stay there despite today's defeat), it was hard to find a satisfied Grobar anywhere. In the short term, it came down to a perceived loss of bragging rights. We had more or less had the league won by Christmas, so Red Star fans had had time to adjust to that reality, and our gloating at their expense had peaked too. We were left with confirmation that it would be another Zvezdino Proleće, and Red Star would almost certainly win the cup too. In the two games to go, we had to hope for a couple of miracles.

Looking further ahead, it was a familiarly uncertain time for fans of the club. If we were to believe everything we read in the papers, we would start next season with only two of the regular first 11 – Stojković and Volkov – still at the club, and a new chairman

(Mr Bogičević, whose attempted putsch had failed over the winter). Maybe a new manager as well. Some of these might be welcome developments, but some of them wouldn't, and all could potentially be destabilising. Not many clubs benefit from that much change at once.

Dušan speculated that a change of board would almost certainly mean a change of boss and a big exodus of players too, particularly those whose agents were close to the board. I was sceptical initially when the lads swore that officials of almost every Serbian club had an active interest in a regular turnover of players, in order for them or their associates to benefit personally from the various signing-on fees and sell-on percentages. It was one of those things that everyone 'knew' rather than ever being talked about publicly or documented. It was easily conceivable in a country where corruption levels were this high, but it was only now (knowing that he was about to be shown the door) that David Manga would complain publicly at the end of the season that he was told in terms early in his Partizan career that if he changed his agent to one 'approved' by the club, he would get picked for the first team more often.

Elections took place the day after the Red Star game. This meant I was preoccupied with 'real' politics more than football politics, and not able to give the transfer gossip my full attention. But fortunately both the first and second rounds of elections were on Sundays, so I still had the Saturdays free enough to see our last two games with the current crop.

League table after the 28th round:
1. Partizan 74 (+53)
2. Red Star 65 (+38)
3. Radnički 47 (+13)

Vince Clarke's Sinister Synth Riff

THE footballing elements of the electoral campaign had about as little effect on the voters as the rest of the political sound and fury over the past six weeks. The whole campaign seemed at times a big ruse to disguise the fact that none of the parties had a detailed manifesto. The thing was, they did have policies. They just didn't make much effort to communicate them to the voters, preferring to concentrate on their own personalities and the flaws of their rivals.

The results were pretty much as the opinion polls had suggested they would be: Boris Tadić went into a second round run-off for the presidency holding a small lead over his challenger Tomislav Nikolić. Nikolić's Progressive Party, meanwhile, became the largest party in parliament, but seemed unlikely to be able to form a coalition and a new government, especially after Ivica Dačić's Socialist Party (the one with the most influence at Partizan) did a deal with Tadić's Democrats to deepen their existing cooperation and form the core of the next national government – which would therefore look quite a lot like the current one. Dačić had been the biggest net winner in the elections, doubling his party's share of the vote, making them a clear third force in Serbian politics.

It was fitting then that the next match was away at Radnički Kragujevac. Kragujevac, which sits slap bang in the middle of Serbia, had been the central battleground for most of the electoral campaign. Nikolić's home town, it was nevertheless a stronghold for yet another party, the United Regions of Serbia, previously part of the government but not in favour with Tadić anymore.

A couple of months previously, a multi-million euro investment by Italian car company Fiat had begun to bear fruit in the form of new jobs in the city, as production began of a new model at a revamped manufacturing plant. In a country desperately needing foreign investment, this was the sign of positive things to come that Tadić, and the government, required to justify four more years of their rule to the voters. Politicians from all parties had been climbing over each other to come to Kragujevac and claim credit for Fiat being there and the prosperity it would bring, or to rubbish the government's claims and uncover the huge subsidies being paid to Fiat to relocate production there.

Uroš, a native of Kragujevac though a resident of Belgrade, was our unofficial tour guide for the day. He hadn't noticed much economic difference from the factory's opening yet, though there were rumours that the influx of Italian executives into the town had led to a proliferation of new pizza and pasta joints. All he had really spotted was that those lucky few who'd got jobs in the new factory had taken to wearing their Fiat uniforms as they walked to and from work, or around town at lunchtime. 'They're basically saying "Look at me, look at me, I've got a job!"' said Uroš mournfully, reflecting the pain of de-industrialisation that Kragujevac had experienced. He brightened briefly to add, 'It's a pretty good way to get girls' attention.'

Radnički's ground is a pleasant enough open-air bowl set in parkland just outside the city centre, and a few thousand Crveni Djavoli [Red Devils] were in good voice as we arrived. With some justification: even though they had only been promoted this season, they were in third place and a potential Europa League spot. But with Vojvodina, Jagodina and Sloboda right behind them, they needed to get a good result against us to keep them firmly in the hunt. Almost inevitably, this led to yet more rumours that we would chuck the game in return for first dibs on one of their best players.

Just one part of the ground sat empty, conspicuous by the fact that, despite an iridescent line of stewards on either side, no one was sitting or standing in the sector. The Zabranjeni had been banned again. Half of our group had been scooped up among the Zabranjeni buses and their car prevented from even getting on the motorway, a full hour away from Kragujevac. They had been unlucky, in that Vili was ill and couldn't take his car, and the lifts they had cadged had been with people not as wise as Vili, and who had taken the main road instead of the less-policed back roads.

Goran and Dario had kept Dušan updated via text as they tried to make the game, while we enjoyed a leisurely and traditionally heavy Serbian pre-match lunch of a kilo and a half of prasetina [roast pork] between the three of us. Firstly the police had insisted that there was no way that the ticketless Zabranjeni were going to be allowed to travel down to Kragujevac. But slowly but surely, a series of negotiations took place in which the police allowed the Zabranjeni to travel down, and then held them again just outside the city, before further relenting and allowing them to buy tickets on the door.

By the time they got to the ground, there were just three minutes left in the first half. 'It's a dangerous tactic,' said Dušan, 'keeping them for that long. They've probably been held like cattle for four hours, bored and drinking. They're asking for trouble.' No one was likely to have minded that they'd missed another dull half of football, even one briefly enlivened by a smartly-taken goal by Stefan Babović.

They did mind that, as soon as they had all assembled in their pen and the players had come out for the second half, a few Alcatraz hotheads barged to the front of their enclosure (some 20 metres away) and yelled some random abuse at them. As the first few Zabranjeni dropped down on to the athletics track and made to move past the yellow-bibbed stewards, a phalanx of gendarmes stormed out of the players' tunnel and rushed towards them. Ten, twenty, thirty, forty. The column just kept on coming.

Not one of the Zabranjeni fancied the fight. A couple of them braved a brush with a Perspex shield in order to launch one last verbal salvo, but for the most part they turned and legged it back to the sanctuary of their stand, the front row a sea of limbs as the guys who had stayed back hauled their mates back off the track.

It wasn't over, though. As the tail of the police crocodile reached the Zabranjeni stand, they fanned out to form a three-deep line, enough to be a serious deterrent to any future incursions. This was deemed to be too much of a 'provocation' by a section of the Zabranjeni, who launched a few seats at the police in front of them, the clonk of plastic on plastic audible even above the cacophony of whistling and booing from all around the ground. The police remained unmoved, choosing to bide their time and not antagonise the hyped-up Zabranjeni any further.

Although he'd had considerable electoral success the night before, doubling his party's share of the vote, Ivica Dačić had clearly not received many votes from the Zabranjeni constituency. He might have had some cause for surprise at this – Partizan had formed part of his campaign publicity late on in the campaign. Because of their debts, unpaid subscriptions, and various crowd behaviour issues, Partizan (and Red Star) were being threatened with their UEFA licence not being renewed, meaning that our place in the qualifying rounds of the Champions League was under threat.

Dačić and Boris Tadić had both written to Michel Platini at UEFA to plead Partizan's (and Red Star's) case, a fact they had persuaded the media to make a big deal of, once it became apparent that both clubs were going to be allowed into European competition and they could present it as a political success, demonstrative of the manner in which they stood up for Serbia's interests in other international fora etc …

The Zabranjeni had not been persuaded that Dačić was acting wholly in the best interests of the club. For them, the political influence over the club went as far as a direct Socialist Party preference for Alcatraz, and a victimisation of the Zabranjeni. The fact that Dačić was pictured toasting his election night success with various trumpeters and Alcatraz leader Aleksandar Vavić added fuel to their fire. A variation of their standard arguments, but with Dačić in the political spotlight as a potential kingmaker, able to influence both the presidential second round and who would be the next prime minister, they chose to muscle in on his publicity.

They unfurled a first banner, directed at Alcatraz: 'What do you think would happen to you if Dačić wasn't there to protect you?' Whether the rank-and-file Alcatraz fully grasped the electoral nuances of the protest against them, I don't know, but they didn't seem too perturbed, continuing their repertoire of songs based around us being champions again. Possession is nine-tenths of the law, even when it comes down to a football club's favoured brand of ultra, and with no sign of a change to Serbia's macro-political environment, there seemed to be an ever smaller chance of the Zabranjeni mounting a coup or securing some kind of fan group equality at this micro level.

In international diplomacy, the process of influencing an unpopular change tends to go in three stages. The first is to use subtle public messaging to try and build a constituency for your argument, or to highlight the likely drawbacks of resisting you. The Zabranjeni were already well into the second stage, in which the consequences of a failure to comply were being made blunter and blunter. Their first banner had been akin to a robust UN Security Council resolution, ultimately quite threatening if you can get through all the preambular paragraphs and know where to read between the lines. Their second banner, with its simple message: 'Dačić, get the f*** out of the south', was comprehensible even to those fans who hadn't read a book since *My first hundred words* when they were five.

Faced with the thick line of police still in front of them, the Zabranjeni were not going to be able to take it to level three and mount an actual invasion to 'liberate' the south stand of its Alcatraz occupiers. But they did launch a major aerial campaign. As keen students of how to enforce a no-fly zone, the Zabranjeni had clearly understood the necessity for stealth technology in order to evade the enemy's defences. Short of radar-absorbent materials and other high technologies, they disguised their plans with a good old-fashioned smokescreen. Every second fan had a flare in his hand when the group simultaneously lit them, creating a thick fog that almost completely obscured them, even from the policemen standing just yards in front of them.

From inside the cloud, all that could be heard was a throaty rendition of the 'Just Can't Get Enough' crno-beli/Zabranjeni chant. It seemed to all intents and purposes that this was just another attention-seeking chance to sing their new favourite song, with the whole stadium turned towards them, including the referee and players. They had been forced to stop the game by the pall extending over them.

In fact, it was the perfect camouflage from which to launch a concentrated bombardment of firecrackers into Alcatraz-dominated territory, causing their rival fans to scatter, panicked, from the areas of their stand within missile range. Their intended victims couldn't see the ordnance as it was launched, only when it emerged from the sky, and neither could the police see which of the few hundred before them were responsible for their launch. In purely military terms, it was quite effective. For the two or three minutes while the barrage was maintained, the same chant continued. I can say categorically that it is the most sinister use of a Vince Clarke synthesiser riff that will ever take place.

As the smoke subsided and the game was able to restart, the stadium announcer warned that any further incidents would lead to the stand concerned being emptied. This was, in my 28th game of the season, the first time I had heard such a threat actually be issued. This made me think further about the effectiveness of security at matches in Serbia. Had this been the UK, the match would already have been abandoned, and several people would already have been arrested just for entering the pitch, and within days banned from attending future matches (and have those bans enforced). But here it had got to the point where 50 or 60 fireworks had to be thrown at people with a reasonable assumption that the assailants wanted to cause injury or mass panic before even the loosest threat to make some arrests was made. Occasional games behind closed doors didn't have the required level of deterrence.

I also contrasted the thoroughness of the pat-downs I was subjected to at pretty much every game, the number of times I had to justify why I had six keys on my keyring or why I needed two mobile phones, or saw fathers with their young kids have their lighters or some other item taken off them for safety reasons, with the industrial quantity of pyrotechnics in the stadium at this game and at pretty much every other one I had seen this season. It was hard to escape the conclusion that the clubs and the police were complicit in allowing this all into the ground. Therein they were contributing to a vicious circle, as we had discussed down in Novi Pazar, in which the only people who really wanted to go to football were the kind of people who wanted to chuck fireworks at each other or fight the police, and the police were unable to stop those people from creating an intimidating atmosphere that put less troublesome people off coming at all, and entrenching the whole situation.

The game finished 1-0, by the way.

Fireworks, though in infinitely smaller quantities, had been thrown at the last derby too. Just not in a way which I had thought excessive by the standards set in previous derbies. But on Monday after the game in Kragujevac, the FSS announced that Partizan would be punished as before by having to play their next home game with no spectators. Dušan was phlegmatic upon hearing the news – if the club pushed hard enough, and made enough promises about it not happening again, they could get this ban suspended. Against my expectations, he didn't see the evil hand of the pro-Red Star Establishment in trying to deny Partizan the formal presentation of the championship trophy, even when I tried to provoke him into saying so. 'No, like I said, this is for form's sake. The club will appeal against the decision and get it overturned or converted into a suspended ban.'

But the appeal never came. The club did ask for special dispensation for a group of a few hundred Serb kids from Kosovo to be allowed to watch the match, as transport had already been arranged, but it didn't try to have the broader decision revoked. Now Dušan had a conspiracy theory to pursue. Dario and others in the Zabranjeni hardcore had told him that they had been planning a big protest against Đurić and the rest of the board to accompany the match, but that the club had got wind of it, and even offered them money to call it off and cease their campaign against him. But they had refused. Could it really be that the club would rather deny 25,000 fans the chance to see their heroes pick up the trophy because it wouldn't brook any dissent? Bearing in mind how the Zabranjeni had reacted in Kragujevac to the police's attempts to contain them, the threat of a 'protest' carried more weight, but if this was true, it was a sad state of affairs.

The trophy presentation was to be put back to next season, to happen before one of Partizan's European qualifiers or at the first league game of the season, so as not to deny the fans a chance to celebrate. But to celebrate with whom if next season's squad only contained a handful of this year's champions?

We would miss several more pieces of history, or at least be forced to watch them on TV. The home game against Metalac would be Avram Grant's last game in charge of Partizan. No one would shed many tears over this. It had been a real marriage of convenience for both parties. Grant had been able to add a Serbian championship to his CV and end a spell of a few years as a nearly man, while on a decent contract. It had put him back in the European spotlight and made him a more attractive proposition for future employers. The Partizan board had been able to present Avram as a sign of ambition in the aftermath of the Stanojević sacking, and he had been a safe enough pair of hands to ensure our success in the league, without requiring a real long-term commitment. It had been good business for both in the short term, but realistically it wasn't what either wanted in the long term.

Avram had never really won the fans over. The way he was appointed (not his fault) hadn't helped, and neither had the repeated failures in the derbies (which were). After a shaky start, the team had played quite well just as often in the second half of the season as it had done in the first, and he had preserved the lead built up under his predecessor to secure the league. But this wasn't enough to erase the pain of how he had arrived, and to compensate for the poor communication between him and the fans.

He ended up being quoted far too often underplaying the importance of events that were important to the fans, and underestimating the strength of feeling around the club. In the last couple of weeks of his reign, he told the press that his wife was always wondering out loud just why he worked for Partizan. It wasn't for the money, that was for sure. And she (he) questioned if all the abuse he took was really worth it. For the bulk of the fans, his reported 400,000 euro per annum salary was beyond their imagination, in a country where the average yearly salary is more like 5,000, if you're in the three-quarters fortunate enough to have a job. Avram said plenty of things that could have endeared him more to us, which weren't always given the same prominence, and he was a target for sections of the media throughout his tenure, but at the same time he always seemed capable of saying one thing per interview that alienated the fans.

A more auspicious piece of history was created in the 45th minute when Lamine Diarra latched on to Babović's pass and tucked away unfussily his 100th goal in Partizan colours. Diarra was one of the favourites to exit the club in the summer, being out of contract, so it looked likely to be his last goal for the club too. Diarra's reaction to scoring was to reveal a self-made version of the Captain Ilić t-shirt, outlining his own 100 goals, four titles and two cups. All of it was true, but as a self-tribute it smacked of arrogance a bit.

One person who didn't get to see Diarra make history, despite being luckier than me and actually present in the stadium was David Manga, in his last game for us. Manga was having a mixed game, busy as ever, missing a great chance in the first ten minutes, forcing a good save shortly afterwards, and then being bundled over two yards out, with an open goal, for no penalty later on in the half.

With five minutes left in the half he chased back into midfield but got into a muddle with Rnić, releasing Metalac's forward to stride forward unopposed into the Partizan half, with just Petrović to beat. Manga overhauled Rnić and set off after the forward.

From six or seven yards back, he got into the box alongside his opponent, and was preparing to slide across in front of him when the recovering Rnić grabbed the Metalac forward's shoulder and pulled him down. The referee was unsure whether to give a free kick or a penalty, eventually being helped by his assistant to give the spot kick. But he was instantly sure that he should send Manga off for the professional foul, despite him making no contact at all. Rnić made no attempt to take the blame for his foul, and let Manga stand there disbelieving before the Central African was compelled to leave the pitch. It was an ignominious end to the brief but shining career in Partizan colours of David Manga Lembe, from burger jockey to employee of the month at one of Europe's most famous football clubs.

Petrović saved the penalty, and we held on until half-time in the lead. The second half was a truly weird experience, in that we were, for the first time this season, hopelessly outclassed by our opponents, who had nothing more to play for than pride, confirmed already as being relegated and as the bottom club.

With no Partizan crowd to try and intimidate them, and only ten opponents, Metalac were a decent side, dominating possession and passing the ball well. It wasn't Barcelona's tika-taka, but it made me wonder how they had contrived to be the worst team in a pretty poor league. Watching us get outplayed but hang on grimly for a 1-0 win was quite liberating. Instead of viewing the players as a bunch of highly talented but fundamentally flawed individuals who laboured to draws in games they should have won easily, they showed that they could knuckle down, work hard and grind out a result when the odds were stacked against them. And I include Stefan Babović in this. Ostojić and Petrović, the kids entrusted with the spine of our defence, both gave cause for optimism.

Combine that with the news coming from Novi Sad, where Red Star managed to lose to Vojvodina, meaning that we were the spring champions as well, and I had the recipe for feeling happier about the world when the final whistle blew than I had been when the match had begun. Dušan texted me within microseconds of Vojvodina's winning goal to allege massive fraud – according to him, Vojvodina's need for points to hold off Radnički and Jagodina and secure third was not enough reasons for them to have beaten Red Star without some kind of deal having been struck. After texting Claire to tell her that we had our weekends back, in reply to Dušan I simply noted Stephen Appiah's goal, and what a great signing he had been.

Jagodina took fourth, giving our man Marković Palma another reason to trumpet the success of his city, and pressgang visiting Europa League fans into testifying on TV that yes, Jagodina really was the city of the future.

It was of course a huge anti-climax for the final whistle to be followed by some adverts and then some anodyne post-match chat from my sofa, when really we should have been in the stadium soaking up the glory of this fifth consecutive championship triumph, while those around us urged our Red Star neighbours to let us impregnate their female relatives. All that would have to wait until next season.

League table after the 30th round:
1. Partizan 80 (+55)
2. Red Star 68 (+39)
3. Vojvodina 52 (+18)

Life Imitates Partizan

EVERY football fan is capable of reading too much into the significance of their club. I once had a Spurs fan swear blind that the economy always grew if Spurs won a trophy. It is said that AC Milan's European Cup success in 1994 brought Silvio Berlusconi to power. Many eastern European clubs were run as an extension of government in the Cold War years, and oligarchs use clubs to expand their 'soft power' reach today.

Partizan fans, on the other hand, consider their club more as a plaything of the rich and powerful, to be used for pleasure, bled of its resources and then discarded. Given that the Grobari fervently believe Red Star to be the club benefiting from the influence and cash of the 'deep State', we could never imagine that Partizan had any measure of control over their own destiny, let alone influence over the wider world. But life, at least in Serbia, seemed to imitate the club during the brief two months off before the start of the 2012/13 season.

Serbia's leadership changed, Boris Tadić losing in a run-off to Tomislav Nikolić and then, over the course of seven weeks of negotiations being forced into the parliamentary opposition, his former partner (and sworn enemy of the Zabranjeni) Dačić taking the prime minister's slot by abandoning Tadić and shacking up with Nikolić's party. Tadić's defeat had caught out all the political specialists in the country (including me), making us look about as stupid as the people who hadn't seen Avram Grant's appointment coming (ie almost all of the sports journalists). We were good company for each other.

Partizan made wholesale changes to the sporting side of the club, matching the politicians stride for stride. Avram's replacement was

Vladimir Vermezović, known as Mr Black because of his lustrous, obsidian and Tom Selleck-esque moustache, a former Partizan defender in the 1980s, and manager from 2004/05. Since then, he had coached in Slovakia, and then South Africa, as manager of Kaizer Chiefs. This was the Partizan way – to respect traditions and arrange a marriage, appointing someone with history at the club, as opposed to our dalliance with Avram, which had had all the 'getting to know you' time of a fling with someone we'd met in a nightclub in Magaluf. Seven of the ten most recent managers (including Vermezović in his first spell) had been Partizan alumni, and while the three outsiders had enjoyed some success, their reigns had either been brief, tumultuous, or both.

Vermezović's director of football would be Ljubisa Tumbaković, a man who held the record as most successful first-team manager ever, having presided over six championships and three Cups in his two spells from 1992–1999 and 2000–2002. The shadow of Tumbaković looming over Vermezović struck me as a recipe for trouble within the club, as befell Manchester United in the post-Busby years when no manager could escape the great man's legacy, nor his far-reaching and interfering tentacles. It had its parallels with Serbia too, where Dačić would have to adapt fast to having increased responsibilities all the while he had a theoretical political ally (but in reality a rival) as his de facto boss.

Dušan, who had been around to see both managers in action in their previous spells, wasn't so concerned. Vermezović was a serious guy and authoritative in his own right. And Tumbaković had been out of day-to-day football management for a couple of years, and out of European football (having been in Saudi Arabia and China) for more like eight. So they would probably get along fine.

The changes placated the fans to a degree, just as Nikolić's surprise election against the backdrop of a political system and media bias skewed against him showed the electorate that Serbia's democracy was in better health than expected. Dušan, unsurprisingly, was not among them. He respected Vermezović's success, but pointed me in the direction of some online materials that suggested he had had (an admittedly minor) role in assisting Partizan chucking a couple of games during his previous spell at the club before becoming manager, allegations denied by all concerned. Our cohort were still broadly dissatisfied with the club's overall management, though, just as across the whole of Serbia the change

in government didn't alter the public's widespread pessimism about the future of the country.

Vermezović set his stall out early on that he wasn't going to tolerate what he described as the indiscipline and laxity of the Grant era. At his first training session, he ordered several players to lose weight, including a demand of Stojković (a man I never felt to be a chubster) to get rid of 14kg of excess blubber. Vermezović also made the players sign a code of conduct that, among other things, required the players to submit a landline number so the club could ensure that they were at home prior to key fixtures. Players not at home when the gaffer rang would be fined. Sweets, booze and fags were banned, along with trips to the splavovi. None of the media reports recorded what Tomić and Smiljanić's faces looked like when they were presented with this reality. 'Don't f*** with Mr Black', Uroš wrote, forwarding us the link to the story online.

Discipline for footballers was a political topic too. Siniša Mihajlović, once upon a time a man who possessed a dynamite left foot and a tongue punished for racism, was in the process of establishing his authority as manager of the national team. He had put together a code of conduct like Vermezović that included a stipulation that all the players had to sing the national anthem. Adem Ljajić, the Fiorentina midfielder and ethnic Bosniak, failed to sing along before Serbia's game against Spain, a pre-Euro 2012 warm-up. Mihajlović, true to his word, sent Ljajić home from the squad, opening up a lengthy debate in Serbia about whether the anthem, chock-full of references to Serb ethnicity, was suitable for a multi-ethnic society, and whether Ljajić was unpatriotic and a bad advert for integration, or had been true to his roots and not betrayed his fellow Bosniaks.

Indicative of the wider problems of minorities, their rights and their responsibilities, it was the first time I had ever been able to write an official communication in the diplomatic service that was mostly about football and genuinely worthy of going on record, rather than my usual practice of shoehorning football references into places no other diplomat would think or dare to put them.

Mirroring Serbia's partial changeover of ministers in the new government, but retention of many of its familiar faces, out went some fringe players like Manga, but also one of the biggest guns, in the shape of Diarra, to Antalyaspor in Turkey. For all his protestations that Belgrade was his city, and Partizan his club (and indeed the fact that he was only months away from acquiring Serbian citizenship), he had been unable to agree a new contract. So we lost him for free.

And who came in to replace them? Just like the ministers, it was a mixed bag. There were a couple of people from other teams, like Branko Pauljević, the Kula full-back who had made Tomić look so ponderous, who was brought in so that he only embarrassed Partizan players in training with his blistering pace (10.7 seconds for 100m, trumpeted the club), and Filip Knezević of Borac Čačak, a decent midfielder.

There were a couple of promising youngsters: Milos Jojić joined Ostojić in being promoted from the youth team; while Darko Brasanac, who had played well against us earlier in the season, came back from his loan spell with Smederevo. There were returnees, like long-time émigré Goran Lovre, most recently at Barnsley, who returned home like Ilić and Vukić had before him. And finally, there were family links, as Marko Šćepović's older brother Stefan, only 22 but having played in Italy, Belgium and Israel already, joined.

Our 'marquee' signing was Libyan international forward Mohamed Za'abia, signed from the Kuwaiti side Al-Arabi. None of the fans were particularly impressed by the quality of the signing, but there was lots of debate about whether he had been for or against Gaddafi during Libya's civil war. The consensus on the forums, with their deep knowledge of Middle East and North African politics and the intricacies of Libya's tribal and clan system, decided that he was a pro-Gaddafiist, had taken up arms to defend the colonel, and indeed had to play overseas now because he wasn't welcome in Libya anymore. Not a shred of evidence was produced to back up any of these claims, but they made a good story.

It wasn't just the sport and politics sections of the papers that mirrored what was going on at the club. Much of the biggest crime news of those two months was directly related to Partizan too. Some of the men convicted of Brice Taton's killing had their sentences reduced, an outcome that pleased neither the victim's family nor those campaigning for 'justice for the Grobari'. Former Alcatraz leader Kimi got 16 months in prison for his hate speech and intimidation towards the B92 journalist. And the police in northern Kosovo, acting on a warrant issued in Serbia, arrested Damjan Sobić in connection with the murder of Zabranjeni martyr Ivan Perović.

According to the media, Sobić had been hiding down in Mitrovica ever since Perović's murder. It was only now, six months later, that the police had managed to track him down.

There was a broader football reflection in events in Kosovo too. Demonstrations by Serbs continued sporadically in Kosovo during this period, in response to various perceived or more real threats. Every time they needed to show strength in numbers they managed to gather together 3,000 people, some of whom the international peacekeeping forces suspected to be rent-a-mob types recruited from the ranks of Red Star and Partizan's more die-hard hooligans. On work visits to Kosovo, more than one person had told me that there was a link between the clubs' fans (though not the clubs themselves) and the violence. It was a damning indictment of my partiality that I could not hide my smile when I heard the best piece of anecdotal evidence – that they noticed a commensurate drop in protestor numbers and violence levels when Red Star were playing. As long as we weren't the most to blame …

I spoke too soon. As Serbs across the world celebrated St Vitus's Day, or Vidovdan, on 28 June, Partizan fans were back in the news. A group of 50 or so Alcatraz travelled down to Kosovo to celebrate the day, which commemorates the anniversary of the Battle of Kosovo in 1389. Having crossed from northern Kosovo into the mainly ethnic Albanian southern part, they were prevented from attending the main celebration at a place called Gazimestan, where a monument commemorates the battle, about seven kilometres from the original Kosovo field. Having been escorted out of Kosovo by the authorities, they exited their bus and (depending on whose story you believe) started lobbing stones at the Kosovo police.

They were better armed and responded with, at the very least (reports vary), tear gas and rubber bullets, injuring 20 of the group. The Serbs said that they were hit with live rounds. Either way, five relatively senior members of Alcatraz were quite badly hurt, one of them receiving a nasty wound to either the lower back (the line in the media) or to his cock (the immediate Zabranjeni propaganda, reflecting their overwhelming lack of sympathy, later picked up by the media too).

In his comments to the press, Kosovo's own Interior Minister Rexhepi blamed Red Star fans for that incident, and another where the evidence was much clearer. Dušan said he was 99% sure that Rexhepi was a Partizan fan too. Even in the heat of a difficult day for law and order in his country, he had found time to sully the name of the enemy.

Neither Kosovo nor the changes to the make-up of government was the biggest problem facing Serbia at that moment, though the latter was a hindrance to solving the major challenge: the economy. Unemployment continued to rise, the government was about to breach its own deficit and public debt rules, and the dinar was slipping against the euro, itself struggling against the pound and dollar.

Serbia had initially believed itself to be cushioned against the global recession when it took hold in 2008, only to realise that its economy (like everyone else's) was so deeply intertwined with the rest of Europe's that the risk of contagion was real. The same applied to Partizan. Sizeable amounts of Partizan's debt, particularly but not limited to that owed to other clubs for unpaid transfer fees, was owed in euros, not dinars. Every further eurocent that the dinar dropped would hit the club, and could only be recouped by selling players for euros. The club would be forced to act in the opposite manner to the national bank, busy selling off its reserves of foreign currency to try and boost the dinar, instead trying to bring in as much hard currency as possible.

To shore up some of the club's dinar finances, necessary for the day-to-day running of the club, price rises for season tickets were announced. The rise depended on the sector of the ground, but mine went up by a sixth, from 3,000 dinars to 3,500. But such was the dinar's slide that this was still cheaper for me than the year before: £26 had bought 3,000 then but £24 bought 3,500 now. The hike in prices caused less of a fuss than I had thought – Arsenal fans had made more noise about a six per cent rise than they had about the team for most of the season, and this was an increase of over 16 per cent during a time of wage stagnation. But ticket sales were consistent with the previous season, proving that demand for Partizan was more elastic than for anything else in Serbia bar beer and cigarettes.

Serbia's economic problems were bad. But they paled into insignificance compared to their regional neighbour Greece's. In Serbian they have a phrase, 'dužan kao Grk/Grčka' [as indebted as a Greek/Greece], which predates the current crisis by centuries, such is Greece's local reputation for owing money elsewhere. Fortunately for Partizan, we were playing Serbia in this drama, while Red

Star were Greece. The summer passed much more quickly and pleasantly knowing that while our squad was being renewed if not actually strengthened, Red Star were being forced into something of a fire sale to keep their creditors from the door, so out of control had their debts become.

Before I knew it, pre-season had already begun, and we looked forward to the first meaningful action on 25 June – the draw to find out our Champions League second qualifying round opponents. Being seeded would stop us from drawing one of the biggest guns like Dinamo Zagreb, Red Bull Salzburg or FC Basel. The team everyone wanted though was Shamrock Rovers. Ivan Ivanov was in the papers so often, desperate for revenge against the Dublin side, that he must have been ringing editors every five minutes to get so many column inches. But Ivanov and the rest of us were to be disappointed – we would face the winners of FC Lusitanos of Andorra, who bore a similarity to Shkendia in that they were the ethnically Portuguese team of Andorra, and Valletta FC of Malta, with the first leg away.

My journey as a trainee Partizan fan had nearly reached its anniversary. Dušan decided to mark the occasion by getting married. To a Red Star fan. While I was trying desperately to find flights to Malta that didn't include three changes and cost €1,000, he was planning the rest of his life with a woman who considered herself a Delije. There was only one logical conclusion for our irrational behaviour: it must be love.

Epilogue

BY the time it looked likely that this book would actually get published, the winter break of the 2012/13 season was already drawing to a close. Some things were terribly familiar. We were six points ahead of Red Star and top of the league, with Jagodina and Vojvodina close behind but almost certainly going to fade. But the home crowd was still horribly fractious, and demands for Vermezović and Đurić to leave rang out weekly.

Vermezović had led the team to the top of the league, averaging three goals a game, and into the group stages of the Europa League, where Partizan had performed creditably against Inter Milan and Rubin Kazan but not had the quality to go through. For most of the fans, he was too defensive-minded.

The complaints against Đurić followed the pattern of 2011/12, but now Alcatraz would initiate some of the demands for regicide, instead of the Zabranjeni having a monopoly. The two groups were still at odds, with the Zabranjeni having decided to relocate from the Istok to the Sever so they could stand even further away from their enemies. The parallel chanting of the same songs at different times was as pathetic and demotivating as ever.

On the pitch, the team veered as it always had from brilliance to mediocrity. The same team which out-played Inter Milan in the San Siro before conceding a late goal to lose 1-0, which slammed Vojvodina 3-0 away, and which was so dominant at home to Borča that goalkeeper Stojković was allowed to take and score the penalty that gave us a 7-0 win, also managed to lose away to newly promoted Donji Srem, a club so tiny that they weren't allowed to play at their own ground, and limp out of the cup against Borac Čačak.

There were differences though. The club's debts meant that most of the familiar faces from last season were gone. Babović, Tomić, Vukić and Rnić were all ex-crno-beli. I asked Dušan who he was going to shout abuse at now that so many of his sworn enemies plied their trade elsewhere. 'It'll give me more time to concentrate on Đurić, so don't worry,' he replied. But some of our favourites, like Aksentijević, Diarra and Medo (to Bolton Wanderers) were gone too. Youngsters promoted from the youth team, like Ninković, Ostojić, Jojić and the 18-year-old giant Aleksandar Mitrović were proving much better than the old guard, and spent less time in the splavs too.

Allegations of corruption round the club hadn't gone away. In early 2013, the difference was that these allegations were actually being investigated. By the police. Since coming to power in August, Deputy Prime Minister and anti-corruption tsar Aleksandar Vučić had embarked on a vigorous campaign to have previously untouchable tycoons and politicians prosecuted. In its early days, the campaign faced allegations from those targeted that it was politically motivated and that evidence came out in the media before in the courtroom. But it challenged the belief that some people were indeed "untouchable", and made people believe that the country might actually be able to turn a corner and begin reducing corruption. It also galvanised parts of the Serbian system into looking into corruption more systematically, including Partizan's transfers under Đurić.

After months of investigation into Partizan, it still wasn't clear if anyone would be prosecuted, and Đurić had been clear throughout that he welcomed the investigation and that he and the club had nothing to hide. But there was hope among some fans that the mystery of Partizan's perpetual player sales and perennial debt might be solved.

Football stopped being just a hobby. Partizan and Red Star's travails (and theirs were worse than ours, I noted with satisfaction) were a frequent front page story, and politicians from all parties were queuing up to offer State support to both clubs. So football started to encroach into my work more regularly.

None of this encroachment prepared me properly for what happened on 16 October, when England's Under-21s played away at Kruševac against Serbia. I wasn't at the game, but both the ambassador and Dušan were. The racist abuse suffered by England's black players during and after the game has been well documented, and after a number of months UEFA eventually delivered their harshest penalties ever for those incidents – though they still appeared disproportionately low compared to the punishment meted out to Nicklas Bendtner for wearing unauthorised branded pants during a Euro 2012 game.

Britain's and Serbia's prime ministers both commented on the racism that had taken place, placing the match at the top of the news agenda in both countries, and becoming a significant bilateral issue. We spent days and weeks patiently trying to extract information from the Serbian system when the local authorities decided to charge two England players and Under-21 assistant coach Steve Wigley with criminal offences in relation to the post-match fracas. Eventually the Serbian prosecutor declared that it would send the case to the Crown Prosecution Service for processing in the UK, something usually only done for the most serious offences, including crimes against humanity, not a bit of shoving.

Dačić and his Minister for Sport, Alisa Marić, launched an intiative to try and eradicate violence and intolerance from Serbian sport, but there was a much heavier focus on the former. Several liberal commentators and ordinary members of the public expressed revulsion at the racism that the England players had experienced, and the prevalence of racism in society, but just as many at the different end of the political spectrum, including some in the footballing authorities, were in denial.

I lost count of the times that I heard 'there's no racism in Serbia'. In a conversation with an official at the Ministry of Sport, I asked him how he could say that when in just one season in Serbia I had heard Albanians, Bosniaks and Hungarians all invited to f*** themselves or do something else unpleasant purely on the grounds of their ethnicity. His answer was that national identity and race weren't the same thing, so he was sticking to his statement.

The truth is that even with his narrow definition of race (ie the colour of someone's skin), he was still wrong. At Novi Pazar disgusting epithets had been aimed at Medo, as well as actual phlegm, just because he's black. And not just there – there had been booing of our black players on a couple of other occasions as well. Racism in Serbian football wasn't actually as bad as I had presumed before I arrived there, but it was definitely still present. And it followed a fairly clear pattern – if the small club we were away against didn't have any black players, then the chances that some of their fans would boo our black players increased.

We at the embassy organised an event in December, bringing over Danny Lynch from Kick It Out to speak on a panel alongside Serbian government representatives and other commentators. Again we heard that there was no racism in Serbia, and that the government's initiative would increase tolerance in school sports. The latter was a noble enough sentiment, but officially for Serbia fair play seemed to end at not physically attacking your fellow players – there was little mention of trying to reduce racial intolerance.

We found sections of the Serbian media working against us too. Instead of discussing the issues, the bulk of the media instead decided that allegations of racism in Serbian football were just an English plot against the country. So they would print endless stories about racist incidents around English football and accuse us of hypocrisy. Dušan tirelessly pointed editors towards two facts – firstly that no one in Britain, from the prime minister down, said that racism had been eliminated in Britain, indeed we were clear that we had a lot more to do, and secondly that the media in Serbia were not reporting the second half of any of these stories – where the perpetrators of racist abuse were banned from football or sentenced in court.

Away from football, my life changed too, for the better. I assume for reasons unconnected to Kula and Smederevo, Claire decided she didn't want to be with me anymore, and ran off to Norway with some bloke she had met on holiday. This directly preceded Partizan being drawn against FC Tromso of Norway in the Europa League qualifiers, an irony that wasn't lost on me. Partizan lost 3-2 inside the Arctic Circle but we still had a chance to go through to the group stage thanks to our away goals.

I can honestly say I've never wanted us to win a game more than that return leg. If there was one thing that was going to help me deal with what was still a pretty raw feeling, it was getting one over those pesky Norwegians. For 70 minutes it looked like Partizan weren't going to give me what I wanted, huffing and puffing but refusing resolutely not to blow Tromso's house down. Then, with our umpteenth corner, Ninković swung the ball into the box and Ivanov rose highest among half a dozen to head the ball through the keeper's hands and in. We had done it, and I at least had some temporary Scandinavian revenge.

The next day, I was at a party on a splav and got talking to a girl called Jenny, whom I'd met a couple of times before. She'd been at the Tromso game too. Supporting the away side. Because she's a Norwegian who lives in Belgrade. As were were talking, and I realised how much I liked her, I wondered just how much irony the world could chuck at me. But I ignored the coincidences, and eventually I got round to asking her out. And it was the best decision I ever made – we fell in love quickly and started making plans for the future, because we already knew we would be together for a long, long time.

And when the season restarted, conscious of the fact that Dušan was going to have to make fewer away trips in light of his impending fatherhood, Jenny said, 'You know, I can always come with you if you like.' Even to Novi Pazar. It really must be love.

2011/12 Season Statistics

League

Novi Pazar (h)*	5-0	Eduardo, Tomić, Ilić, Marković L, Babović
Sloboda Point Sevojno (a)*	1-2	Aksentijević
OFK Beograd (h)*	3-0	Marković L, Diarra (2)
FK Jagodina (a)*	1-0	Tomić
Hajduk (h)*	2-0	Tomić (2)
Rad (h)	1-0	Eduardo
Vojvodina (a)	2-1	Marković L, Šćepović
Spartak (h)*	2-0	Vukić (2)
FK Javor (a)*	2-0	Marković L, Vukić
Smederevo (h)*	3-1	Vukić, Šćepović, Marković L
BSK (a)*	1-0	Šćepović
Borac (h)*	5-1	Tomić (2), Marković L, Vukić, og
Red Star (a)*	2-0	Vukić, Šćepović
Radnički 1923 (h)	3-0	Vukić, Anderson, Ivanov
Metalac (a)*	3-0	Eduardo, Babović, Vukić
Novi Pazar (a)*	1-1	Diarra
Sloboda Point Sevojno (h)*	0-0	
OFK Beograd (a)	2-1	Tomić, Ivanov
Jagodina (h) – closed doors	4-0	Ilić (2), Diarra (2)
Hajduk (a)*	2-0	Tomić (2)
Rad (a)*	4-1	Ivanov, Diarra (2), Babović
Vojvodina (h)*	4-1	Tomić, Vukić (2), Volkov
Spartak (a)	2-1	Eduardo, Vukić
Javor (h) – closed doors	2-1	Vukić, Tomić
Smederevo (a)*	2-0	Ilić, Manga
BSK (h)*	2-0	Diarra, Vukić

Borac (a)*	4-0	Marković S, Ivanov, Diarra (2)
Red Star (h)*	0-1	
Radnički (a)*	1-0	Babović
Metalac (h) – closed doors	1-0	Diarra

Serbian Cup

Novi Pazar (a)	3-0	Tomić, Ilić, Vukić
Metalac (h)*	3-1	Vukić (2), Babović
OFK (a)	2-0	Diarra, Marković L
Red Star (a)*	0-2	
Red Star (h)*	0-2	

Champions League

FK Shkendia (h)*	4-0	Vukić, Eduardo, Šćepović, og
FK Shkendia (a)	1-0	Jovančić
KRC Genk (a)	1-2	Tomić
KRC Genk (h)*	1-1	Tomić

Europa League

| Shamrock Rovers (a) | 1-1 | Tomić |
| Shamrock Rovers (h)* | 1-2 aet | Volkov |

* Denotes match I attended

Final league table

		P	W	D	L	F	A	GD	Pts
1	Partizan	30	26	2	2	67	12	+55	80
2	Red Star	30	21	5	4	57	18	+39	68
3	Vojvodina	30	14	10	6	44	26	+18	52
4	Jagodina	30	14	9	7	34	20	+14	51
5	Sloboda	30	15	6	9	42	35	+7	51
6	Radnički	30	11	14	5	38	27	+11	47
7	Spartak	30	11	10	9	31	31	0	43
8	OFK	30	12	4	14	34	36	-2	40
9	Javor	30	11	6	13	28	32	-4	39
10	Rad	30	10	7	13	33	31	+2	37
11	Hajduk	30	9	6	15	28	44	-16	33
12	BSK	30	7	9	14	18	39	-21	30
13	Smederevo	30	9	2	19	22	42	-20	29
14	Novi Pazar	30	6	10	14	21	41	-20	28
15	Borac	30	4	7	19	16	45	-29	19
16	Metalac	30	2	9	19	14	48	-34	15

Partizan goalscorers

	League	Cup	Europe	Total
Zvonimir Vukić	13	3	1	17
Nemanja Tomić	11	1	3	15
Lamine Diarra	11	1		12
Lazar Marković	6	1		7
Saša Ilić	4	1		5
Stefan Babović	4	1		5
Eduardo Pacheca	4		1	5
Marko Šćepović	4		1	5
Ivan Ivanov	4			4
Vladimir Volkov	1		1	2
Saša Marković	1			1
Nikola Aksentijević	1			1
Anderson Marques	1			1
David Manga	1			1
Vladimir Jovančić			1	1
Own goals	1		1	2
TOTAL	**67**	**8**	**9**	**84**

Map of Serbia

Serbian Pronunciation Guide

Letter	Sound	Pronunciation Example
A/a	a	a as in car
B/b	b	b as in bat
C/c	ts	ts as in cats
Č/č	tʃ	ch as in chalk
Ć/ć	tɕ	ch as in church
D/d	d	d as in dog
Dž/dž	dʒ	j as in jumper
Đ/đ	dʑ	ge as in George
E/e	ɛ	e as in bet
F/f	f	f as in football
G/g	g	g as in game
H/h	x	h as in heaven
I/i	i	ea as in east
J/j	j	y as in yogurt
K/k	k	k as in kick
L/l	l	l as in love
Lj/lj	ʎ	ll as in million
M/m	m	m as in mother
N/n	n	n as in nut
Nj/nj	ɲ	ni as in onion
O/o	ɔ	au as in autumn
P/p	p	p as in point
R/r	r	r as in Fred (rolled a bit)
S/s	s	s as in sound
Š/s	ʃ	sh as in shoot
T/t	t	t as in time
U/u	u	oo as in shoot
V/v	v	v as in violence
Z/z	z	z as in zone
Ž/ž	ʒ	s as in leisure/pleasure